Agrarian Crisis in India: The Case of Bihar

70°
75°
80°
85°
90°
25°
20°
15°
10°
5°
Brahmaputra R.
Ganga R.
(Ganges)
Bihar
Calcutta
India
BAY OF BENGAL
ARABIAN SEA
BIHAR - LOCATION IN THE
INDIAN SUBCONTINENT
Ceylon
SCALE:
0 100 200 300 400 500
miles

Agrarian Crisis in India

THE CASE OF BIHAR

by F. Tomasson Jannuzi

UNIVERSITY OF TEXAS PRESS, AUSTIN AND LONDON

The publication of this book was assisted by a grant from the Andrew W. Mellon Foundation.

Library of Congress Cataloging in Publication Data

Jannuzi, F Tomasson, 1934–
Agrarian crisis in India.

Bibliography: p.
1. Land reform—India—Bihar (State) 2. Land tenure—Bihar, India (State) 3. Bihar, India (State)—Social conditions. I. Title.
HD879.B44J35 338.1'0954'.2 73-19811
ISBN 0-292-76414-6

Printed in the United States of America
Composition by G&S Typesetters, Austin
Printing by The University of Texas Printing Division, Austin
Binding by Universal Bookbindery, Inc., San Antonio

For Vera Anstey

CONTENTS

MAPS

TABLES

FIGURE

PREFACE

Bowed by the weight of centuries he leans
Upon his hoe and gazes on the ground,
The emptiness of ages in his face,
And on his back the burden of the world.
Who made him dead to rapture and despair,
A thing that grieves not and that never hopes,
Stolid and stunned, a brother to the ox?
Who loosened and let down this brutal jaw?
Whose was the hand that slanted back this brow?
Whose breath blew out the light within this brain?

O masters, lords and rulers in all lands,
How will the Future reckon with this Man?
How answer his brute question in that hour
When whirlwinds of rebellion shake the world?
How will it be with kingdoms and with kings—
With those who shaped him to the thing he is—
When this dumb Terror shall reply . . .
After the silence of the centuries?[1]

It must be said at the outset that this is not a work designed to incriminate the leadership of India or the leadership of one Indian state, Bihar. It is written with appreciation of the magnitude of the problems that have confronted that leadership persistently in the years since India established its independence. Inevitably, however, it is a book that contrasts the articulated goals and ideals of those who led with the results now observable. It is judgmental

[1] Edwin Markham, "The Man with the Hoe." Markham also wrote that the theme of the Hoe-Man is as old as the world and as deep as the world's injustice.

therefore of the persisting gap between plans and needs. It is judgmental also of the gap between plans and their fulfillment.

This book is dedicated to the Indian peasantry, particularly to the landless laborers and sharecroppers whose numbers are in the millions and who, until recently, remained passively inarticulate in the countryside, acted upon by forces over which they had little, if any, control. Now they may be the instruments of change. It is they who can be expected increasingly to place demands on the Indian political and economic systems. They are no longer prisoners of a traditional society, immobilized or silent. In a land of universal adult suffrage, their numbers matter and cannot be taken for granted by any party or group that seeks to manipulate or control them. There is latent anger among them, and promises of future benefits, future improvements in income and quality of life, cannot be counted upon for long to contain that anger. The promises of the past have not been fulfilled for the majority of them. Yet, they have observed carefully the processes by which social and economic reforms have been enunciated and then distorted in implementation to benefit the few, rather than the many. No one knows when and how the latent anger among the peasantry will be transformed into militant action. But it can be asserted now that the peasantry of India or those who manipulate them will determine the future course of events in that country. It is they or those who manipulate them who will inherit India from the colonial legacy elites to whom the British transferred power.

The continuing mobilization of the peasantry of India is not a phenomenon easily explained or documented. Nor is it a phenomenon attributable to a single cause. This book recounts something of the background to peasant mobilization in only one of India's states, Bihar. No assumption is made that the events of Bihar have been duplicated or will be duplicated elsewhere. Yet, events in Bihar, particularly as they are related to agrarian reforms that were promised and subsequently diluted or denied, can be considered illustrative of processes going on in many regions of India in which those low in the inegalitarian, agrarian hierarchy have begun to be agents of change.

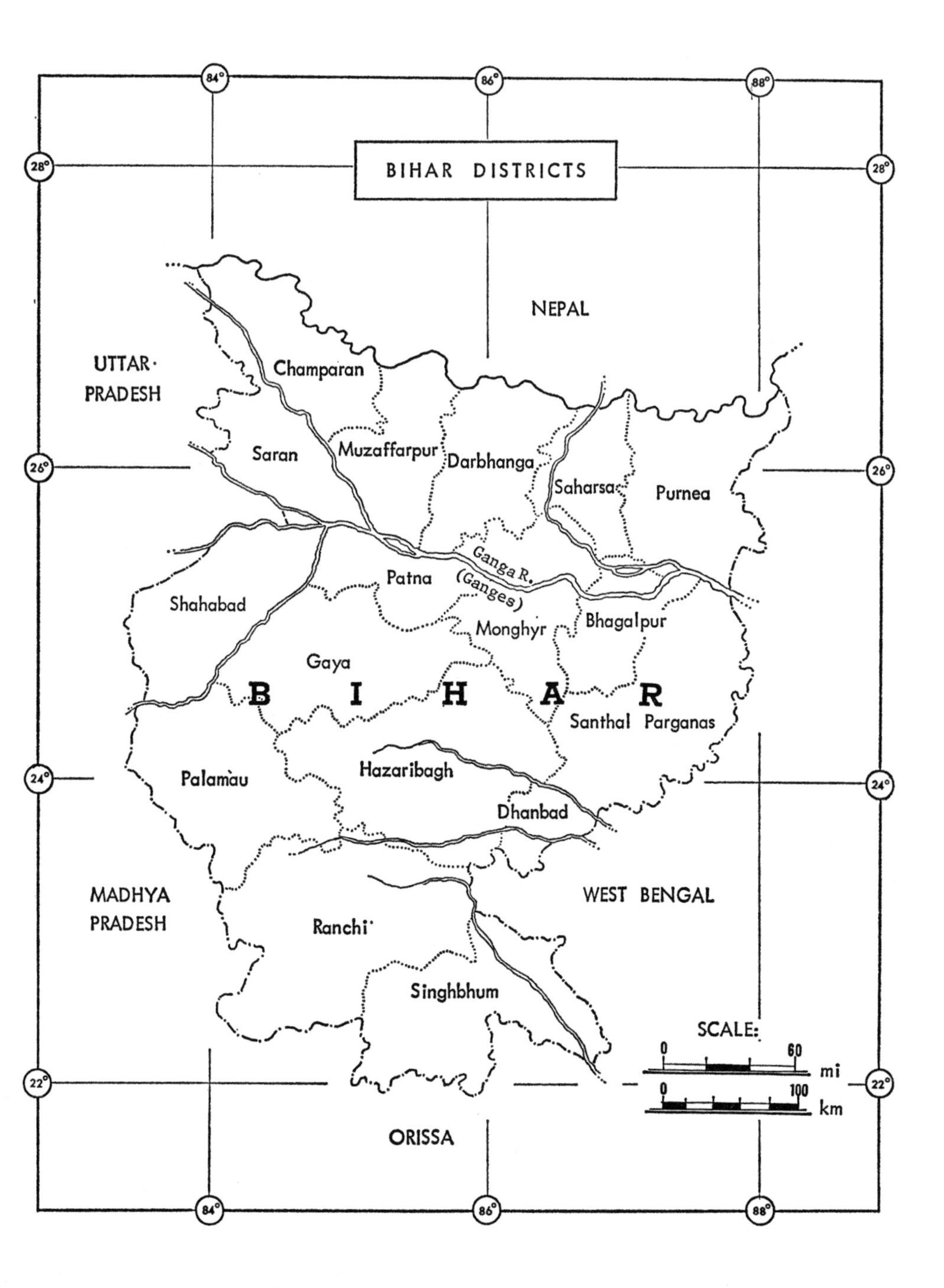
BIHAR DISTRICTS
84°
86°
88°
28°
26°
24°
22°
NEPAL
UTTAR PRADESH
Champaran
Saran
Muzaffarpur
Darbhanga
Saharsa
Purnea
Ganga R. (Ganges)
Patna
Shahabad
Bhagalpur
Monghyr
Gaya
B I H A R
Santhal Parganas
Palamau
Hazaribagh
Dhanbad
MADHYA PRADESH
WEST BENGAL
Ranchi
Singhbhum
SCALE:
0
60
mi
0
100
km
ORISSA

Agrarian Crisis in India: The Case of Bihar

1. *The Commitment to Agrarian Reforms*

Among the goals enunciated by the Congress movement prior to the achievement of independence from the United Kingdom was that of comprehensive agrarian reforms.[1] It was easier then, as now, to reach apparent consensus on the need for such reforms than it was to make explicit the meaning of "agrarian reforms" to various interest groups within the Congress coalition. Inevitably, the nature of the commitment to agrarian reforms varied enormously among the disparate groups comprising the Congress.

For some, particularly the westernized intellectuals within the movement, the general commitment to agrarian reforms was associated loosely with the development of a socialist India in which the ideals of equality and social justice might be realized. Within the Congress party, the most committed to radical agrarian re-

[1] The term "agrarian reforms" is used in this work to refer to a constellation of programs designed to effect structural changes in the agricultural sector of Bihar. Thus used, "agrarian reforms" is a comprehensive term applying to "zamindari abolition," "ceilings," "consolidation," or other such reform programs. The term often has extended meaning in Bihar, implying the total transformation of rural society, especially the removal of basic inequalities between landholders and weaker sections of the peasantry.

forms, including basic land reforms,[2] were the Congress Socialists,[3] who, prior to independence, were comprised of such men as Jaya Prakash Narayan, Rammanohar Lohia, and Minoo Masani. Occupying a position apart from this group, but expressing similar concern regarding the need for agrarian reforms, was Jawaharlal Nehru. In general, it can be said that the proponents of radical agrarian reforms were mainly men whose origins were urban and whose education had involved exposure to Western liberal thought. They tended not to follow the guidelines of the more traditional elites, whose values were rooted in sacred texts and myths and the inherited mores of the countryside. For many of these westernized intellectuals, agrarian reforms had symbolic and extended meaning; they were to be part of a still nebulous program leading to a restructuring of the Indian economic, social, and political systems.

There were others in the Congress fold whose origins were more rustic and whose beliefs were more traditional and conservative. Such men as Rajendra Prasad, later to be the first president of the Republic of India, were representative of this segment within the Congress. And it was this segment, more often than not, which held the balance of power within the policy-making echelons of the movement. Even Gandhi, whose influence generally bridged the gap between radicals and conservatives, was probably ambivalent on the question of agrarian reforms. Though deeply concerned with peasant problems and capable of winning over to the Congress a number of peasant reform movements organized "from about 1920, especially in the heavily settled regions of Bengal, Bihar, the United Provinces, and the Punjab,"[4] Gandhi was also closely associated with the landed middle classes and large industrialists, particularly Marwari and Gujarati businessmen, the principal financiers of the Congress movement. Possibly in an effort to extend the influence of the movement to all classes, "Gandhi's own attitude was that no one class should benefit at the expense of another but all should unselfishly work together. Landlords and industrialists, peasants and workers should not treat each other as enemies but should practice mutual forbearance and tolerance. The one should not

[2] "Land reform" is a term used to suggest basic changes in the distribution of land holdings. It is a term used narrowly in this work to refer to changes in the agrarian structure that shift control of land resources from one owner to another.

[3] The Congress Socialist party was established within the Congress in 1934.

[4] W. Norman Brown, *The United States and India and Pakistan*, p. 227.

withhold rent or go on strikes; the other should provide good living and working conditions, take only a just amount in rent, and pay fair wages."[5] Yet, the critical comment has been made that "under the application of this teaching the landlords lost nothing and the peasants gained nothing."[6]

Even by the late 1920s the Congress had not established a definitive agrarian policy, and the radical initiative on the question of the relationship of the peasantry to the land was captured, at least temporarily, by the Communist party of India which in 1930 published a "Draft Program of Action" calling for "confiscation without compensation of all lands and estates, forests, and pastures of the native princes, landlords, moneylenders, and the British Government, and the transference to peasant committees for use by the toiling masses of the peasantry . . . immediate confiscation of all plantations . . . immediate nationalization of the whole system of irrigation, complete cancellation of all indebtedness and taxes . . . the peasantry and agricultural proletariat to engage in all kinds of political demonstrations, and collective refusal to pay taxes and dues . . . refusal to pay rent . . . refusal to pay debts and arrears to government, the landlords, and the moneylenders in any form whatsoever."[7]

The Congress conservatives did not respond to this Communist challenge, and radical voices within the Congress were muted. Instead, under Gandhi's leadership, the Congress followed a rather pragmatic course with respect to the peasants and agrarian policy. It vigorously defended peasant interests, as in Champaran District, Bihar, in 1917[8] "so long as peasant interests were adversely and directly affected by government (or by British landowners). . . . But where peasant interests were circumscribed by landed interests, the Congress under Gandhi counseled mutual trust and understanding."[9]

Increasingly frustrated with the Congress's unwillingness to

[5] Ibid.

[6] Ibid.

[7] Ibid., p. 228.

[8] For an account of Gandhi's campaign in Champaran, see Mohandas K. Gandhi, *An Autobiography: The Story of My Experiments with Truth*, pp. 404–425.

[9] Walter Hauser, "The Indian National Congress and Land Policy in the Twentieth Century" (mimeographed paper prepared for the December 1962 meeting of the American Historical Association), p. 4, as quoted by George Rosen, *Democracy and Economic Change in India*, p. 62.

make explicit its land policy and, more generally, to follow a more revolutionary strategy in the independence struggle, a group of idealistic radicals stepped forward in 1934 to found the Congress Socialist party.[10] Functioning within the Congress, and in concert with a number of peasant associations, this Socialist party within a party advocated drastic reforms. In Bihar their suggested reforms included abolition of the zamindari system[11] and the elimination of agrarian debt.

It was not until 1936 that the Congress party as a whole produced an election manifesto, which, according to Nehru, included a statement advocating "a reform of the system of land tenure and revenue and rent, and an equitable adjustment of the burden on agricultural land, giving immediate relief to the smaller peasantry by a substantial reduction of agricultural rent and revenue now paid by them and exempting uneconomic holdings from payment of rent and revenue."[12] What is more, following the 1937 elections, when the Congress established its first ministries, it made some attempts to introduce agrarian reform legislation. Yet power within the Congress, especially in a state such as Bihar, remained in the hands of landholding conservatives who were not prepared to commit themselves to meaningful reforms. Leftist pressure was resisted and an agreement was reached between proponents and opponents of radical agrarian reforms to dilute the reform legislation that was passed in Bihar. Thus, in a fashion that was to become typical of the Congress, a means had been found to preserve the fragile unity of the party by permitting the language of radical economic and social change to be incorporated into its policy resolutions, while assuring that no action would be taken to unduly upset conservative landed and industrial interests within the party. Even after independence was achieved, radical language on land policy, followed by conservative action, became standard practice within the Congress throughout India, and especially in Bihar.

Successive documents of government have referred to agrarian

[10] The Praja Socialist party in contemporary India is directly descended from the Congress Socialist party. For additional background on the Congress Socialists, see Acharya Narendra Deva, *Socialism and the National Revolution.*

[11] The zamindari system of landholdings and tenure relationships is explained in chapter 2.

[12] Jawaharlal Nehru, as quoted by W. Norman Brown, *The United States and India and Pakistan*, p. 228.

reforms as necessary to assure favorable conditions for increases in agricultural production within an environment of social justice. Successive leaders of the ruling Congress party have employed the language of agrarian reforms in parliamentary debates and when confronting appropriate sections of the electorate. There have been periodic directives from New Delhi to the states to both legislate and implement reforms consistent with the "Directive Principles of State Policy" within the *Constitution of India.* The states have been advised repeatedly to assure "that the ownership and control of the material resources of the community are so distributed as best to subserve the common good" and "that the operation of the economic system does not result in the concentration of wealth and means of production to the common detriment."[13] However, the central government has found itself lacking in effective power to make certain that legislated reforms were consistent with such "Directive Principles of State Policy" and, if so, could be implemented within the political context in which decision-making takes place in the Indian states. Thus, a gulf persists in 1971 between reforms that have been verbalized and those that have been implemented in the constituent states of the Republic.

That there should be such a wide gulf between articulated ideals and solid accomplishment is, in part, understandable with the realization that the Republic of India is a union of states each of which has retained certain prerogatives and functional responsibilities under the Constitution. Within this constitutional framework, the responsibility for enacting and implementing agrarian reforms has rested with the states. In these circumstances, whatever the directives from New Delhi to the states on agrarian reforms, there has been implicative diversity of response. What has been accomplished in the states has been in spite of numerous obstacles, not the least of which has been the widespread opposition of landholding interests on whom the Congress party has relied for the maintenance of its political power in many regions of the country. Moreover, since India's agricultural history is one of complex land tenure systems and agricultural problems, differing extraordinarily from province to province, district to district, and even village to village, the tasks of the state governments have been unenviable.

The central purpose of this work is to provide deeper under-

[13] India, Ministry of Law, *Constitution of India*, Article 39.

standing of the recent history of agrarian reforms in one of the largest states of India, Bihar. Bihar (with one-tenth of the people of India within her borders) assumes special significance because it was the first state to initiate agrarian reforms through the enactment of legislation to abolish the zamindari system, and possibly the least successful of all in implementing that and other agrarian reforms. Nowhere in contemporary India is the gulf between articulated ideals with respect to agrarian reforms and solid accomplishment more conspicuous than in Bihar.

Not only has Bihar failed to implement agrarian reforms, the misery and poverty of her landless laborers, sharecroppers, and small farmers are extreme even in a country where per capita incomes are less than one hundred dollars per annum. To live at the margin of subsistence is the way of life for the majority of Bihar's peasantry. In real terms this means that some customarily need to consume undigested grain picked from the excrement of cattle as they struggle for survival.

Nowhere in India is there a greater gulf separating the landholding elites and the masses of the peasantry than in Bihar. Yet official reports tell us little about existing relationships of men to land or between various landholding classes and the tillers of the soil. Such reports tend to conceal the dynamic power relationships between those who control land resources in Bihar and those who lack the means to control those resources. Such reports give no indication of the manner in which existing laws governing the relationship of men to the land have been bent and abused in calculated attempts by the traditional landholding elites to retain control over the land and to deny new rights in land to those below them in the rural hierarchy. Such reports give little indication of the growing tension in rural areas between haves and have-nots.

This book examines the legislative content of such agrarian reforms as have been enacted in Bihar. It provides necessary background to an understanding of the degree to which official commitment to agrarian reforms in Bihar has not been translated into meaningful reforms. It provides insight into the traditional and changing relationships between the landholding elites of Bihar and the peasantry who have been so long subservient to them. It should make self-evident why programs of rural development, including attempts to promote new technology in agriculture (associated with what has been referred to popularly as the "Green Revolution"), have been less successful in regions such as Bihar than in the Punjab. Finally, this book incorporates certain policy recommendations that grew out of fifteen years of direct and indirect association with those who now struggle to achieve an agricultural revolution in Bihar.

2. The Abolition of Intermediary Interests ("Zamindari Abolition")

History

Prior to the Bihar Land Reforms Act, 1950, there had grown up in Bihar an intricately stratified system of relationships of people to land. In the Permanent Settlement areas of the state, especially, there were numerous kinds of landholdings.[1] At the apex of the hierarchy was the state. Below the state were the zamindars,

[1] These Permanent Settlement areas resulted from the Settlement of 1793 that was applicable to parts of Bengal, North Madras, and Bihar. The Permanent Settlement was made with the zamindars by the East India Company with the understanding that the revenue due to the company would be fixed in cash, in perpetuity. The unalterable revenue demand, fixed as payable by the zamindars, was supposed to represent nine-tenths of what the zamindars received in rent from the tenants. The remaining one-tenth was left to the zamindars as remuneration for their collection responsibilities. The zamindars were allowed the right to fix their own terms with tenants. At the time of zamindari abolition in Bihar (1950), there were 205,977 revenue paying, permanently settled estates, representing 90 percent of the total area of the state. These figures are based mainly on records made available through the courtesy of the Revenue Department, Government of Bihar, June 1957. See also J. Allen et al. (eds.), *Cambridge Shorter History of India*, pp. 637–640.

tenure-holders, and under-tenure-holders (those who had rent-collecting powers). At the base were the peasants with limited rights to land and the landless laborers, wage laborers with no rights to land.[2]

FIGURE I
Hierarchy of Interests in Land

The State of Bihar
(the "super-landlord")

The Zamindar (legally, a "proprietor," but acting as an intermediary of the state in the collection of rent from tenants)	The Tenure-holder* (acting as an intermediary of the state in the collection of rent from tenants)
The Occupancy Raiyat† (a rent-paying holder of land having the right of occupancy on the land held by him)	The Non-occupancy Raiyat (a rent-paying holder of land not having the right of occupancy on land temporarily in his possession)

The Under-raiyat

(a rent-paying holder of land having temporary possession of a holding under a raiyat)

The Muzdur

(a wage laborer having no rights in land)

*"Tenure-holder" means "primarily a person who has acquired from a proprietor or from another tenure-holder a right to hold land for the purpose of collecting rents or bringing it under cultivation by establishing tenants on it, and includes also the successors-in-interest of persons who have acquired such a right." Bihar Tenancy Act of 1885 as reprinted in Government of India, Ministry of Food and Agriculture, *Agricultural Legislation in India,* VI, 34.

†"Raiyat" is legally defined as "primarily a person who has acquired from a proprietor or from another tenure-holder a right to hold land for the purpose of cultivating it by himself, or by members of his family or by hired servants or with the aid of partners, and includes also the successors-in-interest of persons who have acquired such a right" (ibid.).

[2] The numerous and complex relationships of people to land in rural Bihar are best enumerated in the tenancy acts that are applicable to the state: Bihar Tenancy Act of 1885; Santal Parganas Tenancy Acts of 1872, 1886, and 1949; and Chota Nagpur Tenancy Act of 1908. See India, Ministry of Food and Agriculture, *Agricultural Legislation in India,* VI, 31–174.

The hierarchy of interests in land existing in rural Bihar at the time of the vesting of all intermediary interests in the state is shown in the following illustration. The illustration is representative only of the stratification of interests in land; there were many unusual relationships that existed according to local custom. Moreover, many with interests in land combined roles, functioning simultaneously, for example, as a tenure-holder (rent collector) over a portion of their holding and as a raiyat (rent payer) over another portion. In practice the distinction between a tenure-holder and a raiyat was often hard to draw. For this reason there was provision in the Bihar Tenancy Act of 1885 that local custom would be a determinant in defining the nature of a tenancy.[3] There was the stipulation also that, where a raiyat held more than one hundred bighas (62.5 acres), the tenant (raiyat) would be presumed to be a tenure-holder until the contrary had been shown.[4]

The government of Bihar made its first post-independence legislative attempt to abolish the zamindari system in Bihar by passing the Bihar Abolition of Zamindari Bill in 1947. This bill was then reserved for the consideration of the governor general of India under the provisions of the Government of India Act, 1935, and was returned to the government of Bihar with amendment suggestions pertaining to provisions dealing with mineral rights in that state. The bill was amended, approved by the governor general on June 6, 1949, and published as the Bihar Abolition of Zamindari Act, 1948 (Bihar Act XVIII of 1949). The constitutionality of the Bihar Abolition of Zamindari Act, 1948, was challenged in the courts "and the Courts issued injunctions restraining the State Government from implementing the scheme. Subsequently, it was felt that the act did not make [sufficient] provision for land reforms and it was therefore decided to repeal it and to bring forward a more comprehensive legislation in its place. The Bihar Abolition of Zamindari Act was accordingly repealed and a new [piece of] legislation, called the Bihar Land Reforms Bill, 1949, was introduced."[5] In 1950, the Bihar Land Reforms Bill, 1949, was passed and was transferred for the consideration of the president of India under Article 31 (Clause 4) of the Constitution of India.[6] It re-

[3] Ibid., p. 40.

[4] Ibid.

[5] H. D. Malaviya, *Land Reforms in India*, pp. 205–206.

[6] "If any Bill pending at the commencement of this Constitution in the Legis-

ceived the assent of the president and was published as an act, the Bihar Land Reforms Act, 1950 (Bihar Act XXX of 1950). The act, however, was challenged in the courts, and the Patna High Court declared that the act contravened Article 14 of the Constitution of India.[7] Whereupon, the central government introduced and the central legislature passed the Constitution (First Amendment) Act, which validated the Bihar Land Reforms Act, 1950.[8] At this, zamindari interests in Bihar challenged the constitutionality of the First Amendment in a suit brought before the Supreme Court of India. But the Supreme Court unanimously held that the constitutional amendment was valid. At which, legal proceedings, designed to test the constitutionality of the Bihar Land Reforms Act, 1950, were once more initiated by interested Bihari zamindars and the matter eventually reached the Supreme Court. In 1952, the Supreme Court of India finally upheld the validity of the Bihar Land Reforms Act, 1950.

Five years had been purchased by those who vigorously opposed any legislation that promised "to replace the Zamindari system of land tenure by a Raiyatwari system under which raiyats will hold their lands directly under the Provincial Government [of Bihar] and to transfer to the Provincial Government all the rights of proprietors and tenure-holders in land, including rights in forests, fisheries and minerals."[9] The zamindari interests used every means at their disposal to prevent, delay, or dilute the legislation.[10] In

---

lature of a State has, after it has been passed by such Legislature, been reserved for the consideration of the President and has received his assent, then notwithstanding anything in this Constitution, the law so assented to shall not be called in question in any Court" (India, Ministry of Law, *Constitution of India*, Article 31, Clause 4).

[7] "The State shall not deny to any person equality before the law or the equal protection of the laws within the territory of India" (ibid., Article 14).

[8] "No law providing for (a) the acquisition by the State of any estate or of any rights therein or the extinguishment or modification of any such rights . . . shall be deemed to be void on the ground that it is inconsistent with or takes away or abridges any of the rights conferred by Article 14, Article 19, or Article 31" (ibid., Article 31A).

[9] The wording is that of a draft of "The Bihar State Acquisition of Zamindaris Bill, 1947" provided to the author in March 1968 by Shri K. B. Sahay, a former chief minister of the government of Bihar who, as revenue minister, was responsible for introducing the bill.

[10] The public record of the activities of the zamindars during this period remains incomplete, but the files of the Bihar Pradesh Congress Committee con-

addition to the legal maneuvers mentioned above, direct appeals were made to higher authority in the hope that national leadership might be induced to intervene to delay zamindari abolition legislation. In 1947, for example, one group of zamindars cabled Rajendra Prasad as follows.[11]

PROVINCIAL GOVERNMENT BENT UPON PASSING LEGISLATION REDUCING LANDLORDS SUBSTANTIAL AND STATUTORY SHARE WITHOUT COMPENSATION ACTING FIRSTLY AGAINST CONGRESS HIGH COMMANDS DIRECTION OF SUBMITTING ALL INDIA PLAN OF CHANGING LAND TENURES BEFORE LEGISLATION AND SECONDLY ACTING AGAINST ALL ASSURANCES OF COMPENSATION GIVEN TO DEPUTATIONS OF LANDHOLDERS AND TENANTS AND RUINING ENTIRE LANDHOLDERS CLASS BY SINGLE STROKE OF LEGISLATION. GREAT CONSTERNATION.

Another group sent a briefer plea to Prasad:

HON'BLE RAJENDRAPRASAD NEW DELHI IN HONOUR GANDHIJAYANTI APPEALING PEACE KINDLY DROP ABOLITION ZAMINDARI SAVE COUNTRY CIVIL WAR.

Still others submitted long memoranda to various officials of the government of Bihar, including the paramount official, then known as the "prime minister of Bihar," Shri Krishna Sinha. One such memorandum, dated March 25, 1947, was forwarded to the prime minister of Bihar by Maharaja Pratap Udai Nath Shah Deo, maharaja of Chota Nagpur. The maharaja protested the apparent decision of the government to introduce legislation designed "to abolish all the zamindaris in the Province." Continued the maharaja:

The zamindars are an integral part of the present social structure of the country . . . and the whole social fabric is interwoven with the institution of the zamindari. The zamindars are as much a part of the nation as others are and they are never anti-national. . . . Numbers of zamindars have taken part in various national and other progressive movements of the land and have taken active part in building the pres-

---

tain many papers which, if published, would partially document this chapter in Bihar history. Some documents have been made available to the author by officials of the government of Bihar, members of the Congress party, interested scholars, and ex-zamindars of Bihar. In the following pages these materials have been used to supplement published sources.

[11] The late Rajendra Prasad, first president of the Republic of India, was a lawyer, a man of conservative orientation, and a representative of one of Bihar's leading castes (the Kayastha). His general background was such that he was expected to give a sympathetic hearing to the pleas of zamindari interests.

ent nation. . . . The interests of the raiyats and of the zamindars are not antagonistic and they can be adjusted within the present social structure. The rights and interests of the raiyats now-a-days are well protected by codified laws and the zamindars have got no authority over them except the right to realize rent and the rent is an insignificant item in the budget of the raiyat. . . . Hope the wailing of the zamindars in their distress will touch your heart and you will keep a place in the corner of your heart for them also.

Elsewhere in the same memorandum, the maharaja had put forward many detailed arguments in support of the proposition that he not be placed "in the same category with the other zamindars of the Province." The maharaja pointed out that he was the sixty-first of the ancient "sovereign ruling chiefs" of the area, and that the family's credentials had been attested to by the British and recorded in an early edition of the *Ranchi District Gazetteer*. He traced the origins of his "rajaship" to the year A.D. 61 when the inhabitants of the Chota Nagpur region, "who were all aboriginals then, so far as can be gathered from the historical records," established his ancestor, Phani Mukut Rai, "as the Ruling Chief of this part of the country." And he emphasized that his zamindari rights had been recognized by the Moghuls and the British long before the Permanent Settlement of 1793. To cap his argument, the maharaja quoted British authority to the effect that "up to the end of last century, the Maharaja was considered as a Feudal Chief and not a Zamindar."

The various pleas made by the zamindars to national leaders, including Mahatma Gandhi, were not simply dismissed by those occupying leadership positions in the Congress hierarchy outside of Bihar. To some of his elders, K. B. Sahay (then revenue minister in the Bihar government and intent on pressing ahead with the legislation) must have seemed bent on taking much too precipitate action. Rajendra Prasad wrote Sahay a long letter, dated April 27, 1947, from New Delhi in which he (Prasad) chastised the revenue minister for moving so rapidly in the direction of zamindari abolition legislation without consulting adequately the Congress Working Committee. Stating his point of view rather tersely, Prasad told Sahay in that letter:

Any hope that you may have of giving satisfaction to tenants by simply getting rid of the zamindars is doomed to failure unless it is accomplished by some positive steps for the betterment of the tenants' lot, but I gathered . . . that you were not thinking of the next step and that for the present you would be satisfied if you can remove the zamindars. . . . I have never been able to understand the justice or fairness of depriving a man of the management of his property. I can understand abolition of zamindari. The Congress has sanctioned that, but I do not think there is any sanction in the Congress Resolution for forcibly dispossessing people of their property before they have been compensated for it.

In another passage in the same letter, Rajendra Prasad warned Sahay that the proposed legislation would "affect the entire economic life of the Province," and he suggested that more considered, rather than hastily conceived, legislation seemed warranted in the circumstances. In his reply to Prasad, dated May 1, 1947, Sahay did not seem chastened. In a direct challenge to the views of his distinguished senior colleague in the Congress, Sahay said: "So far as I am concerned, I feel that in order to rehabilitate the position of the Congress it is necessary that the Bills [relating to zamindari abolition] should be proceeded with. If you or the Parliamentary Committee so choose, you may send for me and give me a hearing." As if to punctuate that statement, Sahay enclosed for Prasad's perusal "a printed copy of the Bihar State Acquisition of Zamindaris Bill, 1947."

The degree of bitterness underlying the zamindars' legal arguments against the Bihar Land Reforms Act, 1950, has been illustrated effectively in the pages of one of Bihar's leading English-language newspapers, the *Indian Nation.* For ten years, both prior to and after the debate concerning the enactment of zamindari abolition legislation, that newspaper tended to support the intermediary (zamindari) interest groups against the state.[12] The most convenient target throughout that period was Shri K. B. Sahay, revenue minister of Bihar until 1957, who was chiefly responsible for the act's passing the state legislature and being submitted repeatedly to the central government and the Supreme Court for approval. The following extract from an editorial of April 6, 1948, by the editor of the *Indian Nation*, Shri S. Sen, is illustrative of the tone of political commentary during the period.

[12] This statement is based on personal inspection of the columns of the *Indian Nation* for the ten-year period June 1947 through June 1957. (This was made possible through the courtesy of Shri S. Sen, editor.)

The fire of power politics is consuming his whole being. The Revenue Minister is evidently insensible to the fact that the bill when enacted will upset the rural economy. The Revenue Minister is either one-eyed or wilfully blind. Bihar is screeching under the stewardship of an aggressive politician who has no vision and faith, but who is obstinate and petty. He is impatient to see Zamindars out; he is anxious to favour men with countless jobs in the event of the abolition of the Zamindari system; he is shaking with joy that he will be able to reward his followers and purchase his critics. . . . We plead for rational, cool, and calm thinking on this great issue.

After 1950, some of the largest and most conservative zamindars of the state sought association with the Janta party,[13] which was inalterably opposed in the general elections of 1952 and 1957 to any, within the Congress or without, who supported the concept of change in the traditional system governing relations between landlord and peasant.

The political effectiveness of the Janta party was never demonstrated, except possibly in 1957 when it contributed to the defeat of the Bihar Congress revenue minister, K. B. Sahay. It seems that the defeat of Sahay, perhaps the most progressive leader within the Bihar Congress, was achieved through astute political manipulation (by the Janta party, zamindari members of the Congress party, and other interested groups) of caste differences among Congress party candidates in Bihar.[14] Sahay would probably not have been defeated by the Janta party and vindictive zamindari interests alone. Caste coalition infighting within the Congress and the personal rivalry of Sahay and another congressman, M. P. Sinha, also contributed to the defeat of both Sahay and Sinha. Indeed, each was said to have worked against the other.[15] In its inimitable fashion, the Congress party of Bihar in 1957 was engaged more in the

[13] The Janta party was a party of feudal reaction. It represented landlord and princely elements and was, essentially, an instrumentality of the maharaja of Ramgarh. Its strength was concentrated mainly in south Bihar in the district of Hazaribagh. The Janta party secured 236,094 votes in the general election of 1952 and 501,269 in 1957. Later the maharaja of Ramgarh joined the Congress, defected in 1967 to form another party, the Jan Kranti Dal, and, apparently, rejoined the Congress in 1969.

[14] F. Tomasson Jannuzi, "Agrarian Problems in Bihar" (Ph.D. dissertation, London School of Economics and Political Science, 1958). The dissertation was based mainly on information compiled from surveys in five villages.

[15] For elaboration, see the *Bihar Herald*, September 14, 1957.

politics of power within the party than in the politics of confrontation with Congress opponents. Multiple factions of Bhumihar Brahmans, Kayasthas, and Rajputs were struggling for temporary predominance within the ruling group. The machinations of these groups were obvious to anyone on the scene and were reflected in press accounts of the period. The following excerpt from an article that appeared in the *Indian Nation* shortly after the general elections is suggestive of the passion that was generated.

> Facts must, however, be faced, and it is up to the leadership to assess the results judiciously and weigh them in the scales against the trends that they highlight. A little time must elapse before a full and complete review will be possible. But the challenge is much too urgent and implacable to permit of a leisurely survey, either. Certain obvious pointers must be noted immediately. Had conditions been normal, politically, organisationally, emotionally and psychologically, Shri Krishna Ballabha Sahay's defeat at the polls would have been inconceivable. His worst detractor will not deny him a just tribute of admiration for his many sterling qualities and for his splendid record of service, sacrifice and suffering as a patriot. That he should have gone down . . . before a party that has yet to prove its credentials and that there should be persons ready to celebrate the truly regrettable events of his defeat by lending themselves to vulgarity, descending into positive obscenity, open out before all men of patriotism and decency a vast vista for calm and serious reflection. The unprincipled vendetta pursued against Shri Mahesh Prasad Sinha [another Congress candidate in the general election of 1957], culminating in indecent and vulgar crowing over his defeat, and the circumstances of Shri Krishna Ballabha Sahay's reverse and the gleeful enjoyment it provoked among some people, raise fundamental issues of political and human morality. In respect of both, the Congress not only did not prove a happy family, united in purpose and cemented by discipline, but has confronted Bihar with the grim visage of a fundamental feud which has, in the name of party, group and caste, let loose the flood gates of elemental passions whose logical end imagination shudders to contemplate.[16]

In spite of emphatic and persistent appeals made to higher authorities, in spite of legal maneuvers, in spite of efforts made through the Janta party, and in spite of the fact that the zamindari interests were not without representation in the national leadership of the Congress and in the Bihar Congress,[17] the landholding

[16] Murali Manchar Prasad, *Indian Nation* (editorial), March 20, 1957.

[17] For a more extended analysis of the leadership of the Congress party of

interests were unable to prevent the enactment and subsequent validation of the Bihar Land Reforms Act, 1950.

Bihar Land Reforms Act, 1950—Provisions

Through the Bihar Land Reforms Act, 1950, the government of Bihar legally abolished the interests[18] of zamindars and tenure-holders[19] and vested these interests in the state.

Though the principal purposes of the act were those having to do with the vesting of the intermediaries' interests in the state, it was implicit in the act that it provided for the creation of what is, substantially, a raiyatwari system.[20] In so doing, the act also abrogated the Permanent Settlement of 1793 as well as settlements of temporary duration that had existed in Bihar.[21]

Also implicit in the act was a clarification of the state's status as "ultimate" landlord with exclusive proprietary interest in land. The issue of ultimate ownership of land is one that has been, for years, the subject of discussion and controversy. Prior to the Permanent Settlement of 1793, it appears that the zamindars or tenure-

---

Bihar, see Ramashray Roy, "Dynamics of One-Party Dominance in an Indian State," *Asian Survey* (July 1958). In this article, Roy has suggested that "the dominant leadership in Bihar Congress came from the petty and big landlord class."

18 "Interests" as used above refers to interests in land, including interests in trees, forests, fisheries, bazaars, mines, and minerals. See "Introduction: Bihar Land Reforms Act, 1950 (Bihar Act 30 of 1950)." In *The Bihar Local Acts*, III, 2204.

19 "Zamindars and tenure-holders" comprise those classes holding "intermediary" interests between the state, which is the holder of the superior proprietary right, and the peasant.

20 A "raiyatwari system" is one in which the state deals directly with the raiyat, rather than through an intermediary. The raiyat possesses a right to his holding subject to the payment of "rent" to the government.

In the permanently settled areas of Bihar prior to the Bihar Land Reforms Act, 1950, as amended in 1954, a distinction could be made between the terms "rent" and "land revenue": "rent" was paid by peasants to intermediaries who then paid a share of the "rent" to the state; the sum paid by the intermediaries to the state was "land revenue" (revenue received by the state from its interests in land). After the abolition of intermediary interests, the terms "rent" and "land revenue" may be used interchangeably in Bihar to denote sums paid by raiyats directly to the state.

21 There were 739 temporarily settled estates in Bihar in 1950. This figure has been obtained from documents made available through the courtesy of the revenue department of the government of Bihar.

holders had been little more than rent collectors. After the Settlement it was generally assumed that broad proprietary interests in land were held by the zamindars subject to the payment of revenue to the East India Company. The historical rights of peasants to land are confused, also. Throughout Indian history it seems to have been customary for the peasant to pay a share of his produce to someone in authority, a king or his agents. Even so, the peasant's rights to land have tended to be broad—including rights of inheritance and transfer—so long as a share of his produce has been presented regularly to the authorities. In Bihar, much of this confusion with regard to proprietary interests in land was removed, legally at least, by the Bihar Land Reforms Act, 1950. The government of Bihar now holds exclusive proprietary interest in land, excepting certain revenue-free lands accorded to ex-zamindars.[22]

By taking the right of rent collection away from the intermediaries and transferring that right to the state, the act implicitly provided for an increase in the state's income from land revenue—an increase to be realized gradually over time as the government of Bihar progressively assumed its ultimate proprietary rights in land.[23]

Finally, in the opinion of the former revenue minister and chief minister of Bihar, K. B. Sahay, it was anticipated by some that the Bihar Land Reforms Act of 1950 would so weaken the intermediaries and so improve the sense of security of raiyats that an environment would be created in which the majority of cultivators would be encouraged to assume new risks for production purposes. Thus, though the act made no reference to agricultural production goals, it could be argued that ending the alleged exploitation of the peasantry by the zamindari classes could have an indirect and beneficent effect on the state's agricultural production problems.[24]

Bihar Land Reforms Act, 1950—Implementation

In May 1952, having established the validity of the Bihar Land Reforms Act, 1950, the government of Bihar still lacked the means

[22] For further information concerning the history of the Indian land tenure systems, see B. H. Baden-Powell, *Land Revenue and Tenure in British India.*

[23] By assuming for itself the intermediaries' right to collect rent from the peasantry, the state could increase its revenue demand even if rent rates were not enhanced.

[24] Shri K. B. Sahay, interview, Patna, Bihar, November 15, 1957. Shri K. B.

of implementing it fully. (Whether it had the "will" to do so was always in doubt.) Survey and Settlement operations (which involve cadastral surveys and the checking of village records by revenue officers) had been undertaken periodically by the government of Bihar in order to produce up-to-date records of rights in land. When the Bihar Land Reforms Act of 1950 was passed, such records of interests in land as were in the possession of the government were of little value in connection with the implementation of the act because of the passage of time from the dates of completion of the last Survey and Settlement operations in various districts of the state. The latest Survey and Settlement records were nearly thirty years old, and the most obsolete, relating to certain portions of the state, were over fifty years old. This is illustrated in table 1. Revisional Survey and Settlement operations would take time.[25]

Moreover, the state needed to initiate administrative reforms (particularly in the Revenue Department) so that there would be machinery capable of coping with expanded responsibilities associated with the establishment of up-to-date land records and the collection of revenue without the aid of intermediaries.[26]

Having eliminated—within the terms of the Bihar Land Reforms Act, 1950—the intermediaries' right to collect a share of the rent from agricultural land, the government of Bihar estimated that its potential revenue demand from land rent alone would be 85,850,-

---

Sahay was then the former revenue minister in Bihar and leader of the Congress movement (in that state) for land reform and the abolition of zamindari interests.

[25] The Survey and Settlement procedures are painstaking and take considerable time in the best of circumstances. Yet, the delays associated with completing revisional Survey and Settlement operations in Bihar in the period following the enactment of the Bihar Land Reforms Act, 1950, seem to be extraordinary. Interviewed on December 7, 1967, at his residence in Patna, Bihar, K. B. Sahay deplored the slow progress in Survey and Settlement operations, yet inferred that they would have been completed by 1971, had his government not been defeated in the general elections of 1967. It is noteworthy that, as of August 1970, these operations had yet to be completed for the state as a whole, and repeated exhortations from the central government to speed procedures seemed to be ineffective.

[26] For a detailed description of the principal administrative reforms introduced, see V. K. N. Menon, "The New Anchal Adhikari System in Bihar," *Indian Journal of Public Administration* 2, no. 2 (April–June 1956).

TABLE 1
Survey and Settlement Operations in Bihar, 1892–1958

Bihar Districts	Initiation and Completion Dates of Last Survey and Settlement Operations
Patna	1907–1912
Gaya	1911–1918
Shahabad	1907–1916
Saran	1915–1921
Champaran	1913–1919
Muzaffarpur	1892–1899
Darbhanga	1896–1903
Bhagalpur	1902–1910
Monghyr	1905–1912
Purnea	1952–1958
Santhal Parganas	1922–1935
Saharsa	1902–1910
Ranchi	1927–1935
Hazaribagh	1908–1915
Palamau	1915–1920
Dhanbad	1918–1925
Singhbhum	1934–1938

Source: The data contained herein have been supplied through the courtesy of the Revenue Department, Government of Bihar, August 1970.

000 rupees (that is to say, 858.5 lakhs)[27] or possibly as much as 100,000,000 rupees,[28] if one considered the gross rental from agricultural lands, forest lands, royalties from mines, and other miscellaneous sources.

Despite a slow beginning, the Revenue Department reported yearly increases in income from land revenue from 1952, the first year in which the act was implemented—but related expenditures were also rising, as shown in table 2.

On the basis of accomplishments through 1955–1956, the Revenue Department predicted that income from rent collections might move ahead dramatically in 1956–1957 and approach 80,000,000

[27] India, Planning Commission, *Implementation of Land Reforms: A Review by the Land Reforms Implementation Committee of the National Development Council*, p. 42.

[28] *Times of India Directory and Yearbook, 1967*, ed. N. J. Nanporia, p. 410.

TABLE 2
Bihar Land Revenue:
Collections and Related Expenditures

Year	Income[a] (rupees)	Expenditures[b] (rupees)
1952–1953	11,565,807	6,393,992
1953–1954	15,133,356	14,023,631
1954–1955	17,109,118	18,255,980
1955–1956	35,414,331	24,161,419

[a] Actual collections; [b] associated with the costs of managing estates of intermediaries vested in the state of Bihar.

Sources: The income statistics shown are from Government of Bihar, Revenue Department, Land Ceiling Section, "Statement Showing Demand and Collection of Rent, Cess, Education Cess and Miscellaneous Incomes, Rate of Rent, Rent Potential, Compensation and Establishment Costs, Etc." (Patna: Govt. Printing Office, June 30, 1967). The expenditure data are based on rough estimates made available to the author by the Revenue Department, Government of Bihar, in June of 1957.

rupees—close indeed to the published estimate that potential revenue demand (from land rent alone) would be 85,850,000 rupees.

However, the Revenue Department's optimism regarding collections was unwarranted. Collections continued to lag well below estimated potential demand. Actual collections were poor initially (following the enactment and validation of the Bihar Land Reforms Act, 1950) and have varied enormously through the years, as shown in table 3.

The three best years have been 1963–1964, 1964–1965, and 1965–1966 when (current) collections for rent were, respectively, Rs. 56,306,562, Rs. 60,048,956, and Rs. 59,773,450. The worst year was 1966–1967, a time of famine when land rents were remitted by the government on a huge scale and current collections were only 17.2 percent of current demand.

Even allowing for subsequent minor adjustments in the statistics through additions of income under related categories, actual collections of land revenue seem never to have gone beyond 76.3 percent of total estimated demand.[29]

[29] India, Planning Commission, *Implementation of Land Reforms: A Review by the Land Reforms Implementation Committee of the National Development Council*, p. 43.

TABLE 3
Bihar Land Revenue:
Demand and Collections

Year[a]	Current Demand (rupees)	Current Collections of Land Rent (rupees)
1956–1957	51,578,019	34,990,024
1957–1958	56,322,465	30,088,201
1958–1959	60,090,772	41,372,763
1959–1960	63,181,979	40,387,383
1960–1961	67,659,203	44,561,189
1961–1962	70,851,143	42,355,254
1962–1963	72,755,032	53,184,784
1963–1964	75,823,620	56,306,562
1964–1965	76,217,364	60,048,956
1965–1966	76,635,609	59,773,450
1966–1967	77,199,679	13,296,370

[a] As of August 1970 data for years subsequent to 1966–1967 were not available.

Source: Government of Bihar, Revenue Department, Land Ceiling Section, "Statement Showing Demand and Collection of Rent, Cess, Education Cess and Miscellaneous Incomes, Rate of Rent, Rent Potential, Compensation and Establishment Costs, Etc."

The slow progress in collections resulted mainly from the problems encountered in creating new rent records, where previously there were none maintained by the government. All that had been required prior to "zamindari abolition" was a record of the number of zamindars or intermediaries in the state and the rent payable by them. Even these records, however, were not reliable and up-to-date when the Bihar Land Reforms Act, 1950, was to be implemented. With the removal of the intermediaries' right to collect rent, the Revenue Department had to establish direct relations with landholders in more than 68,000 villages. The names of the raiyats had to be recorded together with the nature of their relationships to the land, and the rents payable by them to the state had to be determined. The out-of-date Survey and Settlement records were consulted, but were essentially useless. Field surveys (the process is known as "field bujharat") were initiated, and painfully slow progress was made in creating new rent rolls. Indeed, in 1963, thirteen years after the intermediaries had been legally "abolished" and the state placed in a direct relationship with its "tenants," the "field bujharat" (which is a much less precise business than Survey and Settlement operations) had not been completed and verified throughout the state.[30] What is more, this process had apparently not been completed as of December 1967.[31]

The failure of intermediaries, zamindars, and tenure-holders to provide the government with personal "estate records"[32] further impeded the implementation of the land reforms act of 1950. In many instances, the zamindars withheld (or did not have available) rent rolls pertaining to their intermediary interests. This was in spite of the fact that Sections 56 and 57 of the Bihar Tenancy Act of 1885 had entitled a tenant to a rent receipt on payment of rent and had stipulated that a landlord (zamindar) should "prepare and retain a counterfoil of the receipt."[33] Even if some of the zamindars' ancestors had complied with those provisions of the Bihar Tenancy Act, 1885, the chances were good that, with the lapse of time and in the absence of fully adequate storage facilities, such receipts as may have existed had become unreadable or reduced to dust. Others among the zamindars' ancestors had made no attempt to comply with the provisions of that nineteenth century tenancy act and had maintained for obvious reasons a tradition of "oral" leases with their tenants. In any event, few receipts were available for consultation in forming new rent rolls.[34]

The first phase (from May through September 1952) of the program to "abolish" intermediary interests and vest them in the state

[30] Ibid.

[31] Reliable information regarding the progress of field bujharat in Bihar is difficult to acquire. The government of Bihar may be sensitive on this issue. The author's statement is derived from a personal interview with Shri K. B. Sahay, former revenue minister and chief minister, December 7, 1967.

[32] "Estate records" are documents pertaining to their rights to land.

[33] India, Ministry of Food and Agriculture, *Agricultural Legislation in India*, VI, 66.

[34] Given the difficulties associated with completing field bujharat and with dealing with frequently obstructionist ex-intermediaries, it seemed possible throughout the 1950s and 1960s that new rent rolls would never be completed and authenticated. This seemed especially likely in the period immediately following the defeat of the Congress in the general elections of 1967 in view of pledges of multi-party successor governments to abolish the existing system of land revenue.

affected only 155 zamindars,[35] intermediaries whose gross annual incomes from their estates[36] had been in excess of Rs. 50,000.[37]

Bihar Land Reforms Act, 1950—Amendment (Bihar Act XX of 1954)

Implementation of the Bihar Land Reforms Act, 1950, continued to proceed slowly until 1954 when the Bihar Land Reforms (Amendment) Bill, 1953 (Bihar Act XX of 1954), removed some of the procedural impediments to more expeditious implementation of the 1950 act. Whereas the original act provided for individual notification of "proprietors" or "tenure-holders" that their estates had been vested in the state, the 1954 amendment act made possible the general notification of all intermediaries.[38] Instead of proceeding to "abolish" several hundred thousand intermediary interests in laborious fashion through individual notification, the state was now empowered to publish a proclamation signaling its intention to take over within a specified time all intermediary interests

[35] This information was obtained from documents made available through the courtesy of the Revenue Department, Government of Bihar, June 16, 1957.

In 1957, the Revenue Department estimated that, when the Bihar Land Reforms Act, 1950, was passed, there were at least 205,977 revenue paying, permanently settled estates in Bihar. Later, the Land Reforms Implementation Committee suggested that there were as many as 474,000 intermediaries affected by the act (India, Planning Commission, *Implementation of Land Reforms: A Review by the Land Reforms Implementation Committee of the National Development Council*, p. 43). The later figure may be inflated by the addition of thousands of "petty zamindars" and tenure-holders not included in the Bihar Revenue Department's 1957 estimate. The inflated figure may also reflect the subdivision of estates by intermediaries as a means of adding to the lands they were permitted to hold within the terms of the Bihar Land Reforms Act, 1950, as amended.

[36] "Estate" means "any land included under one entry in any of the general registers of revenue paying lands and revenue-free lands, prepared and maintained under the law for the time being in force by the collector of a district, and includes revenue-free land not entered in any register and a share in or of an estate." See "Bihar Land Reforms Act, 1950," Section 2, Clause (1). In *The Bihar Local Acts*, III, 2206.

[37] This information was obtained from documents made available through the courtesy of the Revenue Department, Government of Bihar, June 12, 1957.

[38] "Bihar Land Reforms Act, 1950," Section 3A. In *The Bihar Local Acts*, III, 2215.

located in any region of the state, or indeed all such interests in the state as a whole.[39]

In an attempt to assure that the intermediaries relinquished documents relating to their "estates" to the appropriate officials of the government, the amendment act provided for penalties to be imposed on those failing to do so. The district collector, for example, was empowered to levy fines—up to Rs. 500—on intermediaries who, following the general notification regarding the vesting of their estates, did not submit the necessary information regarding their holdings.[40]

The amendment act also tightened provisions governing the intermediaries' right to transfer and lease lands held by them prior to zamindari abolition legislation. Where, after January 1, 1946, zamindars were considered to have taken anticipatory action to circumvent the provisions of the Bihar Land Reforms Act, 1950, by transferring or fragmenting their interests for the purpose of defeating any provision of the act or causing loss to the state, the transactions could be annulled by the district collector (after suitable investigation).[41]

Similarly, the collector was empowered to inquire into cases in which zamindars ("at any time after the first day of January, 1946") reduced or remitted rents on their holdings with a view toward denying the state of Bihar its full share of land revenue. And, if the collector found that reductions or remissions of rent had been made to limit the effectiveness of subsequent legislation, he could cancel these and order restoration of the rents at their original rates.[42]

With the authority of the 1954 amendment act, some sections of the Bihar Land Reforms Act, 1950, were soon implemented, though it would be difficult for anyone other than a zamindar to suggest that the government moved precipitately at any stage during the long process leading to what is commonly—if somewhat incorrectly—referred to as the abolition of zamindari interests. In any event, the amendment act of 1954 made possible the general

[39] Ibid., Section 3B.
[40] Ibid.
[41] Ibid., Section 4, Clause (h).
[42] Ibid., Section 4, Clause (hh).

notification by which the remaining intermediary interests in Bihar were taken over, legally, on January 1, 1956. Yet, much remained to be done—in the face of inadequate land records, rent rolls, etc.—to assure meaningful administration of the Bihar Land Reforms Act, 1950, as amended. There continued to be strong opposition from the zamindars to all measures of agrarian reform in Bihar and steps continued to be taken by them to impede implementation of the enacted legislation.

Bihar Land Reforms Act, 1950—Amendment (Bihar Act XVI of 1959)

Within a few years another amendment act, Bihar Act XVI of 1959, was passed and received the assent of the president of India. This amendment act made further attempts to clarify the meaning of the original act and, belatedly, to eliminate loopholes that were impeding implementation of the 1950 act. The 1959 amendment act was another episode in the continuing struggle between the state, acting as the super-landlord to protect its interests, and the erstwhile landlords or intermediaries, whose interests had been assumed by the state. As such, the amendment act of 1959 continued to focus on the primary interests (land revenue and compensation) of the principal antagonists, rather than on the interests of the peasantry having a direct cultivating interest in the land. Nowhere in any of this "land reform" legislation were the interests of the landless laborers or "bataidars" (sharecroppers) considered. Such was never the intent of the act of 1950, or the amending acts of 1954 and 1959.

3. *Post-Abolition Position of "Zamindari Classes"*

Interests as Affected by the Act of 1950, as Amended

It is sometimes suggested, incorrectly, that (through the vesting of all intermediary interests in the state) the zamindars and tenure-holders of Bihar lost all rights in land. Such is not the case. Though the state assumed the right to collect rent directly from its tenants, rather than indirectly through these intermediary classes, and took over the interests of intermediaries in trees, forests, fisheries, minerals, mines, bazaars, etc., in addition to any buildings of an estate used, primarily, for rent collection purposes,[1] Sections 5, 6, and 7 of the Bihar Land Reforms Act, 1950, specifically provided for the retention by intermediaries of certain interests. These sections have not been altered in substance in the amendment acts of 1954 and 1959. The following are excerpts from these important sections of the act as amended.

[1] "Bihar Land Reforms Act, 1950," Section 4, Clause (a). In *The Bihar Local Acts*, III, 2219.

Section 5. (1) With effect from the date of vesting, all homesteads[2] comprised in an estate or tenure and being in the possession of an intermediary on the date of such vesting shall . . . be deemed to be settled by the State with such intermediary and he shall be entitled to retain possession of the land comprised in such homesteads and to hold it as a tenant under the State free of rent:

Provided that such homesteads as are used by the intermediary for purposes of letting out on rent shall be subject to the payment of such fair and equitable ground-rent as may be determined by the Collector in the prescribed manner.

(2) If the claim of an intermediary as to his possession over such homesteads or as to the extent of such homesteads is disputed by any person within three months from the date of such vesting, the Collector shall, on application, make such inquiry into the matter as he deems fit and pass such order as may appear to him to be just and proper.

Section 6. (1) On and from the date of vesting, all lands used for agricultural or horticultural purposes, which were in *khas*[3] possession of an intermediary on the date of such vesting, . . . shall . . . be deemed to be settled by the State with such intermediary and he shall be entitled to retain possession thereof and hold them as a *raiyat* under the State having occupancy rights in respect of such lands subject to the payment of such fair and equitable rent as may be determined by the Collector in the prescribed manner:

Provided that nothing contained in this sub-section shall entitle an intermediary to retain possession of any land . . . in respect of which occupancy right has already accrued to a *raiyat* before the date of vesting.

(2) If the claim of an intermediary as to his *khas* possession over lands referred to in sub-section (1) or as to the extent of such lands is disputed by any person prior to the determination of rent of such lands under the said sub-section, the Collector shall, on application, make such inquiry into the matter as he deems fit and pass such order as may appear to him to be just and proper. . . .

[2] "Homestead" means "dwelling house used by the intermediary for the purposes of his own residence or for the purpose of letting out on rent together with any courtyard, compound . . . and includes any out-buildings used for purposes connected with agriculture or horticulture and any tank, library, and place of worship appertaining to such dwelling house" (ibid., Section 2, Clause [j]).

[3] "Khas possession" refers to land cultivated personally by an intermediary or by his own stock or servants or by hired labor or with hired stock (ibid., Section 2, Clause [k]).

Section 7. (1) Such buildings or structures together with the lands on which they stand, other than any buildings used primarily as offices [for the collection of rent][4] . . . as were in the possession of an intermediary at the commencement of this Act and used as golas,[5] factories or mills, for the purpose of trade, manufacture or commerce or used for storing grains or keeping cattle or implements for the purpose of agriculture and constructed or established and used for the aforesaid purposes before the 1st of January, 1946 shall, notwithstanding anything contained in this Act, be deemed to be settled by the State with such intermediary and he shall be entitled to retain possession of such buildings or structures together with the lands on which they stand as a tenant under the State subject to the payment of such fair and equitable ground-rent as may be determined by the Collector in the prescribed manner.

(2) If the claim of such intermediary as to the possession over such buildings or structures, or lands on which they stand or as to the extent of such buildings, structures or lands is disputed by any person within three months from the date of vesting, the Collector shall make such order as may appear to him to be just and proper.

(3) Where a building or structure, constructed by an intermediary in his estate or tenure after the first day of January, 1946, is used for the purposes mentioned in sub-section (1), the intermediary shall be entitled to retain the possession of such building or structure together with the land on which it stands as a tenant under the State subject to the payment of the rent . . . if and only if the State Government is satisfied that such building or structure was not constructed or used for the aforesaid purposes with the object of defeating any provisions of this Act.

The key words of these "saving" sections were "khas possession" and "homestead." Note that "khas possession" referred not only to land cultivated personally by the intermediary, but also to lands cultivated by his servants, hired labor, or stock. This broad definition of possession allowed the ex-intermediary to claim land that he did not cultivate himself (prior to "zamindari abolition" legislation)—even though that land was in the personal, cultivating possession of a raiyat, so long as the raiyat did not possess the means (monetary or documentary) of establishing his right of occupancy.[6] Zamindari interests were quick to exploit the "khas possession"

[4] The phrase "for the collection of rent" is a paraphrase of the act's wording.

[5] "Golas" are structures used for the storage of grain, implements, etc.

[6] The "loophole" provided by the "khas possession" stipulation in the act has

provision of the act. They not only used this provision to evict, legally, their former "tenants" from lands traditionally cultivated by those "tenants," but also attempted to enlarge on the definition of "khas possession" in order to add "new lands" to the estates they planned to maintain, within the law, following zamindari abolition.

The attempt to enlarge the definition of "khas possession" received support, initially, from the Patna High Court. That court ruled that the term "khas possession" was broad enough to include what was referred to as "constructive possession" of land. This interpretation would have further expanded the right of the intermediary to recover possession of lands that were, in reality, in the actual possession of a raiyat on the date when the intermediary's estate had been vested in the state. Eventually, however, the Supreme Court overruled the "constructive possession" interpretation of the Patna High Court.[7] This fact notwithstanding, the "khas possession" provision has continued to make possible the legal eviction of uncounted thousands of raiyats in Bihar who cannot prove that they possess an occupancy right to the lands they have customarily tilled. In effect, the "khas possession" provision in the Bihar Land Reforms Act of 1950, as amended, has enabled even absentee zamindars to abuse grossly the interests of the cultivating peasantry. The existing social order in Bihar has been such that the peasant cultivators generally have been in a subservient position to the ex-intermediaries—even in a civil court. Moreover, the dominance of the ex-intermediaries outside the court has been indisputable. Pressures have been applied to assure that the "cultivating tenant" recognized that he had been working only as a personal servant of the zamindar, or even as his hired laborer. In this fashion, "actual cultivators" not only have lost possession of the lands they had tilled, but also, ironically, have sometimes continued to till the same lands under new leases that do not jeopardize the absentee zamindars' "khas possession" of the land.

---

been obvious to observers for years. See F. Tomasson Jannuzi, "Agrarian Problems in Bihar" (Ph.D. dissertation, London School of Economics and Political Science, 1958).

[7] See the Supreme Court decision, *Ramranvijoy Prasad Singh et al.* v. *Bihari Singh*, C.A. 195 (1961), decided on April 25, 1963.

In much the same fashion, the "homestead" provision of the act has served the interests of the ex-intermediaries. Note that homesteads could be retained rent-free by ex-intermediaries if the homesteads and the lands integral to them were used as private residences. And, in the event that an ex-intermediary decided not to occupy his homestead, he could rent it to someone else within the terms of the law—so long as he remembered to pay "fair and equitable ground-rent" himself to the state.[8] What constituted "fair and equitable ground-rent" was, in practice, a matter to be "negotiated" between the ex-intermediary and the district collector. Not infrequently, the collector could be persuaded to set the ground-rent at a level considered reasonable by the ex-intermediary. If an ex-intermediary was known to have political connections, a collector might show himself to be particularly amenable to the ex-intermediary's suasion.

To summarize, the saving provisions of the act (*a*) allowed the ex-intermediary to retain certain portions of his original estate as an occupancy raiyat (as a tenant of the state with occupancy rights), subject to the payment of rent to the state and (*b*) permitted the ex-intermediary to retain another portion of his estate rent-free. The loose definitions of the terms "khas possession" and "homestead" have been fully utilized by the ex-intermediaries, permitting some of them to retain all of the lands they held prior to abolition, excepting only those lands to which an occupancy raiyat had incontrovertible, documentary evidence in support of his claim. Consequently, it was possible, as recently as August 1970, to find ex-intermediaries in possession of estates comprised of 5,000 acres or more. Some were held loosely within the terms and conditions of the Bihar Land Reforms Act of 1950, as amended, and in the absence of effective implementation of later laws limiting the size of holdings. Others were evidence of the capacity of some of the more powerful zamindars to circumvent the legislation.[9]

[8] "Bihar Land Reforms Act, 1950," Section 5, Clause (1). In *The Bihar Local Acts*, III, 2224-d.

[9] When queried on this subject on December 7, 1967, the former chief minister, K. B. Sahay, confirmed the existence of such estates and admitted tersely that "the largest zamindars have managed to circumvent the legislation." Added Sahay in defense of his personal record, "I have tried to close some loopholes in the legislation, but my own party thwarted me."

Compensation for Intermediaries under the Act of 1950, as Amended

The Bihar Land Reforms Act, 1950, as amended in 1954, established that intermediaries, having lost the right to collect a share of the rent due the state, would receive compensation. The act set forth an intricate procedure to be followed by a "compensation officer," appointed by the state government, in computing the amount of compensation due an intermediary. The first task of the compensation officer was to determine the "gross assets"[10] of an intermediary's estate; the second was to determine the "net income"[11] of the estate by deducting (from the gross assets of the estate) "any sum which was payable as land-revenue or rent" to the state government for the previous agricultural year,[12] certain taxes when applicable, and a "cost of management allowance."[13] When the net income of an estate was determined, the amount of compensation could be computed according to table 4.

If there were mines or minerals among the interests of an intermediary, additional compensation was prescribed in the act.[14] Fi-

[10] The phrase "gross assets . . . when used with reference to an intermediary, means the aggregate of rents of such intermediary" in the agricultural year immediately preceding that in which the date of vesting falls. See "Bihar Land Reforms Act, 1950," Section 22. In *The Bihar Local Acts*, III. Because a large number of intermediaries did not provide the government of Bihar with documents pertaining to their estates (e.g., rent rolls necessary for the computation of the "gross assets" of an estate), compensation payments, initially, were delayed. Later, there were other factors (to be discussed) that impeded the flow of compensation from the government to the ex-intermediaries.

[11] "Net income" is determined for the year immediately preceding that in which the date of vesting falls (ibid., Section 23).

[12] Ibid.

[13] The "cost of management allowance" is determined by a rate fixed according to the gross assets of an estate as determined for the agricultural year immediately preceding that in which the date of vesting falls (ibid.).

The table used in the computation of the "cost of management allowance" is:

Gross Assets	*Rate*
Rs. 2,000 and under	5 percent
Rs. 2,001 to Rs. 5,000	7.5 percent
Rs. 5,001 to Rs. 10,000	10.0 percent
Rs. 10,001 to Rs. 15,000	12.5 percent
Rs. 15,001 and above	15–20 percent

[14] "Bihar Land Reforms Act, 1950," Section 25. In *The Bihar Local Acts*, III.

nally, the act stipulated that the total "amount of compensation so payable shall be paid in cash or in bonds, or partly in cash and partly in bonds. The bonds shall be either negotiable or non-negotiable and non-transferable and be payable in forty equal annual instalments . . . and shall carry interest at two and a half per centum per annum with effect from the date of issue."[15]

TABLE 4
Schedule for Compensation Payable to Ex-Intermediaries

Net Income	Rate of Compensation Payable
(a) Rs. 500 and under	Twenty times the net income
(b) Rs. 501 to Rs. 1,250	Nineteen times the net income, but not less than the maximum amount under item (a)
(c) Rs. 1,251 to Rs. 2,000	Eighteen times the net income, but not less than the maximum amount under item (b)
(d) Rs. 2,001 to Rs. 2,750	Seventeen times the net income, but not less than the maximum amount under item (c)
(e) Rs. 2,751 to Rs. 3,500	Sixteen times the net income, but not less than the maximum amount under item (d)
(f) Rs. 3,501 to Rs. 4,250	Fifteen times the net income, but not less than the maximum amount under item (e)
(g) Rs. 4,251 to Rs. 5,000	Fourteen times the net income, but not less than the maximum amount under item (f)
(h) Rs. 5,001 to Rs. 10,000	Ten times the net income, but not less than the maximum amount under item (g)
(i) Rs. 10,001 to Rs. 20,000	Eight times the net income, but not less than the maximum amount under item (h)
(j) Rs. 20,001 to Rs. 50,000	Six times the net income, but not less than the maximum amount under item (i)
(k) Rs. 50,001 to Rs. 100,000	Four times the net income, but not less than the maximum amount under item (j)
(l) Rs. 100,001 and above	Three times the net income, but not less than the maximum amount under item (k)

Source: Bihar Land Reforms Act, 1950 (as amended by Bihar Act XX of 1954 and Bihar Act XVI of 1959), Section 24. In *The Bihar Local Acts*, III.

As compensation payments lagged, pressures were brought to bear on the government to provide ex-intermediaries some interim

[15] Ibid., Section 32.

payments. Accordingly, the amendment act of 1959 contained provisions permitting the state compensation officer to make available "a sum not exceeding fifty per centum of the approximate amount of compensation" to intermediaries in circumstances in which prolonged delay in the payment of full compensation seemed likely.[16] Provision was also made for certain ad interim payments at the rate of 2.5 or 3 percent per annum of the estimated amount of compensation due an intermediary.[17] The former rate was to apply in situations in which ex-intermediaries might expect eventually to receive compensation in excess of Rs. 50,001 and the latter when total compensation was estimated to be less than Rs. 50,000.[18]

Notwithstanding the provisions outlined above, there were thousands of ex-intermediaries of Bihar who had not begun to receive compensation payments by the spring of 1968—sixteen years following initial attempts to implement the act of 1950. Precise data regarding this sensitive subject are not available. The Land Reforms Implementation Committee of the National Development Council released a report in August 1966 to the effect that the government of Bihar "appeared" to be making ad interim payments to 308,000 ex-intermediaries—that is to say, about 65 percent of the total number of ex-intermediaries in Bihar.[19] The report stated that these ad interim payments amounted to a total of approximately Rs. 138,500,000 out of an estimated total due of Rs. 200,000,000.[20] The committee had no information confirming the advance payment of up to 50 percent of the estimated amount of compensation to any ex-intermediary. It was able to report that such payments could have been made "only in a limited number of cases as the amount of 50 percent has been determined only in about 36 percent of the total number of cases."[21] The committee's report suggested that the government of Bihar had (by 1966) made payments totaling approximately Rs. 185,000,000 to ex-intermediaries, either as payment of final compensation or as payment of 50 percent of

[16] Ibid., Section 32A.

[17] Ibid., Section 33.

[18] Ibid.

[19] India, Planning Commission, *Implementation of Land Reforms: A Review by the Land Reforms Implementation Committee of the National Development Council*, p. 43.

[20] Ibid., p. 44.

[21] Ibid., p. 43.

the estimated amount of compensation due, while the amount due had earlier been estimated to be in the neighborhood of one billion rupees.[22]

Other sources provide contradictory data for the same general period ending in 1966. For example, the *Times of India Directory and Yearbook, 1967*, suggested that "ad interim" payments to ex-intermediaries amounted to Rs. 178,100,000 and that additional amounts totaling Rs. 318,600,000 (of the estimated Rs. 1,000,000,-000 total compensation due) had been paid in bonds, in cash, or by adjustment of arrears of various government dues. These figures were said to be valid through November 1966.[23]

In August 1970 unofficial records of the government of Bihar provided the data in table 5.

Though discrepancies in the data are obvious, all available sources agree that compensation payments to ex-intermediaries have in no way approached the estimated Rs. 1,000,000,000 total compensation due. Queried on this subject following the general elections of 1967, former Chief Minister K. B. Sahay not only confirmed that the state was far behind in making payments of any kind to ex-intermediaries, but also expressed doubt whether the ex-intermediaries would ever be fully compensated in accordance with the stipulated provisions of the legislation. Speaking apparently with the freedom of a politician out of office and in his twilight years, Sahay said, "We wrote those [compensation] provisions into the bills, but with no feeling for them. I have no doubt that these provisions will be scrapped in due course. And why not? If anything, the ex-zamindars should be asked to pay compensation to the raiyats."[24]

It appears that compensation payments will continue to lag. In an era of unstable governments following the end of Congress dominance in Bihar after the general elections of 1967, there seems little prospect that the complicated business of assessing and paying compensation will be speeded. Instead, as the years pass, it seems increasingly likely that some non-Congress or coalition government will decide to stop all compensation payments to ex-intermediaries.

22 Ibid.

23 *Times of India Directory and Yearbook, 1967*, ed. N. J. Nanporia, p. 410.

24 Shri K. B. Sahay, interview, Patna, Bihar, March 17, 1968.

Assessment of Post-Abolition Status of Ex-Intermediaries

In order to discuss the "post-abolition" status of the ex-intermediaries, some four hundred and seventy-four thousand in number, it is necessary to emphasize differentiations that must be made among them. Some, like the maharaja of Ramgarh, had been hereditary (and largely absentee) rulers of princely estates. By their own account, they were remnants of a traditional society that preceded the British-instituted formalization of the "zamindari system" by the Permanent Settlement of 1793. Other intermediaries with substantial interests in land had been equally removed from direct involvement with the cultivating peasantry and had long since established permanent homes in urban areas; these could be classified simply as "absentee zamindars." Their estates had been managed by servants or hired help. Their interest in the lands they held was periodic. It heightened when it came time to receive a substantial share of the produce. It was inconsequential for the remaining part of the agricultural year. There were, of course, some intermediaries with substantial interests in land who maintained a direct, managerial interest in their holdings. Some maintained residence in rural areas; others worked through estate managers. There were also many thousands of "petty zamindars" whose pre-abolition income from the land had been insufficient to permit them a parasitic life of leisure. In this general category were intermediaries whose "estates" had yielded the rupee equivalent of $200 or less per annum. Many so classified could be considered "resident zamindars" (and tenure-holders) who lived permanently in rural areas and supervised their interests personally, but usually at a distance from the plow. Others so classified had migrated to the cities of Bihar prior to the enactment of the land reforms act of 1950 and had acquired positions in the "services," frequently at clerical grades that permitted few frills and barely allowed the maintenance of an image of "middle-class respectability."

As mentioned above, there were intermediaries having substantial estates who had not remained apart from the land and had exercised relatively tight control over their holdings, either directly or through estate managers in residence in rural areas. In the post-abolition era, such intermediaries have shown an increasing pro-

TABLE 5
Compensation Payments to Former Intermediaries in Bihar

Year	Compensation in Bonds and Cash (rupees)	Interim Payments (rupees)
1953–1954	—	78,000
1954–1955	—	1,530,000
1955–1956	—	3,090,000
1956–1957	—	9,442,000
1957–1958	—	16,882,000
1958–1959	—	14,987,000
1959–1960	—	18,317,000
1960–1961	64,871,000	20,071,000
1961–1962	57,486,000	18,672,000
1962–1963	38,789,000	18,033,000
1963–1964	22,065,000	18,346,000
1964–1965	14,080,000	15,836,000
1965–1966	15,597,000	15,862,000
1966–1967	11,211,000	11,199,000
1967–1968	9,916,000	13,307,000
1968–1969	not available	
1969–1970	not available	
TOTAL	212,888,000	171,146,000

Source: This information was provided to the author by officials of the government of Bihar in August 1970.

pensity to take an interest in the development of their residual lands. Some of these have invested in tube-wells, other minor irrigation works, and tractors. Others have attempted to incorporate their holdings as model or experimental farms, often as a means of acquiring government assistance. Most within this general category have been able to retain large holdings comprised of their best lands (circumventing later legislation that, if it had been implemented, would have placed a ceiling on the amount of land they could hold) and to engage in some form of commercial farming. A few are prepared to admit that their incomes from land are greater in 1970 than in the years immediately preceding the act of 1950 and the vesting of their intermediary rights in the state.[25]

[25] See the case study for Village A for additional information concerning the post-abolition status of ex-intermediaries such as these, chapter 4, pp. 51–54.

There were also thousands of rural, petty zamindars (intermediaries who had had minimum rights in land and annual incomes from those rights of less than 1,000 rupees per annum). Their losses in the post-abolition period have been minimal, when considered in purely economic terms. Yet many in this general category have experienced diminished social status in the rural communities in which they live. Some of high caste claim that they have less command over labor than in the past. And, a few of these high-caste ex-intermediaries (retaining minimum post-abolition interests in land) envision the day when they will have to engage in manual labor themselves, rather than depend on the efforts of hired laborers. It is this threatened loss of status, more than the loss of income, that is most disturbing to them.[26]

The urban, absentee zamindar who derived a substantial amount of his annual income from his zamindari interests has been hard-pressed to maintain his earlier standard of life—the saving sections of the land reform act of 1950 notwithstanding. Even when he has successfully claimed possession of a portion of his former estate, he has generally experienced diminution of income from the land. He is no longer entitled to an intermediary's share of the produce, irrespective of the nature of his interest in the land, though he can derive income from lands that remain in his cultivating possession within the liberal terms of the legislation that is currently in force.

There are some urban ex-zamindars, of course, who can afford to take a positive view of their "post-abolition" status in society. Among them are those whose pre-eminence in the community has been due to long-established status in interest groups which have made the decisions that help to determine the nature of life for the people of Bihar, rich and poor alike. Ex-intermediaries such as these have managed to maintain a substantial measure of prestige and, on occasion, to enter business ventures with the active support of associates in the ruling elite. These ex-intermediaries have adjusted to the changed circumstances by severing their tenuous links with the countryside. For them, it has been sometimes expedient to give verbal support to various kinds of land reform, while main-

[26] See the case study for Village B for supplemental data concerning the impact of zamindari abolition on petty zamindars resident in rural areas, chapter 4, pp. 54–61.

taining that they have been unaffected by such changes in their traditional status as have occurred and that therefore they would not object to further changes.

Some urban ex-intermediaries have attempted to maintain their earlier standards of living by taking a closer interest in managing the lands they still hold. Especially in the late 1960s, a growing number of urban ex-intermediaries in Bihar began to engage in commercial farming (utilizing hired labor) on the lands they continued to hold in the post-abolition era. This trend may be associated with a growing awareness of the potential income to be derived from farming for those landholders with access to new inputs (chemical fertilizers, insecticides, hybrid seeds, etc.) and to urban markets—an income not yet subject to a national agricultural income tax.[27] However, in Bihar the numbers of urban, absentee ex-intermediaries who have begun to take a direct interest in the landholdings they retain are relatively few.

It has been more common for the urban, absentee zamindar (or ex-intermediary) to remain apart from the countryside—removed utterly from the decision-making that relates to the lands over which he exercises legal control, and from which he continues to derive some income. Having depended in the past on income from inherited zamindari interests, it has been difficult for him to accept the idea of becoming a "gentleman farmer." It has been equally difficult for him to adjust to the problems of deriving income from other means. His immediate concern, generally, has been to maintain outwardly the evidence of prosperity in the absence of his customary, intermediary's share of income. Delays in the payment of compensation, as earlier discussed, have made more formidable the problem of maintaining his earlier standard of living and social prestige. In some instances, savings have been consumed in order to preserve, at least for a time, an accustomed standard of consumption.

The following case study provides a personalized account of the behavior of an urban, absentee ex-zamindar who had depended, almost completely prior to the legislation, on income derived from

[27] In other parts of India—notably in the Punjab, Haryana, and western Uttar Pradesh—substantial numbers of urban, absentee landholders have begun to take an active personal interest in commercial farming. The trend is conspicuous in these states after 1965.

his zamindari interests. His is neither a "typical " nor "atypical" case, but it is nonetheless believed to be broadly illustrative of changes that have occurred in the lives of many urban, ex-intermediaries of Bihar.

Zamindar X—A Case Study[28]

Prior to abolition, Zamindar X was considered to be a man of substance. His family had held zamindari interests in Bihar for generations, and he had inherited portions of these interests worth Rs. 50,000 in net annual income. By 1950, Zamindar X was thirty years of age; he had married and had four children. He and his family lived in his ancestral home, a monolithic cement structure located in the "old city" of Patna, the decaying successor city to ancient Pataliputra, renowned in Indian history. Patna City had long since ceased to be reminiscent of Pataliputra in the days of Chandragupta Maurya. It was a congested urban slum comprised of crumbling buildings, narrow twisting streets, and open sewers—and was no longer a place in which to raise children, in the judgment of Zamindar X.

Several miles to the west was more spacious Patna, a British appendage to the old city and the seat of government in Bihar. In this new locality, in 1950, Zamindar X built a spacious, airy home with modern plumbing, western-type bathrooms, and terrazzo floors; it was outfitted for comfortable living in the style of the departed British administrators whom Zamindar X tried his best to emulate. Attached to the new house, he built a garage for his vintage American automobile. Though he owned another car, a Ford Prefect, the American car was a coveted possession, a symbol of affluence.

Zamindar X had a well-ordered and leisurely existence. He dabbled in the law. He spent a few hours at the old English club and attended an occasional meeting of the local unit of the international Rotary movement. The routine was punctuated, at specified times, by visits of his hired clerk or "patwari"—Zamindar X's rent collector and principal link with his lands and the peasantry who tilled them.

[28] This case study is based on numerous personal interviews with Zamindar X, his family, his associates, and his servants in the years following the partial implementation of the act of 1950, as amended.

In 1952, the orderliness of Zamindar X's life was changed abruptly. On August 17th of that year his intermediary interests were officially vested in the state. There were difficult adjustments to make, particularly in the year immediately following the date of vesting. Zamindar X began to take his law practice somewhat more seriously, but it remained an insubstantial source of income. His net annual income was reduced during that first year from more than Rs. 50,000 to less than Rs. 3,000. Moreover, he made no progress toward realizing compensation within the terms of the Bihar Land Reforms Act, 1950.

In 1953 his daughters finished school and were marriageable. According to the custom and because of his status in the community, it was expected that his daughters would be married with large dowries to prominent young men. The fact that abolition had deprived Zamindar X of his usual income would be incidental in determining the amount of dowry—unless the girls were to be married beneath their station. So, the girls were married, and with them went a joint dowry worth Rs. 150,000—a sum worthy of Zamindar X's pre-abolition status.

Fortunately for Zamindar X, there were no more daughters to be married. A portion of his savings was intact; he owned his urban home, and had been able to retain his khas and homestead lands in the country. There were also two automobiles, and, though the American car was a few years older and tended to burn too much oil and petrol, it remained a symbol of better days.

From 1954 through 1957, Zamindar X continued to live roughly in the manner to which he had been so long accustomed. His net annual income in those years remained less than Rs. 10,000, but he dipped into his savings when necessary to meet his social obligations.

As the years passed, Zamindar X talked about attempting to grow cash crops, particularly sugar cane, on his lands. But when he learned that the conversion to cash crops would necessitate investment by him, he preferred not to risk his own capital on the land and to continue to accept his customary share of the traditional produce from the lands in his "cultivating possession." Meanwhile, his link with the land and the peasants who tilled it remained the patwari, who supervised the cultivators and extracted his and the zamindar's share of the output. Something more than half of the produce went to the patwari and the ex-intermediary, the rest to the sharecroppers who worked the land.

In the 1960s Zamindar X began to receive some "ad interim" compensation payments, as prescribed in the 1959 amendment act, but he was increasingly conscious of the need to regulate strictly his expenditure. Though he continued to maintain his principal servants, four in number, he asked each to accept a reduction in salary. He reduced household expenditure for food. He even talked about selling his American car "because, after all, it is getting rather old."

How long Zamindar X can continue to maintain his traditional status in the community, while apparently making continuing adjustments toward a lower standard of living, is speculative. His law practice remains a questionable source of income in a country and region oversupplied with lawyers. His income from the lands he retains is less than it might be, but he has shown no inclination to assume the risks of investing in the land and becoming personally involved in its management. In essence, he remains as he was—an urban, educated, absentee landlord, though his economic and social status would appear to be slowly declining. His brightest hope may lie with his sons. Their educational advantages may someday qualify them for positions bearing both social prestige and high remuneration. Yet even this hope may prove illusory if we are witnessing the beginning of the end of a somewhat stable social system in Bihar in which the landed elites could assume a continuing predominance over the masses lower in the socioeconomic hierarchy.

4. Rural Reactions to Zamindari Abolition

Villagers' Expectations

The general purposes of the Bihar Land Reforms Act, 1950, as amended, together with the specific provisions of the act, were not well known in villages of Bihar intensively surveyed by the author.[1] Nor is there evidence that specific information regarding the meaning of agrarian reforms legislation has ever been disseminated purposefully in rural areas of the state by the government of Bihar. This seemed to be the situation in 1956–1957,[2] and there is no evidence that the government made attempts in the intervening years through August 1970 to inform the peasantry about the meaning of such reforms as were from time to time enacted into law. While new systems for the collection of land rent, the previously men-

[1] Generalizations made in the text regarding villagers' opinions of the Bihar Land Reforms Act, 1950, are based in part on interviews conducted by the author in selected villages in 1956–1957, 1966, 1967, 1968, and 1970. See Appendix for a description of the villages selected and a discussion of the selection criteria.

[2] F. Tomasson Jannuzi, "Agrarian Problems in Bihar" (Ph.D. dissertation, London School of Economics and Political Science, 1958), Chapter IV.

tioned process of field bujharat, and rumors (generated particularly during political campaigns) have undoubtedly made obvious to the peasantry that changes in the traditional land system are being made, it is significant that "no systematic attempt appears . . . to have been made to inform them in detail of the rights conferred upon them and the action they should take to avail of these rights."[3]

Having learned about land reform legislation mainly through nonofficial channels of communication, those who lived within the surveyed villages entertained confused notions about the meaning of the legislation. It was widely known that the government had "abolished zamindari interests," but there was imperfect understanding of what this meant. Some, particularly the few who were literate, had high expectations. These can be summarized as follows: first, it was understood that "forced labor"[4] on lands of the zamindar or tenure-holder had been abolished; second, it was understood that "high rents"[5] would be lowered; third, it was understood that the land reforms act would bring with it sweeping tenancy reform.

Among the enumerated expectations, the understanding that zamindari abolition would bring tenancy reform seemed to be most commonly held. Tenancy reforms meant different things to various classifications of villagers. The occupancy raiyats,[6] whose rights to land had been protected by the Bihar Tenancy Act of

[3] India, Planning Commission, *Implementation of Land Reforms: A Review by the Land Reforms Implementation Committee of the National Development Council*, p. 44.

[4] Whether large numbers of intermediaries in Bihar customarily used forceful methods on laborers working their (the intermediaries') estates is not known. However, forms of "forced labor" have existed in Bihar and were in evidence in some of the surveyed villages. Some landless laborers have been scarcely more than indentured servants, with rights akin to those of slaves on American plantations prior to the Civil War.

[5] The phrase "high rents" refers to the villagers' attitude toward rent in the rural areas surveyed.

[6] An "occupancy raiyat" has the rights that would usually go with ownership of land. However, the state retains legal ownership of land with the right to collect rent from the "occupancy raiyat." An occupancy raiyat cannot be ejected legally from his land except "in execution of a decree for ejectment passed on the ground that he has used the land in a manner which renders it unfit for the purposes of the tenancy, or that he has broken a condition consistent with the provisions" of the "Bihar Tenancy Act of 1885," Section 25 (in India, Ministry of Food and Agriculture, *Agricultural Legislation in India*, VI).

1885,[7] were the least concerned about tenancy reform. The non-occupancy raiyats, whose rights to land were insecure,[8] expected the tenancy reform accompanying zamindari abolition to mean that they would receive occupancy rights. Even the landless, who generally derived the major portion of their incomes from labor in the fields of a noncultivating zamindar or tenure-holder, had some expectations, generated by rumor, that they would be granted occupancy rights over some parts of the lands they cultivated as wage laborers.

Act's "Inadequacies"

Unfortunately for the villagers whose views on the legislation were ascertained, the Bihar Land Reforms Act, 1950, as amended in 1954 and 1959, was not designed to meet their expectations; nor could it have been, if it can be assumed that opposition to the act as passed would have been increased had there been provisions in it affecting meaningfully the occupancy rights of cultivating tenants, sharecroppers, and landless laborers. The record of long and difficult political and legal struggle necessary for the enactment and

[7] Ibid.

[8] "Insecure," as used above, refers, especially, to the ease with which the non-occupancy raiyat could be ejected by a zamindar (or the state). The ejectment provisions pertaining to non-occupancy raiyats are included in Sections 44 through 46 of the Bihar Tenancy Act of 1885. Excerpts from these provisions are presented below.

> *Sections 44 and 45.* A non-occupancy raiyat shall, subject to the provisions of this Act, be liable to ejectment on one of the following grounds, and not otherwise, (namely): (a) on the ground that he has failed to pay an arrear of rent, (b) on the ground that he has used the land in a manner which renders it unfit for the purposes of the tenancy, or that he has broken a condition consistent with this Act and on breach of which he . . . is liable to be ejected; . . . (d) on the ground that he has refused to agree to pay a fair and equitable rent determined under Section 46, or that the term for which he is entitled to hold at such rent has expired.
>
> *Section 46.* A suit for ejectment on the ground of refusal to agree to an enhancement of rent shall not be instituted against a non-occupancy raiyat unless the landlord has tendered to the raiyat an agreement to pay the enhanced rent, and the raiyat has, within three months before the institution of the suit, refused to execute the agreement.

If a fair and equitable rent, as determined by a competent court of law, is accepted by the raiyat, "he shall be entitled to remain in occupation of his holding at that rent for a term of five years from the date of the agreement," after which he is liable to ejectment unless he has acquired a right of occupancy (ibid., Sections 44–46).

partial implementation of the act of 1950 provides some documentation for the view that the act was the most progressive measure possible under the circumstances existing in Bihar at the time of the legislation. A state legislature controlled by essentially conservative forces, more concerned with the maintenance of the status quo than with the need for progressive change that might affect positively the relationship of the cultivating peasantry to the land, enacted legislation which was tailored to the interests of the ex-intermediaries and the super-landlord, that is, the state. The mass of the peasantry would have to wait a bit longer for the structural changes in the land system that a few were beginning to want.

Resultant Disillusionment

As information regarding the act began to filter down from the administrative heights in Patna to the districts and villages of Bihar, those who had had high expectations were most filled with disillusionment. New rumors replaced the old. Some observed cynically that the government had no intention of ending systems of forced labor on the lands of ex-intermediaries. Others saw the likelihood that land rent would be enhanced by the state to assure payment of compensation to ex-intermediaries.[9]

Cynicism deepened as time passed and the ex-intermediaries, in claiming khas possession of land, evicted peasants who had previously tilled the land and who had assumed that they had an occupancy right to the land and could not be evicted.[10] Even occupancy raiyats began to feel insecure, and with good reason if they had no

[9] There has been persistent talk among some economists and politicians of the need to tax the peasantry more heavily in order to meet the compensation payments provided for in the Bihar Land Reforms Act, 1950, and to secure additional revenue for state development projects. For example, K. B. Sahay said that land revenue needed to be doubled, at least. As Sahay put it, "The state is almost bankrupt and, despite all that is said to the contrary, I am convinced that the people have the capacity to pay enhanced land rent—but I would be quickly attacked by the opposition for daring to suggest this" (interview with Shri K. B. Sahay, former revenue minister, Patna, Bihar, March 17, 1968). Of course, the rumor mentioned in the text above that land rent would be enhanced as a consequence of the act of 1950 was no more than that; the act neither explicitly nor implicitly provided for increased rents.

[10] To claim khas possession of lands held by non-occupancy raiyats is legally in conformity with the provisions of Section 6 of the Bihar Land Reforms Act, 1950, as originally passed and as amended.

means of proving their right to the land they tilled personally or with hired labor.[11] Cynicism was soon replaced by fear as evictions grew in number and no man knew whether he had security of tenure. All evictions, whether achieved within or outside the law, were threatening to the peasantry and came to be considered by raiyats and under-raiyats alike to be infringements on their assumed "right" to hold indefinitely lands in their cultivating possession. An eviction notice was especially feared by the bataidars (sharecroppers), who realized that their only option was to join the ranks of the landless laborers.

Showing apparent responsiveness to the fears being articulated by a section of the peasantry, some legislators introduced a bill in 1954 which, if enacted, might have given increased security of tenure to a number of the weaker peasantry, especially those classified officially as "non-occupancy raiyats." In commenting on this proposed legislation, Daniel Thorner noted:

> The bill aimed to protect this group of very weak tenants against unlawful dispossession . . . [mainly]. As soon as these provisions were announced serious opposition developed, particularly to the clause conceding to the under-raiyat the right to obtain a summary inquiry for restoration of possession. The employees of the Secretariat of the Government of Bihar held a meeting to voice objection to the measure. Local bar associations attacked it as a threat to "proletarianize the middle classes." A prominent Congressman and Bhoodan worker, Mr. Baidyanath Choudhary, expressed fear that the land owners might lose their "right to cultivate the land themselves at any minute they may like. . . . Under the proposed legislation they would not be able to claim their land once let out to bataidars." (*Times of India*, 17 December 1954). Although the Chief Minister described the opposition to the bill as reactionary, and the Revenue Minister was reported to have said he would stake his career on the issue, the landlords carried the day. The measure was sent back for revision, i.e., put into storage.[12]

Evictions continued and fear was unabated in the countryside.

[11] To claim khas possession of lands held by occupancy raiyats is forbidden by Section 6 of the Bihar Land Reforms Act, 1950, as passed and subsequently amended. Hence, occupancy raiyats were legally protected if they could produce documents to support their claim. In the absence of such documents, they could, of course, be evicted—and many were.

[12] Daniel Thorner, *The Agrarian Prospect in India*, p. 33.

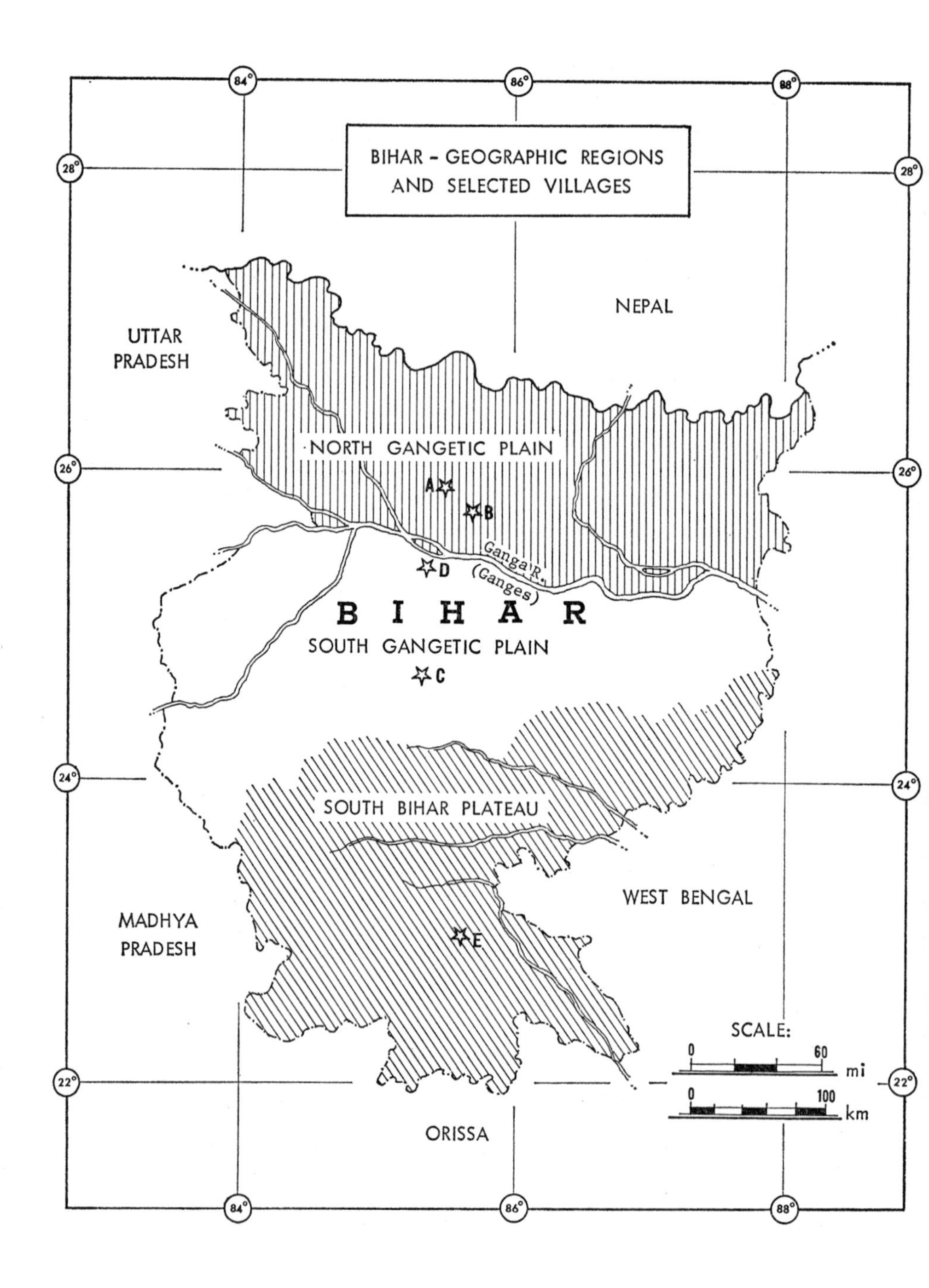
BIHAR - GEOGRAPHIC REGIONS
AND SELECTED VILLAGES
84°
86°
88°
28°
26°
24°
22°
NEPAL
UTTAR
PRADESH
NORTH GANGETIC PLAIN
A
B
D
Ganga R.
(Ganges)
B I H A R
SOUTH GANGETIC PLAIN
C
SOUTH BIHAR PLATEAU
WEST BENGAL
MADHYA
PRADESH
E
SCALE:
0
60
mi
0
100
km
ORISSA

Case Studies[13]

Village A: Muzaffarpur District—North Gangetic Plain

Prior to the act "abolishing" intermediary interests in Bihar, a single zamindar held an exclusive intermediary right over all land (six hundred acres approximately) in Village A. This zamindar, though a nonresident, had exercised full authority through his agents over the people who lived in the village and tilled his lands. Apparently because he was numbered among the leading zamindars of Bihar (having gross annual income from his several estates[14] in excess of Rs. 50,000), he was among those whose interests were first vested in the state in September 1952. In other words, he was one of the 155 zamindars in Bihar who were affected in the first phase of activity associated with attempts to implement the Bihar Land Reforms Act of 1950.

In December 1956, more than four years after the zamindar's interests were said to have been vested in the state, the situation in Village A was as follows.

First, the ex-intermediary had lost roughly 100 acres of his pre-abolition holding when some of his "tenants" were able to retain at least temporary possession (subject to the outcome of pending litigation) of lands they had tilled. These former tenants, representing sixty-one households, considered themselves to be "occupancy raiyats," and had begun to pay rent directly to the state. Their self-classification as occupancy raiyats did not eliminate the harsh reality that few among them were in possession of viable holdings; the size of an average holding per household was 1.65 acres.

Second, in accordance with the "saving provisions" of the Bihar Land Reforms Act, 1950, as amended, the ex-zamindar retained (either "rent-free" or under nominal rents not exceeding Rs. 7.00 per acre) 500 acres of land together with his "village residence" (in fact the home of his estate manager).

Third, whereas the villagers' total holding of 100 acres was divided into 361 separate units for cultivation, the ex-zamindar's homestead holding of 500 acres was unitary—comprised of contiguous plots.

[13] See Appendix for a fuller description of the villages from which the following data are drawn.

[14] "Estates" is used in this instance to refer to Zamindar A's holdings in Village A together with other holdings in north Bihar.

Fourth, twelve households, formerly tenants of the zamindar, had been evicted from his "homestead lands" and had become landless laborers with no option but to till the zamindar's lands for wages.

Fifth, neither the sixty-one landed nor the twelve landless households in the village had managed to achieve economic independence of the zamindar. It remained necessary for both groups to work for some portion of their incomes as wage laborers on the homestead lands of the ex-zamindar. Moreover, daily wages for men had been lowered from 1 rupee, 2 annas (the rate prior to zamindari abolition), to 10 annas since the enactment of the reform legislation. Where daily wages for women had been 12 annas in 1952, they were 8 annas in 1956. And wages for child labor had been reduced from 6 annas to 3 annas.[15]

Sixth, whereas, prior to 1952, some portions of the zamindar's holding had been used for the production of rice and wheat, in 1956 the ex-zamindar's entire holding was cropped in tobacco and sugar cane—favored cash crops in that period.[16]

Finally, of the sixty-one raiyats who had begun to pay rent to the state for the lands they claimed, forty-one had paid rent in 1955 and 1956 at newly assessed rates said to be 6 percent higher than those paid previously to the zamindar. Since rents paid by the raiyats were not to have been increased within the terms and conditions of the 1950 act, but were to have been continued at the same level, there had obviously been some confusion surrounding the amount of rent due. The confusion may have derived from the process of commuting rent in "kind" into rent in "cash." It is possible, also, that the revenue collector had begun to assume illegally an "intermediary's" share of the rent (a practice requiring

[15] In 1956, the landed families had per capita gross annual incomes of approximately Rs. 76, the landless, only Rs. 51. Though income data were not compiled for the households of Village A during revisits in 1968 and 1970, the author's impression was that the standard of living of the people had not improved; wages for labor, paid mainly in kind, were constant at 1956–1957 levels; and the condition of the landless in particular seemed to have deteriorated.

[16] In 1968–1970, wheat of a hybrid variety (grown for sale as seed) had become the new cash crop, following the Bihar "famine" of 1965–1967 and the growing popularity in north Bihar of high yielding varieties of wheat.

an increased assessment of rent, if the collector were to turn over to the government the full rent shown on newly created rent rolls). However explained, the fact was that the former tenants of the zamindar were convinced that the government was raising land rents.

The villagers interviewed in December 1956 viewed "zamindari abolition" with mixed feelings ranging from bitterness to apathy—bitterness from disappointment that the ex-zamindar retained 500 acres of land and a dominant place in the community, bitterness from discovering that they had to continue to pay rent at rates at least equal to those previously paid to the zamindar, and apathy from the belief, reinforced by the experience of some, that they had not been affected tangibly by "zamindari abolition." Though thirteen respondents (ten representing landed households and three landless) suggested that they had benefited indirectly from zamindari abolition, their views were based, at least in part, on the belief that Village A's ex-zamindar (a Congress member of the Bihar State Legislature) would be denied the right, eventually, to retain land as a nonresident of the village. In other words, they were anticipating the ex-zamindar's divestment of his homestead and khas lands and the subsequent distribution of those lands among the villagers. Their wishful thinking was in some measure induced by a local representative of the Communist party of India (C.P.I.). It seemed more than coincidence that the thirteen respondents who saw beneficial effects flowing from zamindari abolition claimed to be communists.

Fourteen landed respondents were of the opinion that the effects of zamindari abolition had been personally injurious. These respondents supported their views by citing the facts of increased rents[17] and lower wages for labor on the lands of the ex-zamindar. They linked such developments to zamindari abolition.

The majority of the respondents (forty-four out of seventy-three) considered the effects of zamindari abolition to be neither injurious nor beneficial. The majority view was partially summed up by the village elder who said, "Our condition is one of not having enough in our bellies to have the strength to be concerned about

[17] As previously noted, an increase in rent due to the government was reported in the village.

our position. Lower wages for labor, higher rent for land—these make little difference. We are already poor."

Table 6 summarizes the views of villagers (as disclosed in a complete enumeration survey in which the headman of every household was interviewed) in Village A as to whether zamindari abolition affected them personally.

TABLE 6
Zamindari Abolition: Opinion in Village A

Number of respondents		Column I[a] (beneficial)	Column II[b] (injurious)	Column III[c] (neither)	Column IV[d] (no comment)
Landed	61	10	14	37	0
Landless	12	3	0	7	2
	—	—	—	—	—
TOTAL	73	13	14	44	2

[a]In column I are recorded the views of respondents who considered zamindari abolition to be (in its broad effect) personally beneficial.

[b]In column II are recorded the views of respondents who considered zamindari abolition to be (in some way) personally injurious.

[c]In column III are recorded the views of respondents who considered zamindari abolition to be (in its broad effect) neither personally injurious nor beneficial.

[d]In column IV are recorded the views of respondents who expressed no opinion on the subject of zamindari abolition.

Village B: Darbhanga District—North Gangetic Plain

Prior to the abolition of all intermediary interests in Bihar, thirty families in Village B[18] had enjoyed intermediary rights, either as tenure-holders or as petty zamindars, to collect rent from tenant cultivators. With the basic right of collection went some measure of social prestige. Indeed, to the intermediary classes of this village, the status value was greater than the economic value of their interests. None of those holding intermediary interests in the village received a net annual income from them of more than Rs. 50. Even so, the intermediary classes of the village were distinctly predominant, both economically and socially. In addition to rights in land,

[18] There were ninety-three households in the village. Fifty-two were landholding households.

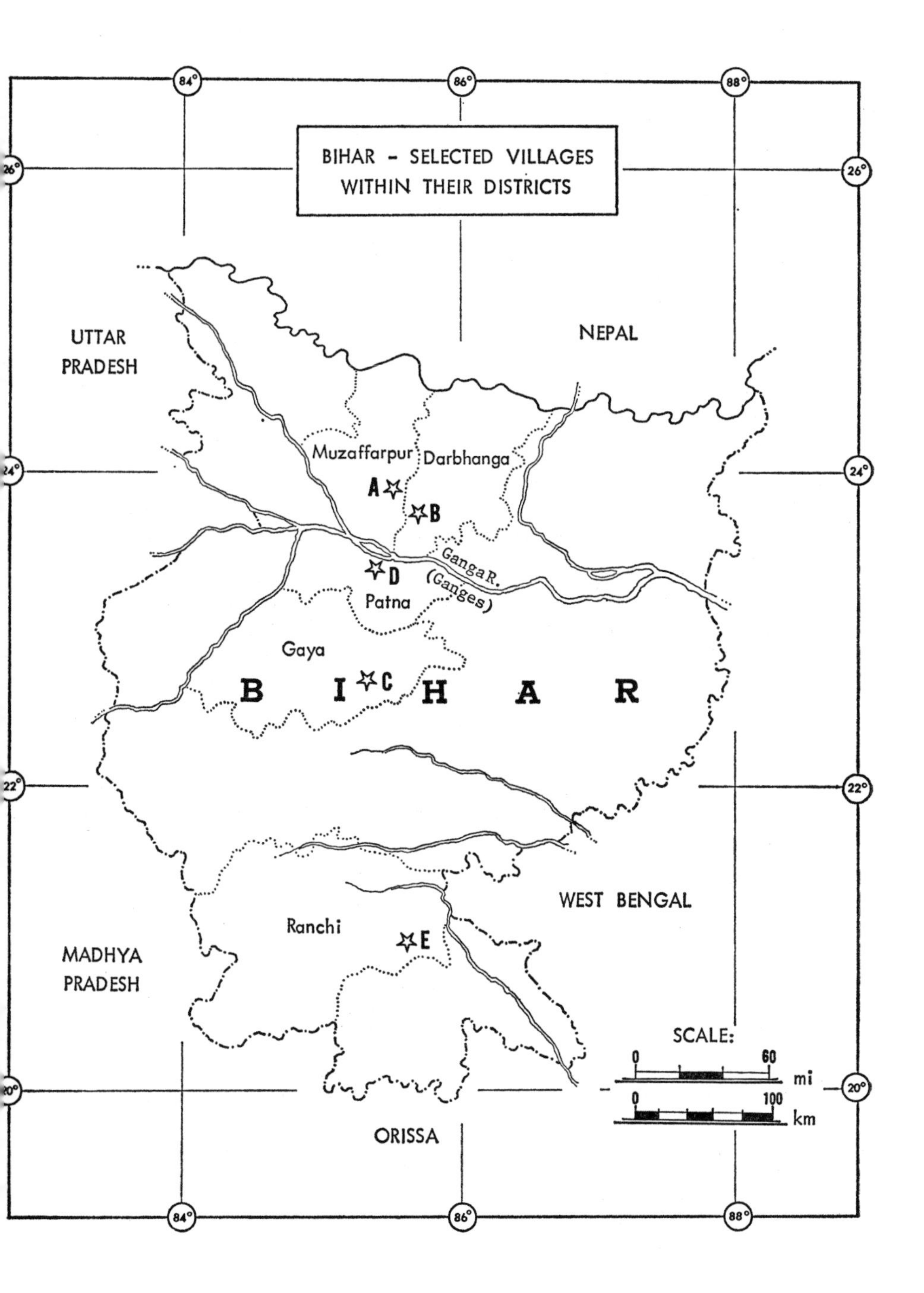
BIHAR - SELECTED VILLAGES
WITHIN THEIR DISTRICTS
84°
86°
88°
26°
24°
22°
20°
UTTAR
PRADESH
NEPAL
Muzaffarpur
Darbhanga
A
B
D
Ganga R.
(Ganges)
Patna
Gaya
C
B I H A R
WEST BENGAL
Ranchi
E
MADHYA
PRADESH
ORISSA
SCALE:
0
60
mi
0
100
km

the intermediaries had savings and money to lend; for them, moneylending was a subsidiary means of income. They owned the most substantial homes. Moreover, the intermediaries were of high caste; twenty-eight of the thirty were Brahmans; two were Koiriis.

The intermediaries' advantages, both social and economic, were enhanced by the large supply of available, cheap labor in the village, especially among the lower castes. No Brahman needed to prejudice his status by touching a plow or engaging in other forms of manual labor. There were forty-one households of landless laborers[19] available to till the lands of the intermediaries and to perform other agricultural functions at daily wages of seldom more than twelve annas per person.[20]

"Zamindari abolition" had affected the lives of the people of Village B, although the effects were not obvious in 1956–1957. As a group, the ex-intermediaries claimed a continuing right to 172.25 acres of their total pre-abolition holding of 221 acres.[21] Twenty-two households (formerly tenants of the thirty intermediaries, now claiming to be raiyats with a responsibility to pay rent directly to the state) had succeeded in establishing (with the intermediaries) their right of permanent occupancy on a total of 48.75 acres. Nevertheless, the ex-intermediaries appeared to have maintained their social and economic predominance in the community.

The landless laborers were still lowest in the socioeconomic hierarchy and earned the major portion of their incomes from work in the fields of the ex-intermediaries or other landholders. The relative difference in standard of living between landed and landless was apparent. In the agricultural year immediately preceding the survey of the village, the landed had a per capita gross annual income of 115 rupees as compared to a per capita gross annual income of 47 rupees for the landless.

Few in Village B (only six respondents) felt that they had gained from the abolition of zamindari interests, while a substan-

[19] The landless laborers were mainly of low caste; therefore, it was not unusual for women and children to work with men. Among higher castes, women and children tend to be non-earning dependents.

[20] In 1956–1957, the men received approximately twelve annas a day, while women and children could seldom expect to get more than ten annas. Seasonal wage fluctuations were reported to be small.

[21] The retained lands were claimed as "homesteads" or "khas possessions" within the terms of the act of 1950, as amended.

tially greater number (nineteen respondents, seventeen of them former intermediaries) considered zamindari abolition to be personally injurious. A majority (fifty-six respondents among a total of ninety-three) considered the effects of abolition to be neither particularly beneficial nor injurious to them. The remaining respondents, twelve in number, registered no views on the subject. Table 7 shows the views of villagers (as disclosed in a complete enumeration survey in which the headman of every household was interviewed) as to how or whether zamindari abolition affected them personally.

TABLE 7
Zamindari Abolition: Opinion in Village B

Number of Respondents		Column I[a] (beneficial)	Column II (injurious)	Column III (neither)	Column IV (no comment)
Ex-intermediaries	30	2	17	10	1
Other landed	22	1	2	17	2
Landless	41	3	0	29	9
	—	—	—	—	—
TOTAL	93	6	19	56	12

[a] See notes to table 6.

The fact that the majority of the landless laborers (twenty-nine) reported that they had received neither personal benefit nor injury from the effects of zamindari abolition might have been expected. The Bihar Land Reforms Act, 1950, as enacted and later amended, contained no provisions designed to affect them directly. On the other hand, probing the views of the twenty-nine revealed the common opinion that, in the long run, the community would benefit. This widely shared view was based on the assumption that future initiatives of government would provide for the landless of the village some other means of earning a living than working on the fields of the landed. The fact that three landless laborers did feel that they had received personal benefit as a by-product of the abolition of intermediary interests was explained by their clearly enunciated antipathy for the intermediary classes. Discussion with them revealed that they had received no substantial personal benefit, but that they were pleased to see the intermediaries hurt. The fact that none of the landless laborers felt personally injured by abolition was explained in part by the fact that, because the Brahmans (who still held their homestead and khas lands) were unwilling to touch the plow, the landless had not suffered loss of work. On the other hand, some of the landless, having stated that they had neither been benefited nor injured by zamindari abolition, did report that the ex-intermediaries were offering lower wages and demanding higher interest on loans. The nine landless laborers who made no comment concerning zamindari abolition were cooperative, but maintained that their status in the community did not qualify them to answer. Their general position seemed not to be one of self-denigration, but rather one of bewilderment at being asked by an outsider to comment about a subject that seemed remote and for them, as landless laborers, irrelevant.

The interviewed landholders, who were not ex-intermediaries, did not differ substantially from the landless in their reactions to zamindari abolition. Most of them were small cultivators who worked their own fields, occasionally drawing on the landless to supplement their own labor during the planting and harvesting seasons. Among the poorer of the landed raiyats it was customary to work as wage laborers on the fields of the ex-intermediaries in order to supplement their incomes. It should be noted that the largest number of the landed raiyats (17) considered the effects of abolition to be neither personally injurious nor beneficial. This was indicative not only of their personal views, but also of the fact that zamindari abolition had not affected them substantially as a group. Where they had been permanent occupancy raiyats paying rent to the intermediaries, they would now be permanent occupancy raiyats paying rent to the state. Only two of the raiyats, as their views indicated, had been affected adversely when parts of their lands were claimed as khas lands of ex-intermediaries. One raiyat felt that the abolition had been personally beneficial. He had received broad supervisory powers over the homestead and khas lands retained by his Brahman ex-intermediary. The two raiyats who made no comment claimed "noninvolvement."

In 1956–1957, despite the apparent post-abolition predominance of the ex-intermediary classes, many of the Brahman ex-intermediaries felt that their power in the community had diminished. This perspective was reflected in the views of the seventeen who reported that the abolition of their intermediary interests had been the result of discriminatory action against their caste and class. The more articulate of the Brahman ex-intermediaries made no attempt to disguise the bitterness they felt. Zamindari abolition threatened their traditional life style. Barely suppressed rage and fear of change seemed to permeate their attitudes as they associated zamindari abolition with the undermining of their authority in a village context in which that authority previously had not been questioned. Some ex-intermediaries reported that they had already been made an object of abuse by lower castes and classes—even by some of the landless. It was said by others that zamindari abolition infringed on their traditional, and therefore permanent, rights in land. Several Brahmans stated that zamindari abolition had "made the landless more difficult to recruit for work in our fields." One elderly Brahman, referring to the diminished authority of Brahmans in the village (diminished authority directly linked to zamindari abolition in his mind), feared that his son would someday have to cultivate the land himself and lose status in the process. The prospect of continuing diminution in authority and status among Brahmans was clearly more frightening to him than the state's assumption of his rent-collecting right.

Not all Brahman respondents accepted the notion that zamindari abolition meant declining status for the Brahman ex-intermediaries. One-third of the Brahman ex-intermediaries were prepared to argue that the state's acquisition of their intermediary interests had been neither personally injurious nor beneficial. They maintained that their situation in the community was unchanged—that their traditional status was neither enhanced nor diminished by events associated with zamindari abolition. Close inspection of their personal circumstances revealed supporting evidence for their arguments. All seemed likely to hold onto their best agricultural lands following zamindari abolition. None seemed likely to experience a meaningful diminution of income following loss of their intermediary rights. None, in the post-abolition period, had experienced diminished capacity to acquire sufficient amounts of labor to meet their needs. Thus, none had been compelled by changed circumstances to engage personally in manual labor or to touch a plow. For these Brahmans, at least, the traditional pattern of life seemed sustainable—at least for a time.

However, the power of the Brahmans in Village B did wane perceptibly in the years 1956–1957 through August of 1970. Whether their behavior was directly attributable to zamindari abolition or not, lower castes (particularly the Koirii landholders) increasingly threatened the traditional dominance of the Brahmans in Village B. By the early 1960s a Koirii had replaced a Brahman as the generally recognized headman of the village.

In the light of the subsequent ascendancy of the Koiriis, it is noteworthy that the only ex-intermediaries in 1956–1957 who stated that zamindari abolition had been personally beneficial to them happened to be Koiriis. In confirming their position at that time, it had been apparent that no material benefits had accrued to these Koiriis that could be associated with the state's assumption of their intermediary interests. Thus, their recorded enthusiasm for zamindari abolition seemed to be related instead to a complex of factors associated with their expectation that the social and economic gap between themselves and the Brahmans would be more easily narrowed in the post-abolition era—given the Brahmans' sense of diminished status following zamindari abolition; given the caste cohesiveness of the Koiriis in Village B; and given the Koiriis' already developed links (in 1956–1957) with local representatives of government responsible for providing rural development assistance.

In 1956–1957, Village B had graduated (following three years of development work) into the post-intensive phase of the government of Bihar's Community Project schedule. The Koiriis had already been recognized as the leading cultivators (if not the leading caste) of the village, and it had been toward them (rather than the Brahmans with their known aversion to cultivate personally their own lands) that the early efforts of rural development workers had been directed. The ten Koirii households in Village B had received new seeds and implements from the government and had been the first cultivators to try new agricultural techniques, including the then fashionable "Japanese method" of growing rice. Their general receptivity to new ideas and techniques was encouraging to Community Project officials, so the Koiriis received additional benefits. The Koiriis themselves were well aware of their favored status in the eyes of government. Several readily commented on the fact that no faction in the village had received more aid than they. While the Brahmans had also received some assistance, they seemed to be less receptive to new ideas and unwilling generally to innovate on their own lands with their own labor. This no doubt contributed to their lack of rapport with local representatives of government. At the same time, it is possible that the Brahmans not only earned the reputation of being less cooperative and receptive than the Koiriis, but also were the victims of conscious discrimination exercised by rural development workers of low, rather than high, caste. In any event, the flow of government assistance tended to benefit the Koiriis at the expense of the Brahmans, as well as others in Village B.

Such other landholding elements as there were in the village had small, fragmented plots and were unable to take meaningful advantage of local programs of rural development. The landless, of course, had no land on which to apply new ideas or techniques, even if they had wanted to do so. And the landless would not have dared to experiment with new inputs on lands they tilled for ex-intermediaries or others. Such initiatives would have been striking departures from the traditional manner in which the landless related to the land and would have been unlikely even with the encouragement of any landholder who might, in rare circumstances, permit a landless laborer to sharecrop some land with the understanding that (*a*) primary risks of production would be assumed by the laborer, not the landholder, and (*b*) 50 percent or more of the produce would be turned over by the laborer to the landholder.

Given the above circumstances, the Koiriis of Village B were in a strong position in 1956–1957 both to benefit from such assistance as was intruded into the village from outside and to consider zamindari abolition legislation a welcome initiative on the part of the state—an initiative, as they perceived it, curtailing Brahmanical authority and facilitating the growth of the Koiriis' social prestige and economic power.

Village C: Gaya District—South Gangetic Plain

Prior to zamindari abolition, there had been in Village C, as in Village A, a single absentee zamindar. With the implementation of the act of 1950, as amended, the zamindar lost his right to collect rent from thirty households of permanent occupancy raiyats cultivating a total of 99.06 acres. Also, at a time roughly coincident with the implementation of the 1950 act, he donated 44.75 acres of previously fallow (rent-free) lands to the Bhoodan (land gift) movement. Nevertheless, in the post-abolition period, he continued to be both the largest landholder in the village (with khas and homestead holdings totaling roughly 200 acres) and the person above all others consulted on matters affecting the conduct of the community's business. Local wages and rights in land, for instance, were mainly determined by the ex-zamindar in 1957, and his position of dominance was unchanged through March of 1968.[22]

After the implementation of the act of 1950, there were three major groups in the village: the raiyats (thirty households) who, having proved their right of permanent occupancy, held a total of 99.06 acres and were obligated to pay rent directly to the state; the Bhoodan landed (forty-four households) who, having received a total of 44.75 acres of Bhoodan land, hoped to receive government recognition of permanent occupancy status; and the landless (fourteen households). The raiyats, who had a per capita gross income of 95 rupees in 1956, cultivated their own lands, hiring labor occasionally, and earned the major portion of their incomes from the produce of their own holdings. The Bhoodan landed, who had a per capita gross income of 50 rupees in 1956, had average holdings of approximately 1 acre per household and needed to work for the major portion of their incomes as hired laborers on the lands of their neighbors or on those of the ex-zamindar. The remaining group, the landless, worked as hired laborers either in Village C or in neighboring villages. In 1956, the landless had a per capita gross income of only 48 rupees.

Though the zamindar received notice in 1954 of the vesting of his intermediary interests in the state, it was not until April 1957 that the government attempted to assume the right to collect rent in this village. For a period of three years, therefore, no rent was collected in Village C. By 1957, rent-paying raiyats of the village had assumed that a permanent remission of rent had somehow been achieved. The government officer who subsequently appeared in the village to collect rents was rejected initially and for some months the raiyats refused to meet government demands for rent. In time, however, it became fashionable to pay rents on the assumption that government rent receipts would be a means of assuring permanent occupancy rights in land.

[22] This was confirmed during the author's most recent visit to this village in March 1968.

Among the thirty occupancy raiyats of Village C, nine considered zamindari abolition to be (in its broad effect) personally beneficial. None considered the effects to be in any way personally injurious. Sixteen suggested that the effects were neither personally injurious nor beneficial. Five expressed no opinion. The nine who claimed personal benefit seemed to believe that land rent had been "abolished." The sixteen undecided landholders had been hopeful that land rents had indeed been abolished, but were shaken by the persistence of the government rent collector.

Among the forty-four Bhoodan landed respondents, forty-two were of the view that they had personally benefited from the effects of zamindari abolition. It is assumed that their answers reflected two things, mainly. First, the rents due to the government for the Bhoodan lands had not been determined and, hence, had not been collected. Second, the Bhoodan landed associated their receipt of land from the local zamindar with zamindari abolition.

The majority of the landless (nine out of fourteen respondents) suggested that they were neither personally benefited nor injured by the effects of abolition. Four landless respondents were convinced that they had been injured by zamindari abolition. These respondents were from the fourteen landless households who failed to receive Bhoodan lands. Their exclusion from the Bhoodan program seemed to have become confused in their minds with the effects of zamindari abolition.

Table 8 shows the views of respondents in Village C (as disclosed in a complete enumeration survey in which the headman of every household was interviewed) as to how or whether zamindari abolition affected them personally.

Village D: Patna District—South Gangetic Plain

Village D is a community in which small intermediary interests had been held by thirty absentee zamindars and tenure-holders. There were no resident zamindars or tenure-holders in the village. Notification of the vesting of intermediary interests in the state was made here in January of 1956.

The major groups of the village were the landed (sixty households), all of whom claimed to be occupancy raiyats and recognized their obligation to pay rent to the state (at rates equal to those formerly paid to the intermediaries), the landless cultivators

TABLE 8
Zamindari Abolition: Opinion in Village C

Number of Respondents		Column I[a] (beneficial)	Column II (injurious)	Column III (neither)	Column IV (no comment)
Landed (raiyats)	30	9	0	16	5
Bhoodan landed	44	42	0	0	2
Landless	14	0	4	9	1
TOTAL	88	51	4	25	8

[a] See notes to table 6.

(twenty-one households),[23] and the landless non-cultivators (fifteen households).[24]

Table 9 shows the views of respondents of Village D (as disclosed in a complete enumeration survey in which the headman of every household was interviewed) as to how or whether zamindari abolition affected them personally.

The sixteen landed respondents who felt that they had personally benefited from zamindari abolition represented fourteen Rajput and two Yaddava households. Generally, their point of view was expressed by the Rajput headman of the village who said that he had grown tired of paying "tribute" to numerous absentee zamindars and tenure-holders and looked forward to a new era in which he could cultivate his lands with the assurance that he would no longer be pestered by many landlords, each demanding his fractional intermediary's share of the produce in rent. Implicit in the headman's statement, in the view of another Rajput, was the hope that government would collect rent in the village at rates no higher than in the past and that there would be some advantage to raiyats in making a single annual payment to the state instead of having to pay rents annually, at varying rates, to several intermediaries for minute parcels of land.

[23] The designation "landless cultivators" is applied in this village only to the landless who worked for the major portion of their incomes as agricultural laborers.

[24] The designation "landless non-cultivators" is applied in Village D to the landless who owned shops in the local bazaar and did not earn a major portion of their incomes as agricultural laborers.

TABLE 9
Zamindari Abolition: Opinion in Village D

Number of Respondents		Column I[a] (beneficial)	Column II (injurious)	Column III (neither)	Column IV (no comment)
Landed	60	16	15	25	4
Landless (cultivators)	21	0	0	11	10
Landless (non-cultivators)	15	4	0	2	9
TOTAL	96	20	15	38	23

[a] See notes to table 6.

Fifteen landed respondents considered zamindari abolition to be personally injurious. These respondents were convinced that the government would be a more capricious landlord, less lenient, for example, about defaulted payments of rent than the former intermediaries. Several noted that it had been possible under the old system to have payments deferred, if one had a close personal relationship with a zamindar or tenure-holder. For these, apparently, a close or personal relationship with the state or its agents seemed unlikely. Indeed, they worried openly about the implications of the new system when, on some future occasion, a crop failed or famine threatened. They feared that the state's revenue demand would be constant, irrespective of conditions in the agricultural sector, and that their weaknesses in negotiations with the new "super landlord" would be much more pronounced than in earlier dealings with absentee zamindars or tenure-holders.

The majority of the landed respondents (twenty-five) saw some marginal advantages (in 1956–1957) in no longer having to bother with the intermediaries, but also suggested that more time would need to elapse before they could state with certainty whether or not they were personally benefited or hurt by the vesting of intermediary interests in the state.

The landless cultivators (those earning the major portion of their incomes from work as agricultural laborers on the fields of the larger Rajput and Yaddava landholders) claimed no personal benefits from zamindari abolition. At the same time, none of them considered the effects of abolition to be personally injurious. Having no rights in land and little prospect of acquiring any, it made little difference to them whether or not the interests of intermediaries had been assumed by the government of Bihar.

Because the landless non-cultivators in Village D had had no direct experience of the zamindari system, their comments, as recorded in table 9, lacked conviction as well as supporting arguments.

Village E: Ranchi District—South Bihar Plateau

When Village E was first surveyed in 1956–1957, its aboriginal inhabitants lacked basic knowledge of "zamindari abolition" and the Bihar Land Reforms Act of 1950. These villagers, essentially non-agriculturists, were culturally, linguistically, and geographically removed from the plains villages of the Gangetic region of north and south Bihar. Their customary relationships to the jungle plateau lands in which they lived were not only markedly different from those of the mainly Hindu plainsmen to the north, but also were delimited by a different legal code pertaining to rights in land —the Chota Nagpur Tenancy Act of 1908.

Though they had not experienced the zamindari system as it had developed in the "permanently settled" region of north Bihar, the villagers nonetheless had strong feelings about three absentee landlords—non-aborigines from the north who had dubious claims to rights in land in their village.

In this general context, the author's questions regarding the effects of "zamindari abolition" in the village were not relevant except in the sense that they exposed local fear of government and suspicion of outsiders generally. Clearly, if government had the power to abolish landlords, then government had the capacity to alter the aborigines' customary rights in land, particularly the right to forage in forest or jungle lands which had vested in the state. Because it had been the practice for generations of aborigines to depend partially on the wild produce of the jungle for subsistence, and because the people of Village E had vague notions of their khunt-katti rights[25] in land, they speculated that government might

[25] Khunt-katti rights, as defined in the Chota Nagpur Tenancy Act of 1908, are rights in land "reclaimed from jungle by the original founders of [a] vil-

be preparing to deny them their rights in land or to modify other traditional rights in some fashion. A few claimed to have heard rumors that the state planned to restrict their movement in forest lands (controlled nominally by the state), ostensibly as a means of preventing the continuing deforestation of the South Bihar Plateau region. So, in a climate of rumor and suspicion of government,[26] "zamindari abolition" became a "personally injurious" initiative of government for the overwhelming majority of respondents (thirty-five out of forty-one). The concept of zamindari abolition was negatively symbolic, signifying the power of the state to intervene in their affairs, as it had done in the case of the zamindars.

Table 10 shows the views of respondents in Village E (as disclosed in a complete enumeration survey in which the headman of every household was interviewed) as to how or whether zamindari abolition affected them personally.

TABLE 10

Zamindari Abolition: Opinion in Village E

Number of Respondents		Column I[a] (beneficial)	Column II (injurious)	Column III (neither)	Column IV (no comment)
Landed	41	0	35	0	6
Landless	0	0	0	0	0
TOTAL	41	0	35	0	6

[a] See notes to table 6.

Ironically, the aboriginals of Village E claimed to be up-to-date in payments of land rent to the state. It was considered wise to be paying rent to the state at prevailing low rates before Survey and Settlement operations were completed in the district. This was seen as a means of "assuring" that rates as low as one rupee per acre would be confirmed and maintained in the future.

lage or their descendants in the male line" ("The Chota Nagpur Tenancy Act." In *The Bihar Local Acts*, I, 400).

[26] This was reflected in the general elections of 1957 when the people of Village E were said to have voted unanimously for the local Jharkand party, a party that stood against the Congress on the "forest rights" issue and also sought a separate identity for their aboriginal constituents from the state of Bihar.

5. *Ceilings on the Size of Agricultural Holdings*

The principle that there should be in India an absolute limit to the amount of land that an individual might hold was commended in the First Five Year Plan,[1] endorsed by official committees of government,[2] and made national policy. The Second Five Year Plan not only proposed the introduction of ceilings on existing agricultural holdings, but also recommended ceilings on future acquisitions of land.

It remained for the various constituent units of the Republic in the 1950s and 1960s to respond to the central government initiative by framing and implementing ceilings legislation. With the states exercising final authority over the nature, extent, and timing of such legislation, the pattern of response among the states varied enormously. There was no national consensus regarding the purposes of legislation to limit the size of agricultural holdings. Each

[1] India, Planning Commission, *Second Five Year Plan*, pp. 193–194.

[2] See, for example, India, Planning Commission, *Reports of the Committees of the Panel on Land Reforms*, pp. 95–110.

state established its own definition of a maximum holding and its own regulations affecting the implementation of ceilings legislation. Some state governments proceeded, with a minimum of debate, to enact their ceilings laws. Others, such as the government of Bihar, employed various means—procedural and legislative, as well as overtly political—to delay the enactment and implementation of any such legislation that might alter the long-established agrarian structure of the state by eroding the power of the landed elite.

The Pros and Cons of Ceilings Legislation

In Bihar, as elsewhere, various arguments were advanced for imposing ceiling limitations on landholdings. The three most common arguments rested mainly on the assumption that, since the supply of land was limited in relation to the number of people who wanted land, social justice required the redistribution of existing landholdings both to satisfy land hunger and to reduce inequalities in the control and use of land resources.

An extreme position was held by those who believed that economic considerations were subsidiary to the social need for land reform. It followed from this point of view that ceilings legislation should be enacted and implemented mainly to enable government to acquire and distribute to the landless "surplus land" derived from limiting the size of family or individual holdings. In this fashion, it was argued, the hunger of the landless for a plot of land could be met, their dependence for employment on the landed reduced, and the inegalitarian nature of rural society modified. The proponents of this view were in many respects similar in motivation to the ex-socialist and Gandhian intellectuals who supported the Bhoodan movement. Their goals were articulated in similar fashion. Their commitment to the ideal of social justice was similar. Their belief in the need for radical redistribution of the state's land resources was similar, as was their unwillingness or inability to reconcile that belief with the hard facts of Bihar's adverse man-to-land ratio. They glossed over the question of whether "surplus lands" actually existed in Bihar in an amount sufficient to satisfy the land hunger of the peasantry, while stressing the need to satisfy that land hunger. They ignored (at least in their public statements) the economic implications of a land redistribution program —for example, the possibility of decreased production at least in the short run—while stressing existing economic inequalities in rural areas. They presented ceilings legislation as a panacea to the problems of rural India.

A related argument was that there should be no place in the Bihar agrarian scene for large landholders (particularly ex-intermediaries retaining large tracts of "homestead" and "khas" lands) who functioned as absentee landlords and assumed few risks of production while demanding and getting as much as 50 percent or more of the produce from the actual tillers of the soil. Those who assumed the primary risks of production, said the proponents of this argument, should have more secure rights in land. This would be possible if low ceilings were established, and if the legislation were designed to give security of tenure to the many tenants and sharecroppers cultivating lands without protected occupancy rights. Implicit in this argument was that ceilings legislation should directly affect tenancy relations and provide new security to thousands of under-raiyats and bataidars. With security of tenure guaranteed, it was assumed that the former tenants and sharecroppers would have added incentive to produce and, if provided liberal credit facilities, would successfully farm units which at first might appear to be uneconomic. From this point of view, ceilings could be associated with the goal of increased production, as well as social justice.

It was suggested by others that ceilings legislation need not mean the abandonment of the supposed economies of scale associated with production on consolidated large holdings. Surplus lands acquired through implementation of ceilings on existing landholdings could be distributed to landless cultivators and farmed jointly by them. Those who held this view sometimes referred to the likelihood that there would be insufficient surplus lands made available for distribution to the peasantry as a result of ceilings legislation then contemplated. If government were then to attempt to distribute such lands equitably to all who wanted them, the result would be the proliferation of individual holdings, likely to be of uneconomic size, especially when tilled according to the prevailing traditional methods of agriculture in Bihar. Distribution of the surplus land to individual cultivators could be contemplated, they argued, only if attempts were made to assure that the lands were pooled for purposes of cultivation and farmed jointly or cooperatively. The feasibility of establishing joint cooperative farming societies in Bihar was not at issue among proponents of this view. At issue was not only the question of social justice, which they believed could be addressed in part simply by granting peasants individual parchas or titles to land (however small in total area and fragmented the units), but also the question of implementing agrarian reforms that would assure production increases—considered to be possible only if large, consolidated units of land were tilled jointly, and preferably according to capital intensive methods of production.[3]

Briefly, the three most common arguments against ceilings legislation were the following: It was suggested that even the most rigorously enforced, low ceilings on landholdings would not make available sufficient "surplus land" to satisfy the land hunger of Bihar's legions of landless agricultural laborers.

It was suggested that ceilings on holdings might lead to a reduction in the production of foodstuffs by fragmenting economic holdings (from which marketable surpluses were common) and thus increasing the number of uneconomic, subsistence holdings (from which marketable surpluses were rare).

It was suggested, furthermore, that there would be, as a consequence of ceilings legislation, social as well as economic disruption of rural areas. It was thought likely by proponents of this view that the traditional, landed elites would devise means of evading the effects of such legislation, even if it were enacted. This anticipated behavior of those holding land above the ceiling would, in turn, alienate segments of the peasantry who would have been encouraged by the legislation and the rumors surrounding it to anticipate receiving new rights in land. Tensions between landed and landless, high caste and low, would mount, and disruption of the rural economy and the seeming "equilibrium" of the traditional pattern of life would become inevitable. From this perspective, then, to oppose ceilings was to opt for rural stability and order. To favor

[3] Some proponents of joint cooperative farming were members of the Communist party in India, at that time a party united rather than split into rival factions as in contemporary India. Others were not. When the efficacy of ceilings legislation was being debated in the 1950s, it will be remembered that advocates of joint cooperative farming on surplus lands (to be generated by laws setting a ceiling on landholdings) found it convenient, therefore, to allude to Chinese agrarian reforms as they attempted to establish a case for joint cooperative farming in Indian conditions. (See, for example, ibid., pp. 144–170.)

ceilings was to opt for instability and disruption of the traditional mode of life.

Provisions of the Bihar Agricultural Lands (Ceiling and Management) Bill, 1955

The above arguments notwithstanding, a ceilings bill was eventually framed in 1955 and referred to committee. It was called the Bihar Agricultural Lands (Ceiling and Management) Bill. This bill would probably not have been put forward by the government of Bihar but for the pressure generated and sustained by the then revenue minister, K. B. Sahay. In addition to maneuvering behind the scenes within the high command of Bihar's ruling Congress party, Sahay marshaled his own arguments for the public record in favor of ceilings legislation.

> About eighty-six per cent of the total population of this State is dependent upon agriculture for its livelihood. Owing, however, to limited availability of land for cultivation and the existing inequitable distribution [of it] . . . about thirty per cent of the agricultural population of the State is landless and a vast bulk of the rest own fragments which prove far too uneconomic for efficient cultivation. One of the ways to provide land to the agriculturists of this class is to fix ceilings on individual holdings and to distribute the lands in excess of the ceiling to them.
>
> Most of the landholders do not cultivate all their lands themselves and employ sub-tenants to bring the same under cultivation. . . . Such an arrangement, by which large areas of land are cultivated through sub-tenants, is not conducive to efficiency in agricultural production. It has been found by experience that unless the land is owned by the tiller his incentive to production does not reach the optimum point. . . . [If] surplus lands are taken away from the landholders and distributed to landless workers or holders of uneconomic fragments it will contribute to efficiency in agricultural production.[4]

The principal provisions of the Bihar Agricultural Lands (Ceiling and Management) Bill, 1955, are listed below, together with suggestions submitted by the Select Committee to which the bill was referred.

The bill proposed[5] that "the ceiling area of a landholder having a

[4] Bihar, Laws, statutes, etc. (Bills). *Bihar Agricultural Lands (Ceiling and Management) Bill, 1955*, "Statement of Objects and Reasons."

[5] Ibid., Chapter II, Clause 6.

family[6] consisting of five members or less, including himself," should be thirty or fifty acres depending on the locality of his holding. If the members of the family of a landholder exceed five, an area of eight and one-third acres or five acres, depending on the locality of the holding, would be added for each additional member of the family to the ceiling area fixed under this section; but in no case would the total ceiling area so fixed exceed three hundred acres. The bill provided, further, that when a landholder had lands in more than one locality of the state, he would have the option of having his ceiling area in one or divided among several localities.

The Select Committee suggested that the ceiling area should be adjustable according to the quality of the land involved. The ceilings that were recommended varied from twenty-five acres for certain irrigated lands (Class I lands) to seventy-five acres for "hilly, sandy, or other lands not yielding paddy or rabi crop or any cash crops, such as chillies, sugar cane or tobacco" (Class IV lands).[7] If, at the time of the commencement of the bill, the "number of members of the family of a landholder exceeds five, an area of five acres of Class I Land or its equivalent area of any other classes of land specified . . . shall be added for each additional member of the family to the ceiling area of the landholder. In no case shall the total ceiling area of the landholder exceed three times the ceiling area"[8] for the class of land he holds. The committee suggested that, after the commencement of the act, no person shall acquire any land so as to make the total area of his holding in excess of the ceiling for a family of five.[9] In other words, at the commencement of the act, the size of a man's family would be considered a factor in determining his personal ceiling; after the commencement of the act, a man could not increase the size of his holding beyond the ceiling set for a family of five, no matter how large his family might be.

[6] "In this sub-section, the family of a land-holder includes the land-holder, his wife, his son and son's son and their wives, dependent parents of the land-holder, and unmarried daughter and sister of the land-holder and those of his son or son's son" (ibid.).

[7] Bihar, Laws, statutes, etc. (Reports). *Report of the Select Committee on the Bihar Agricultural Lands (Ceiling and Management) Bill, 1955*, Chapter II, Clause 6.

[8] Ibid.

[9] Ibid., Chapter II, Clause 11.

The Select Committee suggested, further, that "any land forming part of a homestead having an area of not more than ten acres, exclusive of the area occupied by any building standing thereon, shall be excluded for the purpose of determining the ceiling area,"[10] and that "lands held separately by different members of the family of a landholder shall be deemed, for the purposes of fixing the ceiling area under this section to be lands held by the landholder."[11]

According to Clause 11 of the Bihar Agricultural Lands (Ceiling and Management) Bill, 1955, it would be possible for a landholder to hold lands in excess of his personal ceiling, so long as he held less than three hundred acres and so long as he farmed his "excess" lands in "accordance with the principle of good husbandry."[12] In other words, the landholder could hold excess lands so long as in the opinion of the prescribed authority, he maintained "a reasonable standard of efficient production."[13] Should the landholder fail to maintain efficient standards of production or to comply with certain directives of the prescribed authorities regulating his standard of cultivation and management, he could voluntarily give up possession of his land to the prescribed authority or "join a registered co-operative farming society, if formed and in operation in the area where his land lies, under such terms and conditions as may be mutually agreed upon."[14] A landholder, having failed to comply with certain directives regulating his standard of cultivation and management and having failed to give up, voluntarily, possession of the land in question, could be dispossessed, temporarily, of the land, the land being taken over and managed "either directly or, on such terms as may be prescribed, through a registered co-operative farming society or through other landholders or landless agricultural laborers."[15]

It should be noted that a landholder who was dispossessed of his land would lose his rights in respect to the land for a period "not exceeding five years,"[16] after which period the land would be re-

[10] Ibid., Chapter II, Clause 6.

[11] Ibid.

[12] Bihar, Laws, statutes, etc. (Bills). *Bihar Agricultural Lands (Ceiling and Management) Bill, 1955*, Chapter III, Clause 11.

[13] Ibid.

[14] Ibid., Chapter III, Clause 13.

[15] Ibid., Chapter III, Clause 14.

[16] Ibid., Chapter III, Clause 17.

stored to his possession.[17] During the period of management of the land by the prescribed authority, "the profits received from the land shall be paid in the first instance towards all rents and liabilities for the time being incurred in respect of the land and the cost of management and cultivation of the land and the residue shall be applied towards the annual payments," as determined by the prescribed authority, due to the dispossessed landholder.[18]

The bill proposed, further, that "where a landholder holds land in excess of three hundred acres, such excess shall be acquired by the State Government on payment of compensation to the landholder. The amount of compensation payable by the State Government to the landholder for lands acquired . . . shall be ten times the amount of rent payable by the landholder for such land."[19]

The Select Committee suggested that under no conditions should a landholder be allowed to hold land in excess of his personal ceiling. If a landholder holds land in excess of his personal ceiling, as determined according to the quality of his land and the number of people in his family, such land should vest "in the State free from all encumbrances and the landholder shall be entitled to compensation, at the rate of seventy-five rupees per acre of Class I Land" and at lower rates for poorer classes of land, the lowest payment being fifteen rupees per acre in the case of Class IV land. The compensation would be payable in three annual installments.[20]

The bill proposed that "where a landholder holds land in excess of three hundred acres, such excess shall be acquired by the State on payment of compensation to the landholder"[21] and shall be settled with landless persons[22] on such terms as may be prescribed.

The Select Committee suggested that, where a landholder holds

[17] Ibid., Chapter III, Clause 21.

[18] Ibid., Chapter III, Clause 22.

[19] Ibid., Chapter IV, Clause 23.

[20] Bihar, Laws, statutes, etc. (Reports). *Report of the Select Committee on the Bihar Agricultural Lands (Ceiling and Management) Bill, 1955*, Chapter II, Clause 7.

[21] Bihar, Laws, statutes, etc. (Bills). *Bihar Agricultural Lands (Ceiling and Management) Bill, 1955*, Chapter IV, Clause 23.

[22] "Landless person" means, in this section, a person "(i) whose main source of livelihood is agriculture or agricultural labor or who undertakes in writing to employ himself on lands settled with him under this act; and (ii) who does not hold any land or holds land not exceeding such area as may be prescribed" (ibid., Chapter IV, Clause 25).

land in excess of his personal ceiling, such lands should be vested in the state and "settled with landless persons on such terms and conditions as may be prescribed."[23]

Shelving of the Bihar Agricultural Lands (Ceiling and Management) Bill, 1955

The Bihar Agricultural Lands (Ceiling and Management) Bill, as proposed or as modified in committee, did not prove to be acceptable to the numerous opponents of ceilings legislation. So deep were the divisions within the ruling Congress concerning the proposed legislation that the government of Bihar was unable for several years to develop support sufficient to pass any version of a law limiting the size of agricultural holdings in the state. The original bill, as proposed and as modified in committee, was put into storage, where it remained until new legislation was framed during the first months of the 1960s.

The shelving of the first ceilings bill gave opponents of such legislation additional time to devise means of circumventing legally future legislation having the same intent. The shelving also gave weight to arguments that broader support for future ceilings legislation would have to be engendered if any ceilings on landholdings were to be enacted. Given the structure of power in Bihar, this meant that Bihar's landholders would be deeply involved in determining the content of future legislation designed to establish ceilings on agricultural holdings. A diluted version of the original ceilings bill became more likely than a version having stringent provisions affecting the interests of the landed elite.

Following the tabling of the first ceilings bill, the energies of Bihar's ruling elite were absorbed in political machinations associated with the impending general elections of 1957. While the maintenance of Congress dominance could be assumed, the future structure of power within that political institution could not be. Accordingly, the most ruthless electoral struggles were among men ostensibly united under the Congress umbrella. The decisive battles went on behind the scenes in "the smoke filled rooms" of Patna. Caste, factional, and personal alliances were established, reestablished, and broken. Not surprisingly, the turbulence within the

[23] Bihar, Laws, statutes, etc. (Reports). *Report of the Select Committee on the Bihar Agricultural Lands . . . Bill, 1955*, Chapter II, Clause 9.

Congress party of Bihar led to a number of electoral upsets. The most prominent casualty within the Congress was the man who had spearheaded agrarian reform legislation in the state and who had introduced the Bihar Agricultural Lands (Ceiling and Management) Bill, 1955. With K. B. Sahay's defeat in the general elections of 1957, it seemed likely that ceilings legislation in Bihar would be further delayed for an indefinite period. The forces opposing ceilings were now fully mobilized and powerful. The ex-intermediaries, having been threatened by the Bihar Land Reforms Act of 1950, were even more determined to oppose future legislation that might erode their rights in land. The Congress itself was fragmented among opposing groups and seemed unable to establish a working consensus that might make possible the enactment and implementation of ceilings on holdings. The proponents of ceilings were limited in number and lacking in power, having not yet realized that their numbers and power might be enhanced if attempts were made to mobilize segments of the peasantry in behalf of agrarian reforms. Opponents and proponents of ceilings were alike in that they waged their struggle apart from the peasant masses, the then "silent majority" in Bihar. Whatever the outcome of the struggle, the peasantry would be acted upon by higher authority. Changes in their social and material condition were to be effected by others above them in the hierarchy.

In these circumstances, the government of Bihar waited until 1961 to put forth a new version of the original ceilings bill—a version with sufficient loopholes to satisfy the most militant opponent of the earlier draft legislation. With a minimum of debate, the new ceilings bill, the Bihar Land Reforms (Fixation of Ceiling Area and Acquisition of Surplus Land) Act, 1961, was enacted into law. The principal provisions of the new law, also known as Bihar Act XII of 1962, are summarized in the following section.

Provisions of the Bihar Land Reforms (Fixation of Ceiling Area and Acquisition of Surplus Land) Act, 1961

The act of 1961 established a variable ceiling on landholdings to be based in each instance on an assessment of the quality of land in the possession of a landholder. Within the terms of reference of the act, the agricultural lands of Bihar were considered to be of five classes. The finest lands (Class I) were those irrigated by flow irrigation works constructed, maintained, improved, or controlled by central, state, or local governmental institutions. Next in quality, Class II lands, were those irrigated by "lift" irrigation works or tube wells constructed or maintained by the central, state, or local governmental institutions. Class III lands were those used for orchards or for other horticultural purposes. Class IV lands were those subject to "diluvian or alluvion on account of any change in the course of a river" or lands between two embankments constructed to control a river, as well as any lands earlier so classified within the terms and conditions of the Bengal Survey Act of 1875.[24] Lands of poorest quality, Class V, were those considered hilly, sandy, or incapable of yielding paddy, rabi, or cash crops.

Having thus classified the lands of the state, the act of 1961 stipulated that a "person" would be permitted to retain possession of no more than (*a*) twenty acres of Class I land; (*b*) thirty acres of Class II land; (*c*) forty acres of Class III land; (*d*) fifty acres of Class IV land; or (*e*) sixty acres of Class V land.[25]

However, there were numerous supplementary provisions in the act designed to permit a landholder to retain lands in excess of the ceiling provisions. For example, a landholder could retain, in addition to his ceiling area, lands forming part of his "homestead" not exceeding ten acres in area. He could retain all established structures together with the lands on which they stood, and such other lands as might be considered by the appropriate local authority (in this instance the collector) necessary for the use and enjoyment of his homestead lands. He could retain any land in consolidated blocks (not exceeding fifteen acres in area) used for growing fodder at the time of the act's commencement and destined to be used for that purpose in future. Moreover, a landholder with more than four dependents could retain lands in excess of his ceiling area[26] pro-

[24] These Class IV lands are also referred to officially as "Diara Land."

[25] For the purposes of the act, 1.00 acre of Class I land was considered to be equivalent to 1.50 acres of Class II, 2 acres of Class III, 2.50 acres of Class IV, or 3 acres of Class V land. See "Bihar Land Reforms (Fixation of Ceiling Area and Acquisition of Surplus Land) Act, 1961," Section 5. In *The Bihar Local Acts*, III.

[26] Under this provision a landholder was permitted to hold lands not exceeding one-fifth of his ceiling area for every dependent exceeding four—so long as he retained no more than twice the area of his ceiling holding, as otherwise specified.

vided that the aggregate of lands held by him would in no case exceed two times his specified ceiling area.

Other provisions of the act permitted a landholder to transfer (within one year following the commencement of the act) any lands held by him as a raiyat to any person or persons who might have inherited the land or have been entitled to a share of it at his death. In other words, either prior to the commencement of the act or subsequent to it within a period of twelve months, a landholder with lands in excess of the ceiling could transfer his excess lands to sons, daughters, children of his sons or daughters, or others within the terms and conditions of the act of 1961—the only limitation being that the aggregate of lands held by the recipients not exceed, in each instance, the ceiling area specified by the act.[27] With this provision, the act permitted a landholder to retain within his "extended" family lands greatly in excess of his own ceiling area.

Moreover, the ceilings act of 1961 was not designed to apply to all who enjoyed occupancy rights in land. Its provisions, for example, were not to apply to (*a*) lands previously donated to the Bhoodan (land gift) movement, (*b*) lands held by educational institutions, and (*c*) tea plantations. Also, by special order of the government as prescribed in the act, properly licensed sugar-cane farms could be exempted from the ceiling provisions.

The act of 1961 contained provisions that permitted landholders to resume for "personal cultivation"[28] lands within their ceiling areas being cultivated at the commencement of the act by tenants or under-raiyats who were unable to establish that they were entitled to permanent occupancy of the lands they tilled. That is to say, any landholder who was himself an occupancy raiyat within the terms and conditions of the Bihar Tenancy Act of 1885 could eject legally any of his "tenants" who were non-occupancy raiyats (as defined by the Bihar Tenancy Act of 1885) and therefore not entitled to permanent security of tenure. Moreover, having ejected his former tenants, he could satisfy the "personal cultivation" cri-

[27] "Bihar Land Reforms (Fixation of Ceiling Area and Acquisition of Surplus Land) Act, 1961," Section 5, Clause 5. In *The Bihar Local Acts*, III.

[28] "Personal cultivation" means "cultivation by a raiyat himself or by members of his family or by servants or hired laborers on fixed wages payable in cash or kind but not in crop-share under his personal supervision or the supervision of any member of his family" (ibid., Section 2, Paragraph [i]).

terion fixed by law simply by having the same under-raiyats till the same lands as hired laborers on fixed wages, rather than as "tenants" or even as sharecroppers.

This right of the landholder to resume lands for personal cultivation from his tenants was not without qualification. The landholder's right to resume lands for personal cultivation from an under-raiyat holding in excess of ten acres was qualified to permit the under-raiyat to retain at least five acres. Similarly, a landholder's right to resume lands for personal cultivation from an under-raiyat holding less than ten acres was qualified to permit the under-raiyat to retain at least half of his total area. Finally, the act's provisions were protective of the right of the under-raiyat to retain the lands on which his grass or mud hut stood together with at least one acre of land or the entire area of such land held by him if it were less than one acre.

In addition to those provisions which permitted a landholder to resume lands for "personal cultivation," broadly defined to permit the use of hired laborers, the ceilings act of 1961 permitted the landholder, under specified conditions, to sublet any land within his ceiling area for a period not to exceed seven years on any one occasion. Having permitted subletting, the act limited the amount of rent in kind payable by the tenant to the landholder or raiyat to no more than one-fourth of the produce, and the landholder was denied any share in the straw or bhoosa[29] that might exist as a by-product of agricultural production on the leased lands. Other important provisions relating to the subletting of land made clear that no sublessee (or tenant) who tilled the lands of a raiyat (whose lands were no more than those permitted by the ceilings legislation) could ever hope to acquire an occupancy right to such lands, irrespective of the duration of his tenancy. The act also made explicit provision for the ejectment of the sublessee by a landholder (*a*) for failure to pay an arrear of rent; (*b*) for using the land in a manner that rendered it unfit for the purposes of the tenancy; or (*c*) on the ground that the term of a lease had expired.

Assuming the effective fixation of ceilings on landholdings as prescribed in the act of 1961, the government of Bihar anticipated acquiring superior rights in all lands in excess of the ceilings. Ac-

[29] "Straw or bhoosa" in this context means jute sticks after the jute has been extracted or maize stocks following the harvesting of maize.

cordingly, procedures were set forth in the act to facilitate the vesting of such surplus lands in the state of Bihar.

The act also stipulated that such surplus lands as were occupied by under-raiyats, when those lands were legally vested in the state, might be settled permanently with the under-raiyats—*if* they made formal application to achieve occupancy-raiyat status and paid a prescribed amount to the state.

Additional provisions of the act empowered the state to entrust the management of surplus lands to village councils or Gram Panchayats (made statutory institutions under provisions of the Bihar Panchayati Raj Act of 1947). The understanding was that the Gram Panchayats would not only manage the land under rules made by the state government but also would attempt to assure the actual cultivation of the land by means of cooperative farming societies of landless laborers.[30] If the Gram Panchayats were unable to establish such cooperative farming societies within twelve months of their assuming responsibility for such an undertaking, the appropriate representative of the state government was empowered to settle the land either with individual households of landless agricultural laborers or, in accordance with specific provisions in the act, with other persons of the village in which the land was situated or of a neighboring village.

The act of 1961 stipulated that every person whose lands in excess of the ceiling were acquired by the state would receive compensation according to a schedule appended to the act. An elaborate and time-consuming methodology for determining the amount of compensation due in each case was also specified, together with provisions prescribing how compensation payments would actually be made.

Assessment of the Bihar Land Reforms (Fixation of Ceiling Area and Acquisition of Surplus Land) Act, 1961 (Bihar Act XII of 1962)

The ceilings act of 1961 was a diluted version of the Bihar Agricultural Lands (Ceiling and Management) Bill, 1955. A careful comparison of the provisions of the bill of 1955 and the act of 1961

[30] See "Bihar Land Reforms (Fixation of Ceiling Area and Acquisition of Surplus Land) Act, 1961," Chapter IX, Section 27, Clause (ii). In *The Bihar Local Acts*, III.

makes obvious that the ceilings legislation now in force in Bihar is much less stringent in its intended effects than the legislation earlier proposed, debated, and tabled. The most obvious modifications in the law have favored large landholders (ex-intermediaries, ex-tenure-holders, and other raiyats with occupancy rights in land). Whereas the bill proposed that a ceiling be fixed on a "family holding" (with "family" defined to encompass the joint Hindu family), the act omitted any reference to family holdings and instead permitted the ceiling to be based on "individual" holdings. Moreover, the act permitted each landholder to transfer portions of his holding to relatives and non-relatives within twelve months following the commencement of the act. By thus ignoring the recommendation of the Select Committee (to which the original bill had been referred) that "lands held separately by different members of the family of a landholder shall be deemed, for the purposes of fixation of ceiling area . . . to be lands held by the landholder," the act of 1961 actually served to encourage largely fictitious, yet legal, transfers of land within joint Hindu families. While such transfers had been made for years prior to the enactment of the ceilings act of 1961, anticipatory to any legislation that might eventually be passed, the legislation actually provided an additional grace period during which further transfers could be made legally, to minimize the amount of land that might eventually be classified as "surplus" —to be vested in the state, settled with an under-raiyat, a Gram Panchayat, or a landless laborer—and therefore lost to the landholder. Benami, or fictitious, transfers of land (sometimes ludicrously to cattle recorded as "persons who would have inherited such land" on the death of the landholder) became the accepted legal method of preserving rights in land far in excess of the variable ceilings established by law.

Other provisions of the act of 1961 assured the individual landholder's right to retain, in addition to his ceiling area, ten acres of homestead land, lands on which established structures existed and which could be considered "necessary for the use and enjoyment of his homestead lands," and consolidated blocks of land used for the production of fodder, so long as these "blocks" were no more than fifteen acres in area.

In certain circumstances the act explicitly permitted an individual landholder to retain up to twice as much land as his ceiling area, as normally specified.

Methods of retaining control of lands in excess of the ceiling area were sometimes suggested by certain provisions of the act of 1961. A landholder could claim that he had promised acreage to the Bhoodan (land gift) movement, which should not be considered in fixing his ceiling—even if that acreage were nominally in his possession and the lands comprising it had not yet been distributed by Bhoodan authorities or formally registered in accordance with state law as Bhoodan land. If the landholder had a licensed sugar-cane farm, he could apply for exemption from the ceiling provisions of the law. And, in the absence of up-to-date Survey and Settlement records in the state, each landholder, either by withholding information from authorities or influencing them when he had the power and wealth to do so, could delay the implementation of the ceilings legislation and limit its impact on him.

By establishing variable ceilings and allowing the landholder to resume lands from his tenants for "personal cultivation," the act permitted the eviction of thousands of under-raiyats or tenants from lands they had tilled for many years, sometimes for generations, without being accorded occupancy-raiyat status. The landholder could select from his best quality lands the area he wished to retain within his ceiling; he could evict the tenants on those lands, reducing them in the process to the status of landless agricultural laborers; and he could, if necessary, give up poor quality lands in excess of the ceiling.

Legal and extra-legal evictions of countless under-raiyats were therefore an inevitable by-product of the act of 1961. Such evictions continued to be commonplace in Bihar throughout the 1960s, despite the fact that the government of Bihar made no sustained effort to implement the ceilings act.

Government's nonimplementation of the act of 1961 had been noteworthy throughout the 1960s. The act came into force on April 19, 1962. By 1964 the state had taken only preliminary action to implement the law.[31] A small staff had been collected

[31] See India, Planning Commission, *Implementation of Land Reforms: A Review by the Land Reforms Implementation Committee of the National Development Council*, p. 47.

"consisting of one upper-division clerk for each district headquarters and one lower-division clerk for each sub-divisional headquarters," but no higher staff had been appointed. Sometime later the state began printing notices (required by the act) asking each landholder in the state to submit returns relating to lands in his possession, but there is no evidence to suggest that these notices were actually issued until the summer of 1970.

Under pressure from the "Land Grab" movement in August 1970, government began to take visible, if rather symbolic, steps to implement its ceilings legislation. One hundred and twenty-five landholders were notified that the ceilings act would be applied to their holdings in the interests of determining whether any surplus lands might be made available for distribution to the landless. Simultaneously, according to the *Indian Nation*, similar notices were served "on at least five big farmers in each of the 587 blocks in the State"[32] and Block Development Officers were ordered to process these cases expeditiously "to enable the government to achieve its target of distributing 100,000 acres of land within the next three months."[33]

Serving notices to the landholders, a process barely begun in 1970, is only the first step of a laborious administrative undertaking that can involve months, even years, of delay before a landholder finally is notified whether, in the judgment of government, he is in possession of lands considered to be within or in excess of his ceiling. Thus, in the summer of 1970, it could be said that the ceilings act of 1961 was unlikely to be implemented fully for many years, even in the best of circumstances (assuming the cooperation of landholders in filing returns regarding lands in their possession and assuming sustained pressure for implementation from the central government and from the political parties which either comprise the government of Bihar or who influence it). The absence of up-to-date Survey and Settlement records alone limits the speed with which government can act to implement ceilings, or indeed agrarian reforms, and few would argue in the light of Bihar's record in the field of agrarian reforms that the cooperation of the landholders is likely. Moreover, it remains to be seen whether the pressures generated by the central government in 1969–1970 will

[32] *Indian Nation*, July 18, 1970, p. 1.
[33] Ibid.

be both sustained and acceded to by a state government within which conflicting interests abound.

Meanwhile, as of the summer of 1970, a situation existed in Bihar in which (*a*) unknown thousands of landholders retained holdings in excess of the ceiling area, few steps having been taken to determine the sizes of their holdings; (*b*) unknown thousands of tenants or under-raiyats had either been evicted from their holdings or continued to till them in fear of imminent eviction; (*c*) no one in government knew how much surplus land would vest in the state (and be available for distribution to landless agricultural laborers to be farmed individually or collectively, as prescribed by the act);[34] (*d*) no surplus lands had been made available for distribution as a direct result of ceilings legislation; and (*e*) no under-raiyats had been recorded as raiyats having a permanent occupancy right, as would have been possible had the act been implemented.

It is an inescapable conclusion that the ceilings act has served no constructive purpose thus far. Indeed, its enactment without implementation has permitted those who wish to circumvent the act's provisions to do so, and with time to spare. Its enactment without implementation has helped to engender a climate of apprehension in the countryside among those under-raiyats who fear eviction. Its enactment without implementation has raised expectations among the landless who, on the advice of representatives of political parties and others, anticipate receiving surplus lands that may prove eventually to be almost nonexistent.

In sum, the ceilings act of 1961 has neither produced an amelioration of agrarian tensions in Bihar by contributing to a more equitable distribution of existing land resources nor provided changes in the agrarian structure that can be considered conducive to increasing agricultural output.

[34] There have been various estimates of the amount of surplus that would be generated if the act of 1961 were strictly enforced. The Planning Commission (in 1964) reported that between 100,000 and 150,000 acres would become available as "surplus" land when the ceiling was enforced in the state as a whole. The original proponent of ceilings legislation, K. B. Sahay, said that no surplus land would become available, even if the act were strictly enforced. (Interview with Shri K. B. Sahay, former revenue minister, Patna, Bihar, March 17, 1968.)

6. *Consolidation of Agricultural Holdings*

History

The central government of India has argued for years in favor of programs designed to reduce the number of widely scattered, uneconomic agricultural holdings. Various efforts have been made to encourage the states to enact consolidation of holdings legislation, as well as legislation fixing a minimum holding below which further subdivision would not be permitted.

Responding to the central government's initiative, a number of states have made considerable progress not only in enacting legislation but also in consolidating previously fragmented holdings. Indeed, consolidation efforts have been associated officially with rural development success stories in the Punjab, Haryana, and Uttar Pradesh.[1]

Bihar is not one of the states that has been able to respond meaningfully to the central government's oft repeated recommendations that consolidation programs be pursued vigorously. There is, it

[1] See, for example, India, Planning Commission, *Fourth Five Year Plan, 1969–74*, p. 181.

must be admitted, a certain consistency in Bihar's lack of responsiveness to central government initiatives having to do with agrarian reforms. In the case of consolidation, it is not that Bihar has deferred enacting legislation. Legislation for consolidation of holdings was drafted in 1955 and enacted at the end of the First Five Year Plan. The problem has been mainly one of implementation of that early legislation. That problem persists in 1970 and will persist for some years to come, as will be apparent from the following discussion.

The Bihar Consolidation of Holdings and Prevention of Fragmentation Act, 1956—Provisions

The Bihar Consolidation of Holdings and Prevention of Fragmentation Act has been in force since September 1956. It enables the government to promote the consolidation of holdings in any area or region of the state. The act established an elaborate procedure by means of which consolidation is to be effected. Landholders within a given area are first to be notified officially that the state intends to devise a means of grouping fragmented holdings in a fashion that renders them more compact and, allegedly, easier to cultivate efficiently. From the date of notification, no landholder within the area notified is to transfer or partition any land, except with government's sanction, and all legal proceedings relating to such lands are to be prohibited or held in abeyance until the consolidation exercise is completed.

Following the establishment of a village advisory committee (or committees in the event that the land to be consolidated encompasses more than one village), the officer in charge of the consolidation operation is responsible for preparing an up-to-date record of rights in land "in respect of all lands comprised in the notified area."[2] This record of rights is to be equivalent in detail to the record produced in official Survey and Settlement operations. Indeed, the record of rights is to be prepared in accordance with provisions of the Bihar Tenancy Act of 1885 which, as of 1970, still govern the handling of government's Survey and Settlement operations in Bihar.

When the record of rights has been prepared—a task that may

[2] "Bihar Consolidation of Holdings and Prevention of Fragmentation Act, 1956" (Act 22 of 1956, Section 8. In *The Bihar Local Acts*, I).

take months or even years in areas in which up-to-date Survey and Settlement records do not exist—the tasks of consolidation have only been initiated. It is then required to produce a separate register of lands belonging to raiyats. This register is to include (*a*) the names of raiyats; (*b*) the areas and serial numbers of the plots of land held by the raiyats; (*c*) a classification of each plot of land according to its produce; (*d*) the market value of each plot; (*e*) the market value of buildings, trees, and wells on any plot; (*f*) any other information considered relevant, including the names of any under-raiyats having occupancy rights to land within the area in which consolidation operations are to be effected.

Next, the act prescribes that government is to publish the prepared register, sending copies of relevant entries to each raiyat or under-raiyat whose holdings are within the notified area. By publishing the register, a practice established during the British period during Survey and Settlement operations, government intentionally makes possible the raising of objections by raiyats or under-raiyats who may feel that their interests in land have been claimed by others or in some other fashion wrongfully recorded or ignored.

When objections have been dealt with on the spot by a representative of government empowered by the act to hear arguments and to settle any dispute in accordance with his best judgment, a draft scheme for consolidating holdings is to be prepared in consultation with one of the village advisory committees established under the act. This draft scheme is to include the following kinds of information, supplementing data earlier collected and published: (*a*) the description and area of any new holding to be allotted to a raiyat as a result of consolidation operations (together with a statement concerning market value of the new holding); (*b*) the amount of compensation payable to a raiyat whose new holding, following consolidation, is considered to be of less value than his original holding; (*c*) the sum of money to be recovered from a raiyat whose new holding is considered to be more valuable than his old one; (*d*) the description and area of lands, if any, to be set aside for the use of landless laborers for constructing mud, thatch, or reed homes.

When the draft scheme for the consolidation of holdings has been completed, it is to be published and the objections elicited are to be dealt with by the local officer of government responsible for the implementation of this program. The same officer of government, having made such amendments to the draft scheme as have seemed warranted, is responsible for submitting the consolidation plan to higher authority, the director of consolidation for the state as a whole.

Once again the scheme is to be published, this time under the authority of the director of consolidation. Again, any objections are to be entertained and dealt with—this time by the director himself through visitation in the village or villages concerned. If the scheme of consolidation is confirmed by the director, this will be made known throughout the notified area. Copies of the scheme will be posted in Gram Panchayat offices, police stations, etc., and the substance of the scheme announced even "by beat of drum in the villages comprised in the notified area."[3] If the scheme is not confirmed by the director, he is empowered to demand that an entirely new scheme for consolidating holdings be formulated, which implies going, once more, through all the procedures discussed above.

When the fragmented lands have been consolidated and new holdings allotted to all entitled to them, each landholder is to receive a certificate of transfer that constitutes his proof of title. The same certificate is to specify the rent payable to the state on the new compact holding.

Finally, when all certificates of transfer have been issued and the raiyats and under-raiyats have been settled on the new holdings, the record of rights concerning the newly consolidated holdings will supercede the old record of rights confirmed at the outset of the consolidation exercise.

The consolidation act of 1956 also stipulates that holdings once consolidated are not to be fragmented or otherwise dealt with "so as to create or leave a fragment."[4]

The Bihar Consolidation of Holdings and Prevention of Fragmentation Act, 1956—Delayed Implementation

The delay in implementing the consolidation of holdings program in Bihar is attributable in part to the nature of the legislation

[3] Ibid., Chapter II, Section 3, Paragraph 2.
[4] Ibid., Section 27.

itself. No program could have been pursued expeditiously that required adherence to the elaborate procedures outlined in the preceding section. To follow such procedures in detail and with concern that the new, consolidated units of land be roughly equivalent to the sum and value of fragments earlier surrendered would require officers of government to spend thousands of hours in the field and would demand of them that they be capable not only of collecting and checking records and mediating and settling disputes, but also of resisting unjustified pressures while acceding to legitimate demands. This would be a momentous undertaking for a well-equipped and efficient bureaucracy comprised of highly trained and well-paid officers. Given a poorly equipped, inefficient bureaucracy comprised of hastily trained and under-paid consolidation officers, the difficulties of the exercise were compounded.

The delay in implementation is associated with government's failure to link the consolidation effort directly with the new Survey and Settlement operations initiated in Bihar in the 1950s. Because the consolidation program requires up-to-date land records, a decision to link the regular Survey and Settlement proceedings with the consolidation survey operations would have limited the need to duplicate survey operations for consolidation purposes in regions such as Purnea District, in which post-independence Survey and Settlement operations have been completed.

The delay in implementation is associated, also, with the normal resistance of landholders to schemes of agrarian reform imposed on them by higher authority. In the case of consolidation, even landholders who are disposed to cooperate with government are prepared to question seriously whether it is in their interest to give up choice plots of noncontiguous lands for a compact holding considered by someone else to be equivalent "roughly" in area and value to their original holdings.

Finally, the delay in implementation can be interpreted as reflecting lack of vigorous support for the consolidation concept among members of Bihar's bureaucracy and the ruling elite.

In the above circumstances, Bihar's achievements in the field of consolidation of holdings have been limited. A number of pilot projects were initiated in several districts in 1957–1958, and government claimed to have consolidated 60,000 acres by the end of the Second Five Year Plan and roughly 80,000 acres by the end of the Third.[5] In table 11 Bihar's performance in the field of consolidation is contrasted with that of other states for which statistics are available.

Bihar's tentative target for the Fourth Plan was to consolidate one million additional acres. Even in the light of Bihar's past performance, the Planning Commission considered that target rather too modest and urged instead a Fourth Plan consolidation goal of three million acres.[6]

Notwithstanding continuing central government interest that Bihar proceed to develop a more efficient system for implementing its consolidation of holdings legislation, it is most unlikely that much progress in this field will be achieved during the Fourth

TABLE 11

Consolidation of Holdings in Selected States[a]

State	Prior to First Plan	During First Plan	During Second Plan	During Third Plan	Total to 1968–1969
Bihar	—	—	60	80	140+
Gujarat	276	260	387	680	1,930
Madhya Pradesh	2,443	483	893	2,004	7,394
Maharashtra	216	432	888	3,861	8,747
Mysore	—	274	721	900	3,245
Punjab and Haryana	—	6,180	8,548	7,822	22,848
Rajasthan	—	—	1,400	2,818	4,274
Uttar Pradesh	—	190	5,204	10,814	21,585

[a] All figures are in thousands of acres.

Sources: All data, with the exception of Bihar's, are based on Government of India, Ministry of Food, Agriculture, Community Development and Cooperation, "Chief Ministers' Conference on Land Reform," p. 21. The data for Bihar are from Government of India, Planning Commission, *Implementation of Land Reforms: A Review by the Land Reforms Implementation Committee of the National Development Council*, p. 53.

[5] India, Planning Commission, *Implementation of Land Reforms: A Review by the Land Reforms Implementation Committee of the National Development Council*, p. 53.

[6] Ibid., p. 54.

Plan period (1969–1974). Central exhortation and escalation of Bihar's consolidation target cannot, by themselves, produce the desired results in a state so deficient in trained personnel, so lacking in up-to-date land records, and so resistant to change in its traditional agrarian structure.

7. The Movement for Bhoodan (Land Gift)[1]

The Origin of Bhoodan

In 1950, the Politbureau of the Communist party of India had adopted a Maoist revolutionary strategy in India. It hoped that the party, acting as the vanguard of the proletariat, could mobilize the peasantry in guerrilla warfare that might lead to the overthrow of the Congress-dominated government of India. An effort was made in Telangana (a region within the former "Princely State" of Hyderabad) to achieve an agrarian upheaval. The rallying cry was "Land to the tiller!" In the midst of this communist-dominated insurrection in Telangana, on April 18, 1951, Vinobha Bhave, leader of a land gift movement called Bhoodan, secured his first gift of land for the landless and thereby demonstrated that some lands might be redistributed peacefully—without resort to class conflict. While it cannot be said that Bhave's demonstration of the efficacy of his nonviolent approach to land reform was a primary factor in limiting the potency of guerrilla warfare in Telangana, the fact that his movement originated in confrontation with a segment of

[1] The substance of this chapter, other than material specifically footnoted, is derived from association with members and leaders of the Bhoodan movement over fourteen years, 1956–1970, and from field studies in the state of Bihar.

the Communist party of India led some observers to view the movement as a deterrent to the Communist party in India and contributed to Bhoodan's popularity in the West.[2] However, the Bhoodan movement, as it was conceived by Vinobha Bhave and as it developed in India, did not identify, positively or negatively, with any political party, communist or otherwise.[3]

Bhoodan, as originally conceived, was dedicated to the simple purpose but complex task of solving the problem of landlessness in India. Vinobha Bhave's first appeal to the people of India was that of a moral theorist. He suggested that the problem of landlessness can be resolved not by violence, not through legislation, and not by means of government schemes, but through the spirit of Bhoodan whereby those holding land can be induced to feel compassion for those who have none and voluntarily to donate land to the landless.

In some respects, Bhoodan was Bhave's attempt to adjust certain Gandhian principles to new circumstances. Whereas Gandhi used expressions of "love" and "nonviolence" as negative instruments against a foreign government, Bhave suggested that the same principles should be reemployed positively as means toward cooperative endeavor. The movement thus incorporated the idiom of the saint with the language of the pragmatist. Its goals became transcendental and difficult to articulate. As the movement grew, its goals—both articulated and implicit—were developed and adjusted to meet an increasing number of practical or theoretical problems.

The Development of Bhoodan's Spiritual Ideals

Bhoodan's inception and growth were more spontaneous than planned. This was at once the movement's greatest strength and its most profound weakness. In its origin it was a simple plan created by a pious man for the solution of a complex problem. It became for some an ersatz religion, having few, if any, philosophical boundaries. It suggested as its credo that through love and nonviolence society might be reformed and man's nature changed. Over the years since 1951, it has been a movement that sought no

[2] Bhoodan's favorable image outside India was most apparent in the 1950s. See, for example, Hallam Tennyson, *India's Walking Saint: The Story of Vinobha Bhave.*

[3] For a discussion of the place of the Bhoodan movement within India's political spectrum, see W. H. Morris-Jones, *The Government and Politics of India,* pp. 59–61.

less than to rid man of his alleged acquisitive nature; to solve the land problem (in a static sense, without reference to the demographic crisis which continues to confront India) by means of a nonviolent revolution; to create a new society with decentralized means of production; and, reflecting the mixed ideological perspectives of Jaya Prakash Narayan,[4] to achieve all these things through popular, but not political, support within a stateless community of self-sufficient villages.

Bhoodan, as a narrowly defined movement for the collection and distribution of land gifts, was soon considered obsolete. To the theoreticians of the movement, Bhoodan became a revolutionary means of making a direct appeal to the masses. The new goal was the creation of "a kingdom of kindness"[5] through changing men's hearts and building a new social order.

In the new social order there would be no government, since governments use danda-shakti (the coercive power of the state) to solve their problems while the Bhavian ideal has been the creation of loka-shakti (popular power) vested in village republics.[6] Because the central government (New Delhi) could "never develop enough intelligence for governing all our numberless villages well and wisely [said Bhave], every village should be enabled to become its own planner."[7] Jaya Prakash Narayan enlarged on this theme. He said, "Power and authority would vest with the people in the true sense, and they would regulate and administer their own affairs. . . . Central authority would be sought to be extinguished, and if it continued to exist, the sphere and extent of its operation would be minimised. The village will have all the authority and jurisdiction

[4] Jaya Prakash Narayan, a Bihari, has been identified at various times in his life as a Marxist intellectual, a leading Congress Socialist, and a Gandhian Socialist. He was widely regarded in the 1950s as a likely successor to Jawaharlal Nehru; but Narayan became disillusioned with politics and, in the words of the late Kingsley Martin, "somewhat rashly swore to dedicate the rest of his life to Bhave's . . . movement." See Kingsley Martin, "The Gandhi Way," *The Atlantic Monthly* (August 1960): 64.

Within the Bhoodan movement, Narayan has been second in rank only to Bhave. It is Narayan who has given extended meaning to the movement by calling for a new social order in India. See Jaya Prakash Narayan, *A Picture of Sarvodaya Social Order.*

[5] Vinobha Bhave, *Bhoodan Yajna (Land-Gifts Mission)*, p. 88.

[6] Ibid., p. 91.

[7] Ibid., p. 93.

required. There will be perfect democracy based upon individual freedom; and the individual will be the architect of his own government."[8]

The vision of a perfect society, drawing on a traditional idealized image of India's ancient village republics as well as on Western concepts, was extended and further verbalized in the draft plan for sarvodaya, an unpublished pamphlet written by Bhoodan's leaders, which gave an elaborate statement of objectives and programs. Reflecting the sometimes utopian mood of its authors, the pamphlet described the new society:

> . . . there will be no classes and no castes; no exploitation nor injustice; an equal opportunity for each for fullest self-development. Man will be the centre of such a society, but self-interest will not be the basis of social organization. Life in such a society will not be onesided but integrated and whole, so that work, art and play will form a unified pattern making possible the growth of an integrated human personality.
>
> . . . In the economic field, all wealth, including land, will be considered as common property to be used for the good of each and profit, rent, interest, and wages will lose their meaning and disappear: everyone will work for society according to his capacity and receive from society according to his needs and in consonance with the needs of his fellow men. Production in such a society will not be for commerce, but for consumption and mutual sharing; and there will be no private accumulations of wealth because all wealth will belong to society and each will receive only according to his needs. Even social accumulations will be limited, remaining only as a safeguard against unforeseen needs. . . . [And finally] there will be no need of coercion in such a society, except the coercion—if it can be so called—of love.[9]

The exhaustive, if unrealistic, nature of the draft plan's provisions can be better appreciated if it is mentioned that in 116 pages the plan not only suggested the means by which Indian society could be refashioned but also described how each village would

[8] Jaya Prakash Narayan, *A Picture of Sarvodaya Social Order*, pp. 1–2.

[9] "Planning for Sarvodaya (Draft Plan)" (New Delhi: Ananda Press, 1957), pp. 16–17. (The principal author, apparently, was Jaya Prakash Narayan, but others directly and indirectly associated with the Bhoodan movement made contributions to the pamphlet. Among those contributing were Acharya Kripalani and M. L. Dantwala.)

have a herbarium in which locally available medicinal herbs would be grown so that indigenous medicines might be made for the treatment and prevention of disease.[10]

As successive mutations in the movement's articulated goals have occurred over the years, it has become increasingly difficult to evaluate the movement and its achievements. For some, the progression in Bhoodan's goals—a progression from an emphasis simply on the eliciting of voluntary land donations to a more complex plan for a new society—may seem but the natural outcome of the maturation of a dynamic institution. For others, Bhoodan's pattern of development represents an increasingly desperate escape into the realm of idealistic or utopian theory, an escape prompted by the movement's failure to meet its original, more practical goals.

An Evaluation of Bhoodan's Practical Achievements

A dual paradox of the Bhoodan movement and its various ramifications has been that it set some targets pragmatically, judging them spiritually, and set others spiritually, measuring them pragmatically—thus, the pre-occupation of the movement with certain targets of land donations, on the one hand, while, on the other hand, the tendency to rationalize "in spiritual terms" the movement's failure to reach such targets. If the Bhoodan movement has been essentially "spiritual," then Bhave's suggestion that statistical evaluations of the progress of a spiritual revolution are meaningless should hold. If the movement was not essentially spiritual, or was both spiritual and pragmatic, then its practical achievements should be evaluated straightforwardly.

One of the principal questions in such an evaluation must be the question of whether the Bhoodan movement provided the solution proposed by its leaders to the problem of landlessness in India. The leaders of Bhoodan, from the time of the movement's inception, have enunciated physical targets of land collection and distribution. They have associated the realization of such targets (or the failure to reach such targets) with the success (or failure) of their efforts. In 1951, for example, Bhave equated the solution of the problem of landlessness in India with the collection, through pledges made to Bhoodan, of fifty million acres of land and the distribution of this Bhoodan land to the landless. He said, "Since there are 300 million

[10] Ibid., pp. 17–18.

acres of cultivated land in India and an average family has five members, I felt that every family could give away one-sixth of its land-holding, accepting the poor landless man as the sixth member of his family. This is a way of bringing about a peaceful revolution in the country."[11] At the same time, Bhave suggested that the collection and distribution of the 50 million acres could be completed by 1957 "if all of us take up this work in the right spirit."[12]

Using Bhave's enunciated goals as a measure and judging by statistics supplied by Bhoodan sources, one must conclude that, on an all-India basis, the movement's efforts have been crowned with something less than complete success. During the period beginning April 18, 1951, and ending June 30, 1956, Bhoodan workers in India collected pledges of land totaling 4,103,744 acres and claimed to have distributed 501,223 acres.[13] By March 31, 1966, Bhoodan was credited with having collected a total of 4,244,991 acres and with having distributed a total of 1,151,378 acres in India.[14]

The record of Bhoodan in the state of Bihar, the area in which the most intensive Bhoodan work has been attempted, also offers a means of evaluating Bhoodan's ability to collect and distribute land. Indeed, when Bhave entered Bihar in September 1952, he resolved publicly to test the efficacy of his movement in that state. Skeptical about the possibility of government's legislating change in the agrarian structure of Bihar, Bhave expressed a sense of urgency about resolving the problem of landlessness within a specified time. He suggested that if his movement succeeded only "in bringing help and relief to some here and there . . . [it would fail to achieve the] object of ushering in a new social order based on justice."[15] To this end, Bhave offered to remain in Bihar until the land problem was solved.[16] He described his decision in the following manner:

> I have been reflecting over the situation to find out how best we should plan our efforts so as to achieve the maximum result in the minimum time; and experience has led me to the conclusion that for

[11] Vinobha Bhave, *Bhoodan Yajna (Land-Gifts Mission)*, p. 21.
[12] Ibid., p. 99.
[13] Jaya Prakash Narayan, *A Picture of Sarvodaya Social Order*, p. 47.
[14] *Times of India Directory and Yearbook, 1967*, ed. N. J. Nanporia, p. 131.
[15] Vinobha Bhave, *Bhoodan Yajna (Land-Gifts Mission)*, p. 111.
[16] Ibid., p. 114.

> some time we should concentrate all our energy on Bihar, and even in Bihar on a few selected districts. If these districts succeed in solving the land problem . . . there is no reason why the same should not happen in other parts of India. . . . People ask me whether it would be in the interest of Bhoodan work, if I thus remain tied to Bihar. Is it a right strategy? I say to them that it would undoubtedly help the cause of our movement if we can accomplish our work in a given area within a specified time. . . . The practicability of our programme will have been vindicated and the rest will then be merely a matter of time and the number of workers required in proportion to the quantity of work to be done.[17]

To solve Bihar's land problem Bhave had estimated that he and his followers would need to collect and distribute 3,200,000 acres of land.[18] When equating the solution of the problem with such a figure, he reiterated his pledge not to leave the province until its quota had been reached.[19]

After two years of intensive Bhoodan activity in Bihar, Jaya Prakash Narayan announced that the movement had not reached its target. On April 19, 1954, at an all-India conference of Bhoodan workers in Bodh Gaya, Bihar, Narayan expressed his disappointment in the following words: "I am ashamed. We Biharis took a vow of 3,200,000 acres in order to solve the land problem of our province. We have kept Baba [Bhave] with us for eighteen months, but still this vow has not been fulfilled. If we have not even enough workers to solve the land problem in Bihar, how can we ever solve it in the rest of India?"[20]

Four months later, in August 1954, Narayan's words were still applicable; even though Bhoodan workers claimed that 2,102,000 acres[21] had been pledged by the landed for the landless, Bhave's quota had not been fulfilled. Nor had it been fulfilled on June 30, 1956, when it was claimed that 2,147,842 acres had been collected for distribution.[22]

In June 1956, Vinobha Bhave left Bihar to carry his message elsewhere.

[17] Ibid., pp. 112–114.
[18] Ibid., p. 114.
[19] Tennyson, *India's Walking Saint: The Story of Vinobha Bhave*, p. 87.
[20] Ibid., p. 141.
[21] Ibid., p. 12.
[22] Narayan, *A Picture of Sarvodaya Social Order*, p. 47.

In Bhave's absence, the movement in Bihar gradually lost whatever momentum it had gained during his presence. The number of active workers in Bihar dwindled until it could be said that the movement scarcely existed. Indeed, almost all activity ceased except on those occasions when J. P. Narayan returned to his home in Patna. By March 31, 1966, the movement had to admit officially that its acreage totals for land collections in Bihar had not increased; instead, they had decreased from 2,147,842 in 1956 to 2,132,787 acres in 1966.[23] By March 1966, the movement claimed to have distributed only 311,037[24] acres of land to previously landless families in Bihar.

Not even a disciple of the Bhoodan movement could claim that reaching only about two-thirds of the stated minimum target for donations in Bihar could be called an unqualified success for the movement. A critic might point out that Bhoodan took until 1966 (nine years after Bhave's target date for the solution of the land problem in all of India) to achieve even this limited success.

Moreover, critics of Bhoodan in Bihar question the accuracy of Bhoodan statistics in that state. Some claim that Bhoodan figures are exaggerated as a means of propagandizing the movement and that much of the land represented as "donated land" in Bhoodan statistics does not exist. Some suggest, more leniently, that the lands exist but are predominantly waste lands. While such views may be contentious, the evidence collected in Bihar supports the view that Bhoodan statistics have definite shortcomings and do not reflect accurately the situation in that state. For example, though Bhoodan authorities in Bihar claimed 2,147,842 acres of land in 1956, it was generally recognized that at least 500,000 acres of the land, mainly the contribution of a single maharaja, was of two sorts, forest land and legally contested land.[25]

More damaging to the image of Bhoodan as a successful movement is the fact that, by March 1966, Bhoodan leaders could claim

[23] *Times of India Directory and Yearbook, 1967*, ed. N. J. Nanporia, p. 131.

[24] Ibid.

[25] Tennyson confirms the fact of the maharaja's donation. See Tennyson, *India's Walking Saint: The Story of Vinobha Bhave*, p. 143.

Information made available in April 1957 through the courtesy of the Revenue Department of the government of Bihar confirms the nature of the land donated.

only 311,037 acres[26] of land distributed to previously landless families in Bihar (less than 10 percent of the announced target) and only 1,151,378 acres in India[27] (less than 3 percent of the national target announced for 1957). The movement's inability to distribute successfully even such lands as were donated is one indication of the fact that, in Bihar as well as on a national level, Bhoodan lacked administrative organization and cohesion. Though Bhave's quiet but charismatic leadership provided a kind of national identity for the movement as a whole and though annual national conferences provided opportunities for contact between various regional and local leaders, Bhoodan lacked the administrative machinery necessary to the coordination of the activities of its workers. There were no direct lines of communication between various parts of the movement. That is to say, its leader, Vinobha Bhave, was usually walking in some far-off state in a remote district near an unknown village, expounding new doctrine as he collected land, while the practical administrative problems went unsolved or were solved by workers who had little or no direction from those above them in the Bhoodan hierarchy. "No one seems to have thought of setting up a coherent national organization. . . . [There is] an odd mixture of faith, fervor, and incompetence, and the sort of arrangement that could only be maintained by the enthusiastic amateur."[28]

In Bhoodan there was nothing which demonstrated lack of planning, coordination, and follow-through more obviously than the means by which the movement attempted to distribute land. This becomes clearer if Bhavian idealism with regard to the distribution of land is contrasted with an example of an actual distribution. In theory, there was an elaborate plan for the distribution of donated land. Bhave had suggested that

> . . . on the appointed day, Sarvodaya workers offering land to the landless visit the village. All the people are gathered there. The workers inquire from them who are the most suitable persons entitled to receive their gifts. They [the people] then indicate their choice. The first priority is given to Harijans and other backward

[26] *Times of India Directory and Yearbook, 1967*, ed. N. J. Nanporia, p. 131.
[27] Ibid.
[28] Tennyson, *India's Walking Saint*, pp. 114–115.

communities. Care is taken to bequeath land only to those persons who are not engaged in any other calling and are in a position to do cultivation work, provided land is made available to them. The workers are accompanied by revenue officials who complete the work of registration and other legal formalities. The man returns home as the proud possessor of land. A new life has begun for him.[29]

However, in practice, Bhoodan workers deviated from the plan. Hallam Tennyson cites such an instance in describing distribution tactics in a village that he had visited:

Normally, when all the evidence had been taken, the landless themselves would have been asked to select those most worthy to receive Bhoodan plots. But as it seemed that not all the landless had turned up . . . Srikannto [the Bhoodan worker] retired with the zamindar, the National Extension officer, the Government Records officer, and the head man of the village to make the decision. They returned surprisingly soon. Two acres of bad and one of good for each landless family present. . . . This left a considerable quantity of land still not distributed. I learned that the same thing had happened the day before. . . . [N]o more than one third of the land had been given away.[30]

Regrettably, with respect to the distribution of Bhoodan lands, neither the Bhavian ideal nor the Tennyson example (in which Bhoodan worker, zamindar, national extension officer, government records officer, and headman were all present and reached easy consensus) became the established pattern. The problem of distributing Bhoodan lands has never been resolved in Bihar. During the initial period of intensive work in Bihar, 1952–1956, Bhoodan authorities did not claim to have distributed more than 142,000 acres of land[31] as compared with the collection figure of 2,147,842 acres. In the ten years that followed through March 31, 1966, an additional 169,037 acres were said to have been distributed to formerly landless families of Bihar. If we accept without question the accuracy and meaningfulness of the movement's statistics, as many as 1,821,750 acres of Bhoodan land remained undistributed in Bihar

[29] Bhave, *Bhoodan Yajna*, p. 25.
[30] Tennyson, *India's Walking Saint*, p. 155.
[31] Narayan, *A Picture of Sarvodaya Social Order*, p. 47.

in 1966, and the situation had not changed, except possibly in marginal fashion, by March of 1968.[32] The prospect is that this land, if it exists in cultivable form, will never be distributed. The primary attention of the movement has long since passed on to what some refer to as an "advanced stage of Bhoodan," called gramdan, in which, ideally, all who hold land in a village voluntarily surrender their individual rights to land and the land of the village is vested in the community as a whole (to be managed by the village panchayat or council).[33]

In addition to the lack of administrative organization and coordination, there have been other reasons for the slowness of distribution of Bhoodan lands in Bihar. First, the donated lands are widely scattered throughout the state, and the Bhoodan committee in Bihar has been small. There were in 1957 less than a hundred full-time workers in the Bihar movement, and few among them had time to devote to distribution-related activities. There is no evidence to suggest that the movement acquired larger numbers of full-time workers in the following years (through March 1968). Second, there were legal problems associated with registering distributed lands in accordance with the provisions of the Bihar Bhoodan Yagna Act, 1954.

The Bhoodan Yagna Act of 1954 makes necessary the registration of distributed lands by an officer of the Revenue Department of the state of Bihar.[34] The registration requirement applies to all Bhoodan lands including those donated and distributed prior to the enactment of Bhoodan legislation.[35] The complication which results from these provisions of the act is that an unknown percentage of donated and distributed Bhoodan lands is not recognized by the state. That is to say, until Survey and Settlement operations are completed in Bihar, those who have received Bhoodan land will not

[32] This judgment is based on information provided the author by Bhoodan workers and confirmed in an interview with Jaya Prakash Narayan, Patna, Bihar, March 1968.

[33] For idealized descriptions of gramdan, see Jaya Prakash Narayan, "The Bhoodan Movement in India," *Asian Review* (October 1958): 272–274; Bishwa B. Chatterjee, "Bhoodan Changes Life," *Yojana*, January 26, 1967, p. 41.

[34] "Bihar Bhoodan Yagna Act, 1954," Section 19. In *The Bihar Local Acts*, I.

[35] Ibid., Section 15.

know whether they have an occupancy right to land in accordance with law.[36]

Statutory Recognition of Bihar's Bhoodan Movement

Purporting to "facilitate the donation of lands . . . and to provide for the settlement of such lands with landless persons,"[37] the state legislature of Bihar enacted the Bihar Bhoodan Yagna Act in 1954. The leaders of the Bhoodan movement accepted the act with apparent equanimity, as they did similar legislation in other states, though to some it appeared anomalous that the movement which earlier had claimed that the problem of landlessness could not be resolved through "legislation or government schemes" should accept legislative intervention in its affairs.

The act's significance lies in three spheres: first, the state's recognition of the Bhoodan means of acquiring land for distribution to the landless; second, the state's intervention in the management of Bhoodan affairs; third, the omission of any provision to legalize Bhoodan lands until such time as those lands can be properly recorded. In other words, the state is unable to legalize either the donation or distribution of Bhoodan lands until Survey and Settlement of those lands is completed.

So far as the state's recognition of the means by which Bhoodan workers have acquired land is concerned, the passing of the Bihar Bhoodan Yagna Act, 1954, for the stated purpose of facilitating the donation of lands to the movement is sufficient evidence.

So far as the state's intervention in the management of Bhoodan affairs is concerned, the act's provisions are far-reaching.

1. The state of Bihar intervenes in constituting a Bhoodan Committee "to administer all lands vested in it for the purposes of Bhoodan Yagna."[38] The committee members are appointed by the state government, subject to the qualification that, during the life time of Vinobha Bhave, members will be appointed on his nomination.[39] The state government may remove from office any member

[36] Ibid., Section 22.

[37] Ibid., Preface.

[38] Ibid., Section 3. "Bhoodan Yagna" means "the movement initiated by Shri Acharya Vinobha Bhave for acquisition of land through voluntary gifts with a view to distribute it to landless persons" (ibid., Section 2, Clause [a]).

[39] Ibid., Section 4, Clause 2.

of the committee "on the advice of Shri Acharya Bhave."[40] The state may, at any time, dissolve the committee "in consultation with Shri Acharya Vinobha Bhave"[41] for specified reasons or if "it is otherwise expedient or necessary"[42] to do so. In all of these provisions it is implicit that the state reserves ultimate power on the death of Bhave.

2. The state of Bihar intervenes in determining what lands may be donated.[43] Section 10 of the act specifies that "any person being the owner[44] of any land may donate such land to the Bhoodan Yagna Committee or to Shri Acharya Vinobha Bhave . . . ,"[45] so long as lands in the following classes are not included: burial grounds, lands held under "service tenures,"[46] certain forest lands, mine and mineral lands, and other lands that the state government may designate. Moreover, the state reserves the right, after suitable investigation, to cancel (with retroactive effect) Bhoodan donations if such donations were made by incompetent donors[47] or "on such other grounds as may be prescribed."[48]

3. The state intervenes in determining the rights of a grantee over Bhoodan lands that have been or will be distributed. According to Section 14 of the act, the grantee of Bhoodan land "shall acquire the same right, title and interest as the donor had in such land."[49] In other words, the recipient of Bhoodan land assumes the rights and obligations of the former owner of the land. However, the grantee of Bhoodan land is denied the right to sublet his land, and his right of transfer of such land is restricted.[50]

[40] Ibid., Section 5, Clause 2.

[41] Ibid., Section 9, Clause 1.

[42] Ibid.

[43] Ibid., Section 10.

[44] "Owner" means "any person who holds any land as a proprietor or tenant and has a lawful title thereto and a transferable and heritable interest therein" (ibid., Section 2, Clause [e]).

[45] Ibid., Section 10, Clause 1.

[46] "Service tenures" are tenures held subject to the performance of a given service by the tenure-holder. For example, a village watchman might receive a "service tenure" from his village in lieu of other emoluments.

[47] "Incompetent donors" means, essentially, donors not having legal title to the lands that they have donated ("Bihar Bhoodan Yagna Act, 1954," Section 11, Clause 4. In *The Bihar Local Acts*, I).

[48] Ibid.

[49] Ibid., Section 14.

[50] Ibid.

4. The state of Bihar intervenes in determining the amount of rent to be paid by the Bhoodan tenant. If the donor of Bhoodan land paid rent for the land donated, the grantee must accept the obligation to pay the same amount to the state.[51] However, until Survey and Settlement operations are concluded, Bhoodan lands for which rents have not been previously determined remain rent free.[52]

5. The state of Bihar intervenes in determining the means by which a grantee of Bhoodan land may be ejected from the land. A Bhoodan tenant who holds land in violation of any provision of the Bhoodan Yagna Act, 1954, can be ejected from the land.[53]

In summary, under the provisions of the Bihar Bhoodan Yagna Act, 1954, the far-reaching powers of the state of Bihar to intervene in Bhoodan affairs are such that, on the death of Vinobha Bhave, the state can assume control of all operations connected with the administration of the Bhoodan movement in Bihar.

As mentioned earlier, the state's capacity to implement some sections of the Bihar Bhoodan Yagna Act, 1954, is limited in the absence of adequate land records. The act's omission of any provision to legalize Bhoodan lands, until such time as the lands are properly recorded, means that there will be delay in implementing the act in full until Survey and Settlement operations are concluded.[54] In the meantime, while (from the viewpoint of the government) the status of a Bhoodan tenant is legally indefinite, apparently the Bhoodan tenant neither pays rent to the state for the land he holds nor is he protected, insofar as protection is afforded to any tenant, by the tenancy laws of Bihar.

Case Studies in Bihar's Villages

The fact that the state of Bihar has given statutory recognition to the Bhoodan movement indirectly raises the question whether the movement was "recognized" or "endorsed" by the rural masses, particularly those of low social and economic status who were to

[51] Ibid., Section 14, Clause 1; and Section 18, Clause 2.

[52] This information was obtained from the Revenue Department, Government of Bihar, in June 1957.

[53] "Bihar Bhoodan Yagna Act, 1954," Sections 21–22. In *The Bihar Local Acts*, I.

[54] Survey and Settlement operations had not been completed in Bihar sixteen

have been the principal beneficiaries of the efforts of Bhave and his followers.

Only limited and somewhat speculative comments can be made regarding the degree to which the Bihar peasantry as a whole ever became aware of the existence of the Bhoodan movement, even though the movement had been described by its proponents as one having potentially revolutionary implications. Nonetheless, in the absence of systematic state-wide public opinion surveys covering Bihar's 68,000 villages, the evidence of personal field research can be put forward as at least representative of the movement's impact on the villagers of the state best known to the author, and possibly illustrative of village opinion elsewhere in Bihar.[55] The data collected support the judgment that the rural masses in Bihar had limited awareness of the movement in 1956, a time just following the peak of Bhave's activity in that state. This may have been due in part to the diffuse and disorganized efforts of Bhoodan workers, to the limitations of Bhoodan propaganda (aimed, as it generally was, at the politically powerful and the urban educated elites), or to reasons unknown.

By interviewing the headman of every household in the surveyed villages, an attempt was made to determine whether the villagers could identify the Bhoodan movement by name or purpose. An attempt was also made to determine whether their knowledge, or lack of knowledge, of Bhave and the Bhoodan movement was related to their awareness of other men or movements outside the village.

In order to collect the relevant information, each respondent was asked whether he could identify the name and/or role of Bhave and the name and/or purpose of Bhoodan, and whether he could identify the name and/or role of either Nehru or Gandhi. The underlying assumptions were these: first, if the respondents showed awareness of Nehru or Gandhi, but not of Bhave or Bhoodan, the evidence would suggest that the purposeful dissemination of information regarding Bhave and Bhoodan (particularly in the years immediately preceding the survey, 1952–1956, when Bhave was himself working intensively in Bihar) had been less successful than

---

years after the passage of the 1954 Bhoodan Yagna Act—that is to say, by August 1970.

[55] No claim is made, of course, that the villages surveyed by the author are statistically representative of Bihar's 68,000 villages.

had the less purposeful process of communication through which news of Nehru and Gandhi had permeated the surveyed villages; second, if the respondents showed greater awareness of Bhave and Bhoodan than of Nehru and Gandhi, the evidence would be considered to support the view that the intensive efforts of Bhoodan workers in Bihar had produced a response in certain mofussil (rural) areas of the state and, possibly, had awakened a substantial number of people to the purposes and possibilities of the movement; third, if the respondents showed no awareness of Nehru, Gandhi, or Bhoodan, the evidence would suggest, mainly, that the villagers were in so remote a region of Bihar that little information from the outside had permeated.

Village A: Muzaffarpur District—North Gangetic Plain

It may be remembered that Village A is the village in which a single, absentee ex-zamindar was the principal landholder. There were seventy-three households in the village; sixty-one were landed; twelve were landless. The holdings of the landed tended to be small and fragmented; the average holding per landed household (excluding the ex-zamindar and his lands) was only 1.65 acres. In the village there was little difference in standard of living between landed and landless. All earned some portion of their annual incomes from labor on the lands of the ex-zamindar.

As of November 30, 1956, no one in Village A had given or received land as a result, direct or indirect, of the Bhoodan movement. Though the ex-zamindar, a nonresident of the village, had been approached by Bhoodan workers, he had not responded. The record of awareness in Village A can be seen in table 12.

Those villagers whose answers have been recorded in section I of table 12 had a relatively sophisticated knowledge of the world outside the village. Nevertheless, only six of those could identify (within the liberal frame of reference given in table 12) both the names and roles of Nehru, Gandhi, Bhoodan, and Bhave. In other words, among seventy-three respondents in the village, only six were able to identify the names and roles of all the men about whom, and the movement about which, they were asked. These six respondents represented landed households.

In section II, note that a majority of the seventy-three respondents could identify at least the names of the men and the movement, but that more could identify the names of Nehru and Gandhi than of Bhoodan or Bhave.

In section III the figures more clearly indicate the villagers' more general awareness of Nehru and Gandhi than of Bhoodan or Bhave. Five landless respondents are numbered among those who could identify neither name nor role of Bhoodan and Bhave; at the same time, these five could identify both Nehru and Gandhi by name, though not by role.

Village B: Darbhanga District—North Gangetic Plain

Village B was the village in which Community Development work had been carried on prior to the survey. There were thirty

TABLE 12

Nehru, Gandhi, Bhoodan, and Bhave: Awareness in Village A

Degree of Respondents' Awareness	Nehru	Gandhi	Bhoodan	Bhave
I[a] Could identify name and role of	11	13	6	6
II[b] Could identify name but not role of	59	58	45	47
III[c] Could identify neither name nor role of	3	2	22	20
Total respondents	73	73	73	73

[a] In section I of tables 12–16 are recorded the numbers of respondents who could identify the name and role of Nehru, Gandhi, Bhoodan, or Bhave. The answers recorded in this section were liberally interpreted. For instance, respondents who suggested that they "knew" Nehru and that his role was that of a "big man" were credited with having identified the man and his role. Similarly, people who suggested that they knew Bhave, a "man who walks everywhere and likes poor people," were credited with having accurately identified Bhave and his role.

[b] In section II are recorded the numbers of respondents who could identify the name but not the role of Nehru, Gandhi, Bhoodan, or Bhave. The answers of respondents recorded in this section also were interpreted liberally. People who said that they had heard a name, but could not place it within context, were credited with having identified the name.

[c] In section III are recorded the numbers of respondents who could identify neither name nor role of Nehru, Gandhi, Bhoodan, or Bhave.

ex-zamindari (landed) households, together with twenty-two landed households and forty-one landless households—ninety-three households in all. Caste stratification was notably rigid in comparison to Villages A, C, D, or E, the other villages surveyed.

In April 1954, a total of less than one acre of land, divided into seven noncontiguous plots, was donated to Bhoodan workers by seven ex-zamindars (six Brahmans and one Koirii, all residents of the village). The lands were found to be fallow when inspected and were considered by the donors to be "waste lands."[56] As of April 1957, Bhoodan workers had not returned to the village; the donated plots continued to lie fallow and undistributed.

The record of awareness in Village B can be seen in table 13. In some respects, the pattern of response recorded in Village B is similar to that of Village A in the preceding case study. In section I of Village B, as in section I of Village A, the more sophisticated answers were given by respondents who were, generally, more conscious of people and events outside the village. These people were predominantly of high caste. All of the respondents whose answers have been recorded in section I represented landed households, with the exception of three landless respondents who knew the name and role of Gandhi.

TABLE 13
Nehru, Gandhi, Bhoodan, and Bhave: Awareness in Village B

Degree of Respondents' Awareness	Nehru	Gandhi	Bhoodan	Bhave
I[a] Could identify name and role of	25	29	22	22
II Could identify name but not role of	65	62	41	42
III Could identify neither name nor role of	3	2	30	29
Total respondents	93	93	93	93

[a] See notes to table 12.

[56] The waste lands donated to Bhoodan were not included in statistics pertaining to cultivable land in Village B.

There is similarity also in sections II and III of Villages A and B; in each, the figures indicate the villagers' more general awareness of Nehru and Gandhi than of Bhoodan and Bhave. All of the respondents whose answers are recorded in section III represented landless households.

Village C: Gaya District—South Gangetic Plain

Among the villages surveyed, Bhoodan activity had been most pronounced and successful in Village C. There were eighty-eight households in the village; prior to the work of Bhoodan, thirty had been landed and fifty-eight landless. The largest landholder of the village, with a holding of two hundred acres, was the nonresident ex-zamindar.

In 1955, the absentee zamindar had been persuaded by Vinobha Bhave himself to donate 44.75 acres of land (classified as waste land) to the Bhoodan movement. In the same year, the donated lands were distributed, though not in accordance with the provisions of the Bhoodan Yagna Act, 1954, to forty-four landless households. In the following years, up to July 1957, the newly landed Bhoodan tenants worked to reclaim and crop their new holdings, though yields per acre were low. In the same period, the Bhoodan tenants received further aid from the Bhoodan movement in the form of seeds and bullocks.[57]

So far as the Bhoodan tenants were concerned, the agricultural year immediately preceding the date of interview had been "fair." Yet the per capita gross income of the Bhoodan tenants was (for that year) substantially the same as that of the fourteen remaining landless households of the village; the per capita gross income of the former was Rs. 50, and for the latter Rs. 48. Moreover, the

[57] The movement failed on many occasions to provide appropriate assistance (in the form of credit, implements, or seeds, for example) to landless families settled on donated lands of poor quality. However, Bhoodan authorities did seek and received funds from the government for such purposes. In 1958 Jaya Prakash Narayan reported that the government of India, in response to a Bhoodan request for assistance in the amount of one crore rupees (10 million rupees), had provided "three crores [30 million rupees] so far to furnish to the landless means of cultivation. We want to give the means of cultivation to those families which are getting what we call waste lands, uncultivated waste lands" (Jaya Prakash Narayan, "The Bhoodan Movement in India," *Asian Review* [October 1958]: 271).

Bhoodan tenant households reported continued dependence, for the major portion of their incomes, on work as agricultural laborers on the fields of the village's well-to-do.

Though the Bhoodan tenants were proud of their lands, which they associated with the attainment of higher social status, the fourteen landless households (who derived their incomes solely from agricultural labor) were anything but enthusiastic about their neighbors' good fortune. Some of the landless explained, by way of rationalization perhaps, that "the Bhoodan lands are useless, anyhow," or that they had been offered, but had turned down, Bhoodan land. Some lived in expectation of the day when additional land might be distributed among them. But the general feeling among the landless was one of resentment of the ex-zamindar, or of Bhoodan, for the failure of either to assuage their thirst for land. Having lived without expectation of change in their condition, they had begun now to aspire for change.

The landed (non-Bhoodan) households of Village C tended to be noncommittal about the work of Bhoodan in the community. Yet one landed respondent was outspoken in a fashion that seemed to betray some fear of change in the traditional structure of the village: "We grow more food than they can grow. We have three times as much good land as they have bad. And, to make ends meet, they still have to work our fields as well as their own. So what has Bhoodan done for them? They have to depend on us to subsist, and they know it."

The record of awareness in Village C is recorded in table 14. The pattern of response in Village C, with regard to the identification by name and role of Nehru, Gandhi, Bhoodan, or Bhave, was the reverse of the pattern in Villages A and B. In Village C both Bhoodan and Bhave were better known by name and role than either Gandhi or Nehru. It is noteworthy, of course, that the level of awareness of all three men, as well as the Bhoodan movement, was high. Only one respondent out of a total of eighty-eight fitted into section III, having claimed no awareness of Nehru.

It appeared that the intensive efforts of Bhoodan workers in Village C had been largely responsible for the people's awareness of the Bhoodan movement, its leader, and its purposes. The villagers' widespread recognition of Nehru and Gandhi, and general knowledge of people and events outside the village, can be attributed, to

TABLE 14
Nehru, Gandhi, Bhoodan, and Bhave: Awareness in Village C

Degree of Respondents' Awareness	Nehru	Gandhi	Bhoodan	Bhave
I[a] Could identify name and role of	29	27	49	44
II Could identify name but not role of	58	61	39	44
III Could identify neither name nor role of	1	0	0	0
Total respondents	88	88	88	88

[a] See notes to table 12.

some extent at least, to the contributions of Bhoodan workers to village discussion and gossip.

Village D: Patna District—South Gangetic Plain

Village D was the community in which urban influences were most pronounced, due mainly to its location within access of river, rail, and road lines of communication. The community was predominantly agricultural, though a number of its households were nonagricultural; there were eighty-one households in the former category and fifteen in the latter. Among the eighty-one households involved principally in agricultural operations, twenty-one were landless households whose members worked as agricultural laborers.

The predominant caste of the village was the Rajput; the headman of the village and the largest landholder were of that caste.

In 1954, Vinobha Bhave spent two days in Village D and made his headquarters in the local school. In the course of his visit, Bhave persuaded three members of the community to donate, among them, slightly less than two acres of previously fallow land. These Bhoodan lands had not been distributed as of February 1957 and had remained fallow since their donation.

The record in Village D of awareness of Nehru, Gandhi, Bhoodan, and Bhave is detailed in table 15. The pattern of response

TABLE 15
Nehru, Gandhi, Bhoodan, and Bhave: Awareness in Village D

Degree of Respondents' Awareness	Nehru	Gandhi	Bhoodan	Bhave
I[a] Could identify name and role of	32	35	16	17
II Could identify name but not role of	62	57	60	62
III Could identify neither name nor role of	2	4	20	17
Total respondents	96	96	96	96

[a] See notes to table 12.

in section I of the table indicates that more villagers knew more about Nehru and Gandhi than about Bhoodan or Bhave. Sections I and II, in combination, show the villagers' general awareness of Nehru, Gandhi, Bhoodan, and Bhave. However, section III shows more clearly that Bhoodan and Bhave were much less well known than either Nehru or Gandhi.

Bhave's failure, in 1954, to persuade more than three members of the community to donate lands in the name of Bhoodan and the failure of Bhoodan workers in the intervening years, up to March 1957, to distribute the less than two acres that Bhave received were frequently cited by landed villagers to support skeptical remarks regarding the movement. Not one among twenty-one landless respondents suggested that they expected to receive Bhoodan lands. This was not surprising, since only five landless respondents could identify either Bhoodan or Bhave by name; none could identify either by role. The landed and nonagricultural households were more aware of the names and roles of Bhoodan and Bhave than were the landless.

Village E: Ranchi District—South Bihar Plateau

Village E was an aboriginal village. Its principal characteristics were isolation (in terms of nearness to urban centers or lines of communication), absence of caste, and absence of pressure of population on land. The community could be described as being socially homogeneous. The concept of individual or private ownership of land was subordinate to the concept of community ownership of land. The villagers were not, primarily, agriculturalists and tended to subsist on the wild produce of the jungle for at least two months of the year. None of the villagers could be considered to be landless.

No Bhoodan lands had been donated or distributed in Village E as of June 1957. No Bhoodan worker had visited the village or its locality.

The record in Village E of awareness of Nehru, Gandhi, Bhoodan, and Bhave can be seen in table 16.

In section III of table 16, note the number of respondents who were unable to recognize the names or roles of Bhoodan or Bhave. While it can be seen also that a number of respondents could identify neither the name nor role of Nehru or Gandhi, the differences in degree of awareness, or lack of awareness, are self-evident. Sections I and II add to the picture of the villagers' low level of awareness of Bhoodan and Bhave, and show also that few villagers were fully aware of the names and roles of either Nehru or Gandhi.

One explanation for the villagers' generally low level of awareness of Nehru, Gandhi, Bhoodan, or Bhave is the remoteness of the community from urban areas. Village E's isolation from the rest of Bihar is linguistic, religious, and cultural, as well as geographical. The fact that the villagers, as a community, seemed to be more

TABLE 16
Nehru, Gandhi, Bhoodan, and Bhave: Awareness in Village E

Degree of Respondents' Awareness	Nehru	Gandhi	Bhoodan	Bhave
I[a] Could identify name and role of	3	7	1	1
II Could identify name but not role of	22	25	7	9
III Could identify neither name nor role of	16	9	33	31
Total respondents	41	41	41	41

[a] See notes to table 12.

aware of Nehru and Gandhi than of Bhoodan and/or Bhave is considered to be the result, partially, of Village E's increased contact with Government of Bihar revenue officers (as these officers took up their duties in conjunction with the administration of the Bihar Land Reforms Act, 1950, as amended in 1954). Also, some of the villagers had had contacts outside the village while working as unskilled laborers in urban areas of south Bihar. Because these villagers' contact with the outside world had been of limited duration and because Ranchi District, in general, and aboriginal areas, in particular, had not yet received much attention from Bhoodan workers, it is not considered unusual that the villagers' contacts had enabled them to acquire some awareness of Nehru and Gandhi, but more limited awareness of Bhoodan and Bhave.

The Shift to Gramdan (Village Gift)

Perhaps the most significant change in Bhoodan policy, since the movement's initiation in 1951, occurred in 1957 at the all-India conference of Bhoodan workers in the state of Kerala.[58] Without referring to problems associated with the implementation of the Bhoodan (land gift) phase of the movement, Bhave used this conference to emphasize the apparent success of gramdan (village gift) experiments. In effect, he shifted the focus of his movement from the established policy, in which individual land gifts had been sought, to a new policy, in which donations of whole villages would be more highly valued. In the terminology of the movement, this meant that the new emphasis would be toward "villagization of the land" through gramdan. Workers were exhorted to work for donations in the aggregate, that is, donations of entire villages.

In the ideal gramdan, the community as a whole would receive title to all land. Representing the community would be a village

[58] This conference was the occasion, also, for informal discussion between Bhoodan's highest leaders, Bhave and Jaya Prakash Narayan, and representatives of the Communist party in India, particularly E. M. S. Namboodripad, then chief minister of Kerala. The author, who attended the conference, witnessed some of these meetings at a distance. What precisely was discussed during them is unknown, but it has been rumored that a limited *modus vivendi* was established between the Bhoodan movement and the Communist party of India (Kerala). It is known, at least, that the Communist party did not harass Bhoodan workers in Kerala, where the movement claimed to have collected 26,293 acres and distributed 5,774 acres of land through November 15, 1966.

select committee or gram panchayat which would try to estimate the amount of land to be tilled jointly by all. The produce from this land would be shared by the entire community in accordance with a formula designed by the village council. Other lands held by the community would be apportioned by the council for personal cultivation, according to need. Need would be determined, primarily, by the size of each family. Decisions of the council would be rendered unanimously. Periodic reviews would occur to determine whether each cultivator had used his land efficiently. As families changed in size, land would be reapportioned according to their increased or diminished needs. Since the occupancy right to the land would be vested in the village itself, and not in the villagers, the problem of redistribution could, hopefully, be solved on the spot.

In later mutations, the gramdan movement permitted landed families to retain possession of nineteen-twentieths of their holdings for personal cultivation, thus limiting at the outset the right of the village council to reapportion all lands vested in the community and considerably restricting the land reform effects of the gramdan movement. As the movement continued to evolve, other requirements were relaxed so that a village could be considered a gramdan even if some families did not vest their lands in the community. In this fashion, gramdans could be collected even when the movement encountered a minority of families opposed to the gramdan concept in a given village.

Within an idealized frame of reference, the gramdan phase of the movement was designed to have extended meaning; that is to say, the gramdan experiment was to lead over time to a restructuring of life in the village. A society fragmented by caste and class conflict would be transformed into a "little community" in which the people would identify common problems and would learn to work in harmonious and disciplined fashion to resolve them. In other words, gramdan became a new path toward the creation of the social order already envisaged to be the ultimate goal of Bhoodan.

As might be expected, the gramdan movement's earliest successes were in villages located in tribal regions of India. It was "not by accident that Gramdan started in Koraput [Orissa], an area largely inhabited by the Khonds, an aboriginal tribe which sets so little store on private property that they believe that land belongs to God, and which has a very homogeneous social structure, free from caste. For them to share a village was easy."[59] For a time, the movement concentrated its attention on aboriginal communities and the number of gramdans claimed grew steadily. According to Bhoodan statistics, there were 2,500 gramdans in India by September 1957, the majority of which were located in tribal areas of Orissa and Bihar. There were said to be more than eighteen thousand gramdans in India by March 31, 1966; most of these were in tribal regions.

A Tribal Gramdan: Gaya District—South Gangetic Plain

The tribal gramdan used for this case study was selected at the suggestion of Bhoodan workers of the permanently established Bhoodan Ashram at Bodh Gaya, Bihar. In April 1957 the gramdan was surveyed in the understanding that it was one of the more successful "village gift" experiments in the state. The total number of gramdans in Bihar at the time of the survey (June 1957) was less than a thousand. These were located, without exception, in aboriginal or tribal regions of the state.[60]

The gramdan was situated in a hilly part of Gaya District near the district's eastern boundary. The nearest hard surfaced or pacca road was nearly ten miles from the village. The village could be reached by traveling by bus to the nearest point of access, then by foot cross-country. During the rainy season, when intermittent streams lying between the village and the nearest road fill, the community was cut off from the outside.

The terrain near the village was irregular; scattered outcroppings of basaltic rock rising two or three hundred feet above the plains were common. Most of the hills in the immediate vicinity of the gramdan were denuded of foliage, though the community itself was situated in a thick wood.

The community's isolation, with respect to nonaboriginal villages of Gaya District as well as other tribal villages, was such that

[59] "Indian Villages in Trust," *The Economist*, September 28, 1957, p. 1038.

[60] This information was supplied by Bhoodan authorities at the Bodh Gaya Ashram in June 1957.

there were approximately two miles separating it from the nearest settlement. The village was not electrified and received no postal service.

The people were socially homogeneous; though minor distinctions in status were evident, there was no caste system; factionalism did not seem to exist to a marked extent. The community was governed by a nonstatutory village council and decisions involving the whole community were made by the council, apparently after consultation with the adults of the village. The council was supposed to meet with the adults of the community in plenary session when especially controversial matters were to be discussed.

The village was small, both in area of cultivable land and in population. Its area was approximately fifty cultivable acres. Its population was only sixty-four. Whether so small a settlement should have been considered (by any definition) a village was considered incidental in view of the settlement's designation as a gramdan by Bhoodan workers.

The absence of population pressure on the land resources of the village arose more from the fact that the community was basically nonagricultural than because the fifty acres of cultivable land provided average holdings per household of 4.5 acres. If the people had not foraged for food in the surrounding woodlands, especially during the lean months of February and March, it seemed that family holdings would have had to be enlarged or the pressure of the community's small population on existing lands might have been felt. As it was, the community subsisted for two or three months of every year mainly on the mahua flower (which could be found in the neighboring woodlands), while also bartering wood for food in distant villages. As nonvegetarians, the villagers could occasionally enhance their diets by slaughtering animals, including domesticated cows and pigs.

There were eleven families in the settlement. The size of an average family was 5.8 persons. The gross annual income of an average family (for the year preceding the field survey) was estimated to be 486 rupees. There were special difficulties associated with calculating a household's income from foraging in the woodlands surrounding the settlement, so the income figures can be considered to be approximate only.

Among eleven households, seven had incurred debt in the year preceding the survey. The amount of indebtedness per household was small, no debt being more than 25 rupees in cash or kind.

In June 1956, the community had been persuaded by Bhoodan workers to reconstitute itself as a gramdan. A permanent Bhoodan worker had been posted in the village. This worker, a widowed Hindu, had lived continuously in the village, except for brief journeys to Bhoodan centers in Patna or Bodh Gaya. She had received a maintenance allowance in the amount of Rs. 25 per month from the Bihar Bhoodan movement.

Her work in the gramdan, as she described it, had been initially to develop more fully in the community the concept of "villagization of the land." To villagize the land, she explained, was to change the pattern of ownership in a community from that of individual to that of group ownership. When the process of villagization of land was complete, the land could be redistributed to individuals according to need. "Eventually, the community owned lands can be farmed cooperatively," she stated.[61]

According to the Bhoodan worker, the gramdan's lands had been "villagized" within two weeks of her residency in the community. She explained that the process had been concluded rather quickly. In her opinion the villagers had been persuaded easily to relinquish their individual rights to land because (*a*) in aboriginal communities, such as this one, communal ownership was more traditional than private ownership; (*b*) in this community, as in similar aboriginal communities, the people were not primarily agriculturalists and therefore did not consider land to be a supreme asset; (*c*) so far as this community was concerned, its size and cultural homogeneity helped to facilitate group discussion and agreement; and (*d*) there seemed to be some expectation generated by the presence of the outsider and her promises of further assistance that it would be in the community's interest to cooperate with a plan

[61] This statement by the Bhoodan worker in the gramdan represented a deviation from the then established Bhoodan policy of stressing "community title" to land, but "private cultivation." However, there were others (including the late Prime Minister Nehru) who felt that gramdan deserved support from government because it was a means of promoting "collective cultivation" (Taya Zinkin, "Collective Villages of Orissa," *Manchester Guardian*, October 24, 1957).

that seemed unlikely to modify negatively the traditional pattern of existence.

The redistribution of village lands had, from all accounts, proceeded smoothly. Though there were said to be "minor complaints about redistribution, these were settled to the villagers' satisfaction by the village council."[62] Because none of the villagers had been landless prior to the process of villagization of lands, the redistribution had apparently caused little trauma or excitement; the process had been one of awarding a small fragment of land to a household and taking away a similar fragment from another household. In fact, no single plot of more than one acre had been transferred, for cultivation purposes, from one household to another. But, the early ritual of gramdan had been performed, and the Bhoodan worker seemed immensely satisfied that all had gone well.

Having accomplished the redistribution of village lands, the resident Bhoodan worker had attempted to introduce a form of cooperative farming in which the villagers were expected to share agricultural implements and till all the lands of the community jointly. This experiment had ended in failure when the villagers apparently refused to join in any kind of cooperative endeavor. No explicit explanation of this failure was put forward, either by the Bhoodan worker or by the villagers. The villagers seemed reluctant to talk about it, and no attempt was made to induce comment.

The most successful project introduced by the Bhoodan worker had been the village school. By suggesting that she would volunteer her services as a teacher, if the villagers donated their time and service as construction workers, the Bhoodan worker had been able to encourage the community to build itself a one-room, mud-walled, and tile-roofed school. Classes were being held daily when the village was surveyed; the children were learning to read and write Hindi and had been given some instruction in basic education—that is, "basic" in the Gandhian sense, meaning instruction in animal husbandry, use of the charka (spinning wheel), etc. Some pride was exhibited by the Bhoodan worker in confirming that fifteen of the older children and women had been trained to use the charka, but she later admitted that none of them had sustained interest. This had been disappointing to her because she

[62] The resident Bhoodan worker expressed this opinion on April 22, 1957.

clearly derived a sense of achievement from adhering ritualistically to a program containing Gandhian, as well as Bhavian, symbolism.

Probably due to contact with the Bhoodan worker, the villagers showed remarkable awareness of Nehru, Gandhi, Bhoodan, and Bhave. The record of awareness in the village follows in table 17.

The people's feelings for Bhoodan (or gramdan) varied, but were generally positive; some expressed mild pleasure at the change they saw in the life of the village; others were more enthusiastic. One saw the possibility of further change in the quality of life in the settlement. Another, less hopeful, was of the view that the village

TABLE 17

Nehru, Gandhi, Bhoodan, and Bhave: Awareness in a Tribal Gramdan Village

Degree of Respondents' Awareness	Nehru	Gandhi	Bhoodan	Bhave
I[a] Could identify name and role of	6	6	10	9
II[b] Could identify name but not role of	5	5	1	2
III[c] Could identify neither name nor role of	0	0	0	0
Total respondents	11	11	11	11

[a] In section I are recorded the numbers of respondents who could identify the name and role of Nehru, Gandhi, Bhoodan, or Bhave. The answers in this section were liberally interpreted; however, because Bhoodan activity had been more intense in the gramdan than in the other villages, except Village C, a somewhat higher standard of answer with regard to Bhoodan and Bhave was expected. For example, to be credited with the identification of the role of Bhave and/or Bhoodan, a respondent had to know that the movement and/or its leader was associated with the distribution of land to the landless, or with gramdan.

[b] In section II are recorded the numbers of respondents who could identify the name but not the role of Nehru, Gandhi, Bhoodan, or Bhave. The answers in this section were also liberally interpreted; that is to say, a respondent's claim of identification was accepted, generally, without further discussion beyond that necessary to determine whether the respondent could also identify the role of the person or movement in question (i.e., whether the respondent's answer should be listed in section I rather than section II).

[c] In section III are recorded the numbers of respondents who could identify neither name nor role of Nehru, Gandhi, Bhoodan, or Bhave.

had no doubt benefited, particularly from the school, "but my position remains as usual."

When gramdan workers attempted to collect pledges in the non-tribal areas of Bihar, it soon became apparent that it was much easier to conceptualize than to actualize the ideal process by which the families of a village would surrender their private rights to land and vest them in the community. Such acts of altruism would be uncommon in most social systems, and certainly could not be anticipated in villages of India known to be comprised of diverse factions lacking a shared sense of community. But the image of the factionalized village was rejected by Gandhi, his disciple Bhave, and their followers. They have idealized the "village republics" of ancient India and romanticized the villages of contemporary India. They have, therefore, endorsed the concept of self-sufficient village republics in which mutual trust and cooperation would predominate and divisions based on caste and community would cease to be. Such conceptions of the Indian village have been the source of much unrealistic thinking in India both prior to and after independence. The late Dr. B. R. Ambedkar, speaking at the Constituent Assembly in November 1948, made a more realistic, if somewhat harsh, generalization about the villages of India when he said: "What is the village but a sink of localism, a den of ignorance, narrow-mindedness and communalism?"[63]

As the gramdan movement evolved, more and more difficulties were encountered in persuading villagers to donate all of their lands to the community. The stratified villages of the Gangetic plain showed themselves to be particularly resistant to the movement's message.

Apart from the obvious problem of creating a sense of community in fragmented villages, the gramdan experiment was sometimes hampered by its need to conform to legal requirements not unlike those imposed earlier on Bhoodan by the Bihar Bhoodan Yagna Act of 1954. For example, according to the Gramdan Act of Orissa (legislation having to do with legalizing gramdans in that state), "unless all land of the villagers living in a revenue village [an administrative unit often consisting of a number of villages]

[63] "Panchayat Raj as the Basis of Indian Policy, an Exploration in the Proceedings of the Constituent Assembly," *AVARD Newsletter* 4, no. 1 (January–February 1962): 4.

has been voluntarily given in Bhoodan, the village cannot be declared a Gramdan and land cannot be entered in the records as belonging to the village council."[64] By October 1957, there were 1,400 gramdans in Orissa that had not yet been registered properly; some of the land still had to be surveyed, and the state government was not cooperating, "partly out of apathy, partly because so many of its representatives are members of the classes which have most to lose."[65] For one or both of the above reasons none of the 1,400 gramdans claimed in Orissa by October 1957 were legally recognized by the state.[66]

There were other problems too. In many instances, for example, traditional moneylenders refused to extend credit to gramdan villagers because the villagers, having relinquished their individual rights to land, had no collateral for loans.

By the middle of the 1960s disillusionment with the gramdan phase of Bhoodan was widespread, even among disciples of Bhave. In these circumstances, Bhave returned to Bihar in 1965, possibly hoping to breathe new life into the movement by building on what he considered to be past successes. He remained in Bihar for several years (1965–1969). It was during this period that further mutations were permitted in gramdan—mutations, as earlier discussed, which were designed to facilitate the process by which gramdans could be claimed even in stratified and factionalized villages where not all villagers could be induced to donate their holdings (or even a portion of them) to the community. The stacks of gramdan pledges, based on relaxed criteria, continued to grow in Bihar. By the end of March 1966, there were said to be 5,812[67] in Bihar and by November 15, 1966, 10,966[68] gramdans were claimed in that state—a substantial increase in villages claimed in only seven and

[64] Zinkin, "Collective Villages of Orissa," *Manchester Guardian*, October 24, 1957, p. 9.

[65] Ibid.

[66] Ibid. Bhoodan claimed 5,241 gramdans in Orissa through November 15, 1966. These were concentrated in tribal villages of the Koraput region. Many of these were written off as failures by March 1968; according to spokesmen for the movement considered reliable by the author, the "Koraput experiment" was then considered no longer viable—no longer to be sustained through infusions of men or capital.

[67] *Times of India Directory and Yearbook, 1967*, edited by N. J. Nanporia, p. 131.

[68] Chatterjee, "Bhoodan Changes Life," *Yojana*, January 26, 1967, p. 41.

one-half months. By May 1969, it was reported that the movement claimed to have collected gramdan pledges from approximately 35,000 of the 68,000 villages of Bihar.[69] Whole districts (for instance, Darbhanga) were said to have given themselves to the movement.[70] Such claims had not been made since the earliest recorded successes of Bhoodan (after Bhave in 1954 had pledged not to leave Bihar until the land problem was solved there).

Regrettably, the more recent claims only strengthened doubts about the movement's veraciousness. The reported new successes have been less publicized than the old. When publicized, they have sometimes been ridiculed as "paper successes," empty of real meaning. Such criticisms can no longer be dismissed.

The Decline of Bhoodan

The Bhoodan movement's shift in emphasis from individual land gifts to gramdan (not to mention other variations on the same theme) implies the leaders' tacit recognition that the Bhoodan movement, alone, could not solve the problem of landlessness, even in areas in which it had succeeded in distributing some land. It failed to solve that problem for a number of reasons.

First, except in widely isolated instances, the donations of land were insufficient to provide all, or even a large proportion, of the landless of a locality with land. Instead, what was done in some areas was to raise new expectations among the peasantry and to instill in them the hope that they might be the beneficiaries of land. In such areas, the landless who did not receive land were left resentful or bewildered—sometimes a source of easily mobilized political discontent. They were jealous of their neighbors who had received land and on occasion bitterly remembered the promise of a Bhoodan worker that all would receive some. Moreover, the newly blessed "haves" were often as bewildered as the "have-nots." Formerly landless, they owned no bullocks or implements with which to till their new holdings. They had no seeds to plant. That they could somehow acquire capital in order to get started was a remote possibility. Under such circumstances, the newly acquired lands

[69] Joseph Lelyveld, "India Finds Gandhi Inspiring and Irrelevant," *The New York Times Magazine*, May 25, 1969, p. 60.

[70] Mr. Jaya Prakash Narayan made this claim to the author in an interview, Patna, Bihar, March 1968.

could be mortgaged and lost, except possibly where Bhoodan legislation was enacted (as in Bihar) to give protection, on paper at least, to the Bhoodan landholder.

Second, even in nominally successful Bhoodan areas, there was little if any change in the traditional agrarian structure. Using Bihar (particularly Village C) as an example, the ex-intermediaries remained in a predominant position; the landed families remained powerful; the recipients of Bhoodan lands still had to earn a crucial portion of their incomes as agricultural laborers in the fields of their more prosperous neighbors.

Third, the movement sometimes divided and embittered the landed. In certain communities, the economic position of the landed who refused to give land, or gave waste land, was markedly better than that of those who actually sacrificed to give. Those who had given sometimes wondered at the injustice of the situation and were perplexed at the community's failure to solve the problem for the solution of which they had given so much. In short, it can be said that the Bhoodan movement failed to create a "revolution through love." Far from removing man's acquisitive instinct, it sometimes strengthened his yearning for the possession of property. Jealousy of one man for another seems to have been as much a product of the movement as has love.

Neither the Bhoodan principles nor awareness of the movement have spread spontaneously from villages where Bhoodan efforts have been concentrated to villages not visited by Bhoodan workers. Nevertheless, the movement received deferential treatment from politicians and officials of government for many years.

When the movement was at its zenith, which in retrospect was probably in 1957, it was fashionable to commend Bhave and his followers for accomplishments in the field of rural development that seemed beyond the capabilities of the government of India. The movement commanded the attention of the powerful so that when a gramdan conference was called by Bhave in Yelwal, Mysore, "the President of India, the Prime Minister of India and at least half a dozen Chief Ministers were present"[71] to lend unanimous support to a resolution "praising this method of tackling economic

[71] Narayan, "The Bhoodan Movement in India," *Asian Review* (October 1958): 273.

problems and social problems."[72] And, through the years, government of India publications, including various five-year plans, extended recognition to the movement. One read, for example in the Third Five Year Plan, that "the Bhoodan and Gramdan movements have greatly helped to create a favourable atmosphere for implementing progressive measures of land reform."[73] In the same document, the planners said that "Bhoodan and Gramdan . . . are an outstanding demonstration of the potentialities which reside in voluntary action stimulated by high idealism and a missionary zeal."[74] Nor was official support confined to words alone; crores of rupees were provided in support of the movement by the central government.[75] But times have changed, and it was no longer fashionable in 1969 to lend official support, verbal or monetary, to Bhave and his followers, even in the year of Gandhi's centenary.

Eighteen years have elapsed since Bhave began his movement. For a time the movement gave hope of mobilizing opinion in India regarding the need for land reform. For a time it gave hope that its achievements might exceed those of government in effecting social and economic change in rural areas of India. For a time it was grudgingly or enthusiastically endorsed by the government of India and major political parties. But, by 1970, Bhave had retired from active work in the field and had gone into spiritual retreat at his ashram at Wardha. Only J. P. Narayan, working with calculated independence of Bhave, remained actively engaged in field work within a single block of Muzaffarpur, Bihar.[76] Now, the whole

[72] Ibid.

[73] India, Planning Commission, *Third Five Year Plan*, p. 221.

[74] Ibid., p. 293.

[75] As mentioned earlier, for example, the government of India provided 3 crores (30 millions) of rupees to the Bhoodan movement to be used to furnish formerly landless Bhoodan land recipients with means of cultivating their new land. Also, the Third Plan contained reference to the provision of central government funds to settle approximately 10,000 landless families of Bihar on Bhoodan lands, as well as funds "for developing a number of Gramdan villages in Orissa" (ibid., p. 376).

[76] The block, Musahari, is one in which militant, Maoist-oriented land grabbers were active in 1969–1970. Earlier the entire block had been claimed in gramdan, but J. P. Narayan admitted to the author on August 13, 1970, at his headquarters in Musahari, that the gramdan claim had been exaggerated by his followers and the basic work of persuasion would have to be undertaken again by him. To this end he vowed to remain in Musahari for one year or more to

8. *The Growth of Agrarian Tensions*

Rural "Apathy" in the 1950s

In Bihar in the 1950s the force of tradition still governed relationships among unequals. Those who held land enjoyed the prerogatives of power and status that have accompanied control of that most primary of resources in agrarian societies. Those without land, those with tenuous rights in land, and those with holdings lacking in quality or size enjoyed few prerogatives—except in relationships with others of even lower social (caste) or economic (class) status.

If one idealized the rural scene, one could still refer to a system of relationships in which mutual obligations existed between inferiors and superiors. Those low in the hierarchy, within this idealized conceptualization, would perform primary agricultural functions and share their produce with those holding superior rights in land. Those with superior status would assume certain responsibilities in relationship to their inferiors—providing them advice, protection, loans at varying rates of interest, and performing ritual services on ceremonial occasions.

However, such idealized relationships involving a system of mutual obligations between superiors and inferiors were not the rule in Bihar, even in the 1950s. Obligations were seldom mutual. Authority was exercised downward in the social and economic hierarchy. Communications were mainly one-way, from superior to inferior. The peasant having inferior social and economic status was in no position to question the authority exercised over him. The peasant's very existence was in the hands of his superior. Whether he could fulfill his elementary needs was determined by someone else, not by him.

To be utterly dependent for life on "superiors" exercising absolute and often capricious authority was the common experience of the Bihar peasant as recently as fifteen years ago. Indeed, it had been his common experience for generations—a recurring experience that no doubt helped to condition him to accept his station in life and to make him largely incapable of expressing his needs or defining his interests.

In the early 1950s, the structure of power in Bihar seemed to be immutable. The traditional society of the village had only begun to be disrupted, and the pattern of life (while in many respects unacceptable to the alien observer) had been so regularized that the Bihar peasant seemed prepared to accept as datum his position in the social and economic hierarchy. His view of the world was limited. His capacity to conceive of change in his relationships with his superiors or inferiors was minimal. His expectation of a higher standard of life was almost nonexistent. A landless peasant could not conceive of himself as a holder of land. An agricultural laborer could not conceive of himself as having employment at wages above subsistence. A raiyat (or under-raiyat) tilling land without security of tenure, subject to eviction at any time, could not conceive of himself as having an occupancy right in land—assured by law and circumstance.

If the prevailing conditions in rural areas were not ideal, the Bihar peasant was in no position to conceptualize a world in which conditions differed. Lacking a basis for comparative judgment, he was prepared to accept his world as it was and as it seemed likely to remain for some time.

A sense of frustration among some peasants concerning the nature and quality of their existence was no doubt incipient, but hardly discernible through scrutiny of peasant behavior. Their condition was one of apparent apathy, as if they were devoid of feelings concerning the forces acting upon them.

Gradual Awakening of the Bihar Peasant

The intervening years since the early 1950s have seen unprecedented penetration of Bihar's rural areas by outsiders acting in behalf of various institutions, both governmental and nongovernmental. Among governmental penetrations, there were the following: (*a*) A rural Community Development program was established in 1952 when sixteen development blocks were initiated.[1] This program was rapidly expanded during the following twelve years until a network of 587 blocks encompassed, at least nominally, all of Bihar's 67,665 villages.[2] (*b*) An attempt was made to develop a viable set of cooperative institutions, and by 1965–1966 government claimed to have extended the coverage of primary cooperative credit societies to 85 percent of the villages and to 23 percent of the rural families in the state.[3] (*c*) An effort was made to decentralize administration and decision-making associated with various developmental programs through the introduction of village self-government (Panchayati Raj) institutions in three districts of the state, Ranchi, Bhagalpur, and Dhanbad. A State Directorate of Panchayati Raj was established, training centers for panchayat functionaries initiated, and legislation enacted in anticipation of the spread of Panchayati Raj institutions to all regions of the state. (*d*) The decisions of the state to pass legislation designed to abolish the right of intermediaries to collect land revenue in behalf of government and to establish the state's own rent collection machinery meant that, from 1956–1957 on, thousands of new employees were re-

[1] The block is the primary administrative unit for the Community Development program. An "ideal" block would consist of 100 villages and 60 to 70 thousand people. A Bihar block has, on the average, 116 villages and a total population of nearly 78,000.

[2] For data showing where (by district) and when (by year) the various blocks were initiated, see Bihar, Directorate of Economics and Statistics, *Bihar Statistical Handbook, 1966*, p. 378.

[3] If one were discussing the quality of the cooperative movement in Bihar, a number of rather critical comments would need to be made. However, the purpose in this instance is merely to show the extent of coverage claimed by government for the cooperative-credit dimension of the program.

cruited and incorporated in state service. Many of those were placed in direct relationship with the peasantry. (*e*) Finally, all instrumentalities of government having responsibility for any facet of rural development (for example, major and minor irrigation, power, flood control, rural electrification) greatly expanded their numbers of employees and posted many of them in the countryside.

Less sustained and comprehensive penetration of Bihar's rural areas was effected by various nongovernmental institutions, such as Bhoodan, and, particularly in 1966–1967, by famine relief agencies, both Indian and foreign.

Added to these penetrations were those of the politicians, mainly at five-year intervals preceding general elections, and the mass media, especially radio with the advent of the transistor.

Whatever the successes or failures of government programs such as Community Development and Panchayati Raj and whatever the penetrative significance of the work of political parties, the mass media, and nongovernmental institutions, the cumulative effects of all have ended the historical isolation of Bihar's rural areas. This is not to suggest that the villages of Bihar, uniformly and without exception, have experienced change produced by the penetration of outsiders. As of 1970, thousands of villages no doubt remain relatively untouched by the programs and policies of external institutions, governmental and private. Tangible or physical change, the result of externally influenced social, political, or economic programs, may not be discernible in such villages. Nevertheless, substantial numbers of people in these villages have experienced the kind of contact with outsiders that contributes to awakening. That is to say, new needs and expectations have been generated among the people, even by programs classified as failures when evaluated in conventional terms. Above all, perhaps, the effects of these programs have been to intrude into the villager's consciousness the concept of the legitimacy and possibility of change in the traditional mode of life. This concept has been endorsed and nurtured by the politician soliciting votes, by the second son who migrates to the city and returns to his village with new perspectives on the world outside, and by government servants charged with implementing development programs.

The source of the idea that change is both legitimate and possible is less important, of course, than its existence and persistent growth in recent years among the rural masses of Biharis. This profound attitudinal change has been set in motion in Bihar among people whose subservience to authority and malleability under pressure had been assumed to be constants by the ruling elite. The irony in this rural transformation is that the ruling elite (unwittingly in most instances) imposed the programs and transmitted the ideas that have contributed to the great awakening.

The general elections of 1967 provided striking evidence of the awakening of the peasantry of Bihar. The election results helped to confirm that the rural masses were no longer docile and lacking in capacity to think and act independently of their superiors in the rural and urban hierarchies. The shattering of Congress party dominance in that election showed the power of previously subordinated groups—often in direct confrontation with Bihar's traditional, high-caste, and landed elites. Symbolic of that breaking of the monopoly of power of the traditional elites has been the emergence of chief ministers in successive Bihar governments (in the period 1967–1970) who have been drawn invariably from backward or scheduled castes, rather than from the landholding, high-caste elites.

Additional evidence of the awakening of the peasantry comes in microcosm from villages first surveyed by the author in 1956 and visited repeatedly thereafter through August of 1970. The people in those villages have been transformed, gradually, over fourteen years. While it is difficult to measure and adequately document the psychological changes that have taken place, there can be no denying that the old equilibrium of the surveyed villages has been disrupted. Even in those villages in which noteworthy physical change has been at a minimum, changes in attitude and expectation among the people are obvious. Where once the physical, social, and economic structure in these villages had been accepted as datum by the people, there was by 1968 a new capacity for even the lowest in the traditional hierarchy, the landless laborers, to articulate the need for change and to become agents for change. Deepening frustration regarding their status and economic vulnerability was evident. The inarticulate were becoming articulate. Many villagers, landless and landholders alike, who earlier had referred to the immutability of their condition were prepared in 1968 to cry out in protest against the circumstances that denied them the ability to provide the barest necessities for their children. In 1968 their expressions of anger were diffuse. Their ability either to assess blame or to scapegoat any individual, faction, or group was limited. Yet, they were in the process of repudiating a traditional life-style, and it seemed only a matter of time before leadership would emerge to give focus to the newly articulated feelings of anger among them.

In the period 1966–1969, incidents of agrarian unrest associated with what the Home Ministry called "the persistence of serious social and economic inequalities"[4] began to be reported with some frequency not only in Bihar but also in Assam, Andhra Pradesh, Gujarat, Kerala, Manipur, Orissa, Punjab, Rajasthan, Tamil Nadu (formerly Madras), Tripura, Uttar Pradesh, and West Bengal.[5] Among the cases of unrest reported in this period were many involving peasants in land-grab type activities. In Bihar, in the period June through December 1967, roving bands of peasants had forcibly harvested standing crops in separate incidents in Purnea, Bhagalpur, Santhal Parganas, and Darbhanga districts. During January–February of 1968 in Champaran District, Bihar, two hundred persons had attempted to encroach upon government lands. Also in 1968, there had been repeated demonstrations[6] in which landless peasants were said to have demanded land from officials of government.

During the same period in the neighboring state of West Bengal, there were frequent, and sometimes violent, outbreaks of agrarian unrest. For a time in 1967, the most militant expressions of this unrest were localized around Naxalbari in West Bengal. By August of 1969 there had been 346 separate incidents of forcible occupation of land in the whole of that state.

Central Government's Recognition of Rural Unrest

By 1969, following careful assessment of evidence concerning all types of peasant agitations in various states, the Ministry of Home Affairs had concluded that steps would have to be taken both by the central government and by the states to reduce tensions in rural

[4] India, Home Ministry, Research and Policy Division, "The Causes and Nature of Current Agrarian Tensions" (unpublished report, 1969), p. 4.

[5] Ibid., Annexure I.

[6] Such "demonstrations" occurred in the districts of Bhagalpur, Monghyr, Gaya, and Chapra.

areas. This could best be achieved, it seemed, by meeting some of the immediate needs of the weaker sections of rural society—especially the needs of the landless, the sharecroppers, and the tenants lacking secure rights in land. The Home Ministry warned that a failure to meet these needs, or even to address them seriously, would leave the field to "certain political parties."[7] These parties, the Ministry noted, had already succeeded in organizing dissident groups of peasants by appealing to their hunger for land and their yearning for better standards of living. While they had not demonstrated "capacity for launching sustained agitations"[8] and might be organizationally weak, these parties (together with their peasant political organs) were considered by the Home Ministry to be capable of continuing to exploit the rural tensions produced by a "widening gap between the relatively few affluent farmers and the large body of small landholders and landless agricultural workers."[9]

The Ministry recognized that twenty-two years of planned rural development had not transformed the agrarian structure in much of India. Land reforms, generally, had not benefited the actual tiller. Superior rights in land were concentrated in the hands of a few. Much of the land was still cultivated by sharecroppers lacking security of tenure and forced to pay exorbitant rents. The Home Ministry report emphasized the fact that "the programmes so far implemented are still more favourable to the larger owner-farmer than to the smaller tenant-farmer. As for the sharecropper and the landless labourer, they have been more often than not left out in the cold. In consequence . . . disparities have widened, accentuating social tensions"[10] and producing a situation requiring urgent action by responsible authorities.

It appears that the prime minister, Mrs. Indira Gandhi, and other concerned officials of government agreed with the Home Ministry's assessment of the seriousness of the tensions growing in rural areas. Mrs. Gandhi addressed a letter to all state chief ministers on August 18, 1969, in which she made plain the view that an effec-

[7] India, Home Ministry, Research and Policy Division, "The Causes and Nature of Current Agrarian Tensions," p. 4.

[8] Ibid., p. 10.

[9] Ibid.

[10] Ibid., p. 32.

tive agricultural development strategy for India would require "not only organization and inputs but also the removal of existing institutional and social impediments to production."[11] She pointed out that small farmers, tenants, and landless laborers had not been sharing adequately in such progress as had been generated as a result of various rural development measures, including land reforms. She alluded to the growth of agrarian tensions—suggesting, for example, that the "landless labourers have been dissatisfied about not getting their due share,"[12] even in circumstances in which agricultural production increases had been recorded.

Mrs. Gandhi urged the chief ministers to implement programs that might benefit the rural have-nots, reduce social tensions, and produce a climate in which rural development could proceed without disruption.[13]

First, she asked that a "fair share of fertilizer, seeds and irrigation facilities" be guaranteed to small farmers. Second, she appealed for measures in the states which would help to assure security of tenure for cultivators threatened with eviction by others more powerful in the rural hierarchy. Third, Mrs. Gandhi asked that ceilings on the size of land holdings be implemented and surplus lands distributed to the landless. Fourth, she asked that consolidation of holdings programs be implemented "within a specified period of time." Fifth, Mrs. Gandhi called for the expansion of employment opportunities outside of agriculture for landless laborers in order to reduce the pressure of population on available land resources. This might be done, she suggested, through establishing "viable programmes of rural works" financed possibly by Panchayati Raj institutions wherever they were active.

Mrs. Gandhi concluded her message to the chief ministers of the states by stressing that the implementation of her recommendations was important not only from the point of view of social justice, but also from the point of view of assuring the spread of improved farm practices to those in the rural hierarchy, such as

[11] India, Ministry of Food, Agriculture, Community Development and Cooperation, "Chief Ministers' Conference on Land Reform—Notes on Agenda," Annexure C, p. C1.

[12] Ibid.

[13] The five proposals as outlined in the text are paraphrased and quoted (in part) from Mrs. Gandhi's letter to the chief ministers (ibid., pp. C1–C2).

sharecroppers, who had been slow to adopt new practices because the agrarian structure gave them insufficient incentive. She left implicit the argument that state action on her various recommendations was important to the preservation of political stability, hopefully through the provision of belated benefits to sections of the peasantry who had been, for the most part, nonbeneficiaries in twenty-two years of rural development.

The recommendations of the central government, transmitted by the prime minister to the state chief ministers, were followed by the convening of a Chief Ministers' Conference on Land Reform in November 1969. At this conference, attention was focused anew by the Center on the states' need to transform "the agrarian structure of the country through speedy, efficient and effective implementation of land reforms."[14] Once again the central government was attempting to achieve through exhortation and the communication of a sense of urgency what had not been accomplished, except in a few regions, in more than two decades of programming for rural development.

Bihar Government's Reaction to Rural Unrest

The period immediately preceding and following the Chief Ministers' Conference of November 28–29, 1969, was one of possibly unprecedented attempts on the part of Bihar state officials (and central government officials during a period of President's Rule) to implement existing agrarian reform legislation and to introduce new legislation conforming in broad outline to various recommendations made by authorities of the central government.

During the last months of 1969 and the first months of 1970, perhaps the most conspicuous activity in Bihar in the broad field of agrarian reforms occurred in the state legislature, where numerous measures were introduced.

That there should have been a flurry of attempts to introduce new land reform legislation in Bihar in 1969–1970, following years of plodding implementation of existing legislation, cannot be interpreted simply as that state's almost immediate response to a new round of central government exhortation, which had been tried frequently in the past and had been mainly ineffective in pro-

[14] Ibid., p. ii.

ducing results at the state level. A more credible, if not complete, explanation for the timing of the introduction of new legislation is that Bihar's ruling "minority" (comprised generally, irrespective of party affiliation, of landed, urban-based, and high-caste communities) was responding symbolically to its instincts for self-preservation as it contemplated the gradual mobilization and politicization of a rural-based majority of economically depressed, backward, and scheduled castes. Fearing that the emerging majority would be led by dissident politicians prepared to exploit land hunger and other parochial issues for diverse purposes (including possibly the destruction of existing institutions and the men who had so long dominated them), the ruling elite acted swiftly to preempt the programs of the dissidents and to demonstrate their own "radical" and "socialist" credentials. From this perspective, the new legislative proposals can be seen as a rather desperate attempt to anticipate peasant demands by demonstrating that lawful changes in the agrarian structure might be effected by a genuinely responsive government before unlawful changes became a prevalent and accepted mode of addressing agrarian problems in Bihar.

The new legislative proposals are discussed in succeeding paragraphs.

Bihar Tenancy (Amendment) Act, 1970

Proposed in June 1970, the Bihar Tenancy (Amendment) Act, 1970—Bihar Act VI of 1970—was enacted by the president of India, during a period of President's Rule in Bihar,[15] to amend Section 109 of the Bihar Tenancy Act, 1885. The amendment act removed from the jurisdiction of Bihar's civil courts certain applications or suits (arising generally from disputes over rights in land) and granted to administrative officers of government the power to dispose of such suits or applications outside of a court of law.

More specifically, the amendment act eliminated from the jurisdiction of civil courts all applications or suits (including those already pending when the amendment act was passed) (*a*) relating

[15] President's Rule can be invoked in certain circumstances specified in the *Constitution of India.* When President's Rule is in effect, the president can assume to himself "all or any of the functions of the government of the State," including legislative functions (India, Ministry of Law, *Constitution of India,* Part XVIII, Articles 354–356).

to government's attempts to produce up-to-date records of rights in land and rent rolls or (*b*) growing out of confusion concerning tenancy rights in land.

This was a bold, if controversial, attempt to assure that land disputes would be settled expeditiously by government officers on the spot, rather than being transferred to civil courts. Interpreted positively, the amendment act offered the possibility of the resolution of controversies over rights in land in a fashion less costly to both disputants and the state.

Even critics of the amendment act, while interpreting its passage as a blow against long-established judicial procedures, had to admit that justice was not being rendered to anyone as long as Bihar's civil courts were so swamped with cases that most decisions trickled out of the courts only after years of delay—delay which contributed to a climate of fear in rural areas and made it unlikely that disputed lands would be improved or farmed efficiently in the period during which court decisions were pending.[16]

The interests of all parties could be served if the Bihar Tenancy (Amendment) Act of 1970 facilitates the quick settlement of land disputes. This is not to suggest, however, that the amendment act's implementation will necessarily assure the rights of the weaker sections of rural society any better than they were assured earlier in civil court cases involving the rich and the poor. In a hierarchical and inegalitarian society, those lowest in the hierarchy are likely to continue to find themselves at a disadvantage, whether land disputes are settled within or outside of a civil court. In such a society even the concept of equal justice under law is illusive.

The Bihar Tenancy (Amendment) Bill, 1970

The Bihar Tenancy (Amendment) Bill, 1970, was designed to amend Section 48C of the Bihar Tenancy Act of 1885. The bill, if enacted and implemented, would deny any under-raiyat the opportunity to acquire the rights of permanent occupancy over certain lands temporarily in his possession "irrespective of the duration of his holding"[17] such lands as an under-raiyat. Under the provisions

[16] In Purnea District alone, for example, there were more than 38,000 litigations pending early in 1970.

[17] Bihar, Laws, statutes, etc. (Notices). "Notice Issued to the Assembly Secretariat for the Introduction and Consideration of the Bihar Tenancy (Amend-

of the Bihar Tenancy Act of 1885, an under-raiyat (or tenant of a raiyat) could acquire such occupancy rights simply by holding land continuously "as an under-raiyat in any village whether under a lease or otherwise . . . for a period of twelve years."[18]

The amendment bill provided that a landlord[19] could hold a minimum amount of land tilled by his tenants (or under-raiyats) without jeopardy of losing it to an under-raiyat's claim. Specifically, the landlord could hold (*a*) at least five acres of land irrigated by flow irrigation, lift irrigation, or tube wells (whether such irrigation facilities were owned, constructed, maintained, or improved by the central government or the state government or were owned and maintained by the landlord) or (*b*) ten acres of "other land" (the understanding being that one acre of irrigated land as described above would be equivalent to two acres of "other land").

The amendment bill provided additional protection to landlords who could be classified as widows, persons suffering from mental or physical disability, or public servants, including members of the army, navy, and air force "in receipt of substantive salary not exceeding six hundred and fifty rupees a month"[20] (while remaining thus classified).

The above provisions, proponents of the bill would argue, were not designed to benefit landlords at the expense of their tenants. Instead, it was said, such provisions were framed to reduce tensions in rural areas between landlords and tenants (tensions that might lead to evictions of tenants in order to remove the possibility of their claiming occupancy rights in land). From this perspective, the amendment bill would protect indirectly the temporary rights of tenants simply by reducing the fear prevalent among landlords that their occupancy rights in certain lands might be threatened by their tenants. However, it can be argued that fears are unlikely to

ment) Bill, 1970" (unpublished: June 12, 1970). A copy of this unpublished document was made available to the author on August 9, 1970, by officials of the government of Bihar. At that time printed copies of the bill were not available.

[18] "Bihar Tenancy Act of 1885," Section 48C. In India, Ministry of Food and Agriculture, *Agricultural Legislation in India*, VI.

[19] The bill uses the word "landlord" rather than the term "occupancy raiyat" to refer to those landholders having permanent occupancy rights in land.

[20] Bihar, Laws, statutes, etc. (Notices). "Notice Issued to the Assembly Secretariat for the Introduction . . . of the Bihar Tenancy (Amendment) Bill, 1970."

be reduced among large landholders by a measure giving added protection to only five or ten acres of their holdings.

The temporary rights of tenants were to be further protected by another section of this 1970 amendment bill. That section stated that an under-raiyat "threatened with unlawful ejectment from his tenancy or portion thereof by his landlord"[21] could be shielded by the intervention of the appropriate district-level official of government, either acting independently or in response to an application submitted to him by an under-raiyat. Similar provisions in the Bihar Tenancy Act, 1885, would have permitted the intervention of an official of government to settle a dispute between a landlord and his tenant only following the "unlawful ejectment" of the tenant, not in response to a "threatened" ejectment.

In general, it can be said that this bill's provisions, even if enacted and enforced, are unlikely to affect established practices by which under-raiyats are seldom "evicted" from lands previously leased and tilled by them, but are forced to surrender those lands "voluntarily" by their landlords. It is the failure of any legislation in the past to protect adequately the temporary rights of under-raiyats that has helped to give substance to arguments of those who are attempting to persuade sections of the peasantry to move outside the structure of the law to seize the lands they consider to be their own.

The Bihar Land Reforms (Amendment) Bill, 1970

The Bihar Land Reforms (Amendment) Bill, 1970, was introduced to make the Bihar Land Reforms Act, 1950, fully applicable to lands in the possession of industrial establishments, such as the Tata land in Jamshedpur, Singhbhum District, Bihar. Under the provisions of the Land Acquisition Act of 1894 some lands (including the "Tata Zamindari") had been acquired to be used as "industrial undertakings"; as "industrial undertakings" these lands have been exempted from the provisions of the Bihar Land Reforms Act, 1950. Through the provisions of the 1970 amendment bill, the lands on which "industrial undertakings" had been established would be vested in the state; that is to say, such lands would no longer be exempted from the provisions of the Bihar Land Reforms Act, 1950.

[21] Ibid.

The Bihar Land Reforms (Amendment) Bill, 1970, does not make specific mention of the Tata interests or of the interests of any other industrialists. Yet, the bill's proponents made no attempt to disguise the fact that their attention was focused mainly on the "Tata Zamindari." It seems clear that the amendment bill was intended to have symbolic meaning to informed, leftist-oriented sections of the Bihar electorate. From this perspective, the bill was a means of affirming the "socialist" convictions of the eight-party coalition government led by the Congress (Ruling).[22]

The symbolic purpose of the amendment bill was underlined time and again by officials of the government of Bihar in interviews in July and August of 1970. These officials (including some who would be responsible for enforcing the bill after its enactment) expressed their doubt that the amendment bill would have other than symbolic significance. However, in August 1970 there was some indication that officials of Tata industries had questions about the amendment bill's potential effects and might be prepared to enter into litigation with the state of Bihar over the matter. Others questioned the amendment bill on the grounds that it would establish a precedent that would make the Bihar Land Reforms Act, 1950, applicable to many forms of urban property on which not only industries but also private residences have been established.

The Bihar Public Land Encroachment (Amendment) Ordinance, 1970

The Bihar Public Land Encroachment (Amendment) Ordinance, 1970,[23] substituted "new sections" for Sections 3, 6, and 11 of the

[22] The government responsible for the introduction of most of the legislative proposals discussed in this section was an eight-party coalition, headed by Indira Gandhi's Congress (Ruling) party. That government was formed following elections in Bihar in February 1970.

[23] An ordinance such as this one has, pending ratification by the Assembly, "the same force and effect as an Act of the Legislature of the State" (India, Ministry of Law, *Constitution of India*, Article 213).

The Bihar Public Land Encroachment (Amendment) Bill, 1970, was issued to the Assembly Secretariat for introduction and consideration on June 22, 1970. The state legislature was not in session when the bill was promulgated by the governor of Bihar as the Bihar Public Land Encroachment (Amendment) Ordinance, 1970, on the grounds that circumstances warranted immediate action.

In July 1970, printed copies of the bill or the ordinance were not avail-

Bihar Public Land Encroachment Act, 1956 (Bihar Act XV of 1956). The ordinance was designed to give government (through its district collectors) the power to initiate proceedings against any person who is likely to make "or is making, or has made, or is responsible for the continuance of, any encroachment upon public land [land vested legally in the state of Bihar]."[24] By means of this ordinance, government district collectors were empowered not only to initiate proceedings against such persons but also to issue, at any time, "a temporary injunction to restrain such encroachment, or make such other order for the purposes of preventing such encroachment"[25] as seems appropriate in each instance until the land encroachment issue is settled. According to the ordinance, the actual settlement of land encroachment cases is to be effected by the district collectors themselves using one of three alternatives: (*a*) by dropping proceedings following appropriate investigation; or (*b*) by issuing a permanent injunction restraining a person from encroaching on public lands; or (*c*) in certain circumstances, by permitting the permanent acquisition of public lands (not to exceed one-tenth of an acre) encroached upon when such lands are contiguous to an agricultural holding of not more than five acres.

The ordinance also contains a provision that permits a landless laborer[26] to retain public lands on which he has encroached prior to the tenth of October, 1955, if it can be proven that that laborer had "no homestead on the date of such encroachment and the encroachment does not exceed an area of one-eighth of an acre."[27]

Finally, the ordinance specifies that "no suit shall lie in a Civil Court in respect of encroachment upon any public land."[28]

---

able. Officials of the government of Bihar made available to the author a copy of the "Notice Issued to the Assembly Secretariat for the Introduction and Consideration of the Bihar Public Land Encroachment (Amendment) Bill, 1970" (unpublished, June 22, 1970).

24 Bihar, Laws, statutes, etc. (Notices). "Notice Issued to the Assembly Secretariat for the Introduction and Consideration of the Bihar Public Land Encroachment (Amendment) Bill, 1970" (unpublished, June 22, 1970).

25 Ibid.

26 For the purposes of the Bihar Public Land Encroachment (Amendment) Ordinance, 1970, a landless laborer is a "person whose main source of livelihood is agriculture or agricultural labor and who does not hold any land or holds land not exceeding one acre" (ibid.).

27 Ibid.

28 Ibid.

In order to apply the provisions of this ordinance, the government of Bihar needs up-to-date and reliable land records. For the most part, such records continue to be lacking in Bihar, as has been mentioned earlier in this work. In the absence of such records, government (in 1970) does not know how much of its land has been encroached upon (or "grabbed") by the stronger sections of rural society.[29] Indeed, in the period leading up to the land-grab movement of August 1970, proponents of the movement commonly argued that they were encouraging the peasants to emulate their superiors in rural areas who had already demonstrated (through encroachments on government land, through forced evictions of peasants, and through fictitious settlements and transfers of land designed to evade Bihar's ceilings legislation) that land grabbing was a "respectable" means of acquiring acreage.

While there is spuriousness in the argument that land grabbing by the poor is justified simply because the rich have already demonstrated that illegal encroachments on public and other lands can be effected without penalty, it must be admitted by responsible men that Bihar's ruling elite have been witnesses to land grabbing (of the sort described in the preceding paragraph) for years. Having tacitly accepted, or, in some cases, willfully abetted such processes, the ruling elite were in a vulnerable position in 1970 from which to condemn the new land grabbers as a potentially revolutionary rabble, lacking in respect for democratic institutions and the rule of law. Put in this context, the promulgation of the Bihar Public Land Encroachment (Amendment) Ordinance, 1970, can be considered a belated and rather ineffective way of demonstrating official concern that the stealthily effected land grabs of the past be rectified.

The Bihar Consolidation of Holdings and Prevention of Fragmentation (Amendment) Bill, 1970

The Bihar Consolidation of Holdings and Prevention of Frag-

[29] In the words of Jaya Prakash Narayan, "In Bihar, the situation is so bad that the Government itself does not know how much vested land it has and what is the extent of encroachment upon it. Government policy and orders have also been such that encroachment, though stealthy and illegal, has been given the appearance of legality" (interview with Jaya Prakash Narayan, Musahari Block, Muzaffarpur District, Bihar, August 10, 1970).

mentation (Amendment) Bill, 1970, was intended to facilitate the implementation of the consolidation of holdings legislation enacted in 1956. The means adopted in the 1970 amendment bill was to permit relatively recent land records (produced by Survey and Settlement operations within five years preceding the date of publication of the notification by government of its intention to consolidate lands within a specified locality) to be considered up-to-date records for the purposes of consolidation operations. Thus, the amendment bill moved in the direction of utilizing, where possible, existing land records produced during post-independence Survey and Settlement operations. Yet, the amendment bill did not respond adequately to the need, noted earlier, to link Survey and Settlement and consolidation procedures so that consolidation tasks might be undertaken immediately following the publishing of up-to-date land records in a given region.

The belated recognition in the amendment bill of 1970 that there are procedural impediments to the implementation of Bihar's land consolidation program can be welcomed. However, the delays associated with the implementation of consolidation of holdings have been due to factors in addition to those which can be considered procedural. Therefore, further delays in the implementation of consolidation of holdings in Bihar can be anticipated following enactment of the 1970 amendment bill.

Whether the continuing delay in implementation of Bihar's land consolidation program will be associated with a rise in agrarian tensions is impossible to predict. The consolidation issue is less clearly linked to contemporary unrest in Bihar than some other issues. It may be that more vigorous action to implement consolidation would be more productive of rural tension than the persistence of a consolidation effort on the part of government that lacks vigor.

The Bihar Privileged Persons Homestead Tenancy (Amendment) Bill, 1970

The Bihar Privileged Persons Homestead Tenancy (Amendment) Bill, 1970, was designed to insert a new section in the Bihar Privileged Persons Homestead Tenancy Act, 1947. The 1947 act had provided a means by which certain peasants (essentially landless, but some with dwarf holdings) could acquire a permanent tenancy right to their "homesteads"[30]—that is, could become "privileged" permanent tenants—if they held these homesteads continuously, at any time, for a period of at least one year while paying rent to their landlords.[31] The amendment bill of 1970 was designed to make such "privileged" peasants tenants of the state, acting in its capacity as super landlord. It was explicit in the bill that the "privileged" tenants would pay rent (at rates comparable to those paid to landlords in the past) to the state, and that the former landlords would receive compensation equivalent to ten times the rent payable in each instance by their former tenants.[32]

Thus, the amendment bill of 1970 would enable the state of Bihar to establish a direct relationship with such "privileged" tenants and would deny former landlords the right to collect rent from tenants who had earlier acquired "permanent tenancy rights" to a homestead.

Among the problems associated with implementing this legislation are two that have hampered the effective implementation of similar legislation. First, in the absence of reliable and up-to-date

[30] These Bihar "homesteads" can be considered, in general, to be huts comprised of jute stalks and straw standing on roughly five-hundredths of an acre of land.

[31] The difficulties associated with becoming a "privileged" permanent tenant should be obvious. Any landlord could deny his tenant such status simply by evicting him before the legislated conditions of "privileged tenancy" were fulfilled or by denying him the right to establish or maintain a "homestead" on any part of the landlord's holding.

[32] In 1970, government estimated that roughly 800,000 privileged tenants would be covered by the 1947 act, as it would be amended by the 1970 amendment bill. Two hundred thousand were considered to be occupants of land that had already vested in the state. The remaining 600,000 were thought to have homesteads on lands encompassing no more than 30,000 acres, the average homestead holding being of minute size. With average rents in the state as a whole considered to be Rs. 3.25 per acre, government estimated that the total rent received by landlords from their privileged tenants in a year would be Rs. 97,500 (30,000 acres times Rs. 3.25). In estimating the amount of compensation payable to landlords, this amount was inflated by 25 percent to allow for rent increases (which have already taken place in certain districts of Bihar under so-called "fair rent settlement proceedings" conducted by government) and multiplied by ten, in accordance with the provisions of the 1970 amendment bill, to provide an official estimate of Rs. 1,218,750 to be paid to landlords in cash in one installment.

land records, government can only estimate roughly the number of "privileged tenants" covered by the bill; where these tenants are located and their exact number was not known in 1970 by anyone. Second, government could not establish reliable records speedily, given traditional procedures, even if full cooperation from landlords were forthcoming.

Even if, following its enactment, expeditious implementation of the Bihar Privileged Persons Homestead Tenancy (Amendment) Bill, 1970, were assumed, the "privileged" tenants would receive negligible benefits from the legislation. Those who could be evicted easily from their homesteads have already been evicted. Those who could not be evicted by their landlords have been enjoying the same permanent tenancy rights to their homesteads that are to be maintained without modification by their new landlord, the state of Bihar. Therefore, any benefits that may be derived by the peasantry from this legislation are obscure and can be classified as intangible. There is no provision for the enhancement of the economic or social status of the "privileged tenant" in this legislation. He is to exchange one landlord relationship for another. His responsibility to pay rent to his landlord for his homestead is to remain unchanged, except that his rent may be increased. Whether the new relationship might provide him greater security than the old remains to be determined over time, and it is obvious that the peasant could be as susceptible to eviction and exploitation under the new relationship as the old, when the state's agents are corrupt.

It is difficult to believe that the 1970 amendment bill would contribute to a reduction in agrarian tensions in Bihar. Too few tenants are covered by the legislation; those that are receive uncertain benefits from it. Another set of petty landlords would become, in a legal sense, "ex-intermediaries," deprived of their right to collect rent from a certain class of tenants. They would lose in status but acquire some benefits in the form of compensation. For its part, government would acquire new responsibilities associated with the administration of the legislation. It would have to determine who its new tenants were, what rents they should pay, and how much compensation is due the ex-intermediaries. There is nothing in the Bihar record to suggest that government has the capacity to fulfill these responsibilities, except in a fashion that pleases no one. Thus, the legislation's effects may be to exacerbate rural tensions, rather than to diminish them, at least in the short run.

Bihar Government's Reaction to the 1970 Land-Grab Movement

Despite the hurried legislative attempts designed, in part, to defuse agrarian tensions, tensions in rural Bihar continued to mount. By the summer of 1970, even the least discerning of observers recognized that substantial sections of the Bihar peasantry were both "awakened" and capable (with assistance from outsiders) of placing new demands before the political elite. Politicians of the left in particular had become increasingly cognizant of the potential power of an aroused peasantry. It had become obvious to them that the issue of land hunger was one around which millions of peasants might be mobilized.

In Bihar, and in India as a whole, tension mounted as the hot season waned and the monsoon began. Rumors abounded. There was increasing talk of a nationally coordinated mobilization of the peasantry—a mobilization designed to effect drastic changes in the country's agrarian structure, by means of force if necessary. People in rural as well as urban areas became fearful about what the future might hold. Landholders with substantial acreage in Bihar began to discuss strategies to meet the threat of a peasant uprising; they began also to carry arms and to demand police protection.

With each passing day, rumors fed the fear of massive, even revolutionary, change, and it seemed more likely that there would be violence in rural areas of Bihar, as well as in other regions of India. A national land-grab movement was endorsed by the Praja Socialists, the Samyukta Socialists, and the Communist party of India, Right (or Moscow oriented). The movement was to be launched everywhere on August 9 (in commemoration of the Quit India movement of 1942) and its first phase was to be completed by August 15.

In Bihar, government displayed concern about what seemed to be happening and pleaded for more time to implement its already legislated package of agrarian reforms. There was no need, argued government leaders, to grab lands unlawfully. Appropriate lawful measures would be taken within three months (*a*) to enforce ceilings, (*b*) to distribute surplus lands among the landless, (*c*) to issue "parchas"[33] to the landless to assure their right to hold the land on which their huts or homesteads stood, and (*d*) to prevent the illegal eviction of sharecroppers from the lands they tilled.

On July 1, 1970, government issued a directive to all Revenue Department officials. It urged them to implement land reform measures on a priority basis. The directive said, in part, that government attached "the highest importance to the speedy implementation of land reforms. . . . As you are aware, delay in implementing land reforms often leads to agrarian unrest and the two are, therefore, interconnected. . . . [T]here would be little or no cause for any agrarian unrest"[34] if full implementation of existing legislation had been effected in the past. The directive concluded by specifying that the land reforms implementation drive should be carried on with immediate effect and should be continued until the 30th of September.

Eight days after the July 1 directive, on July 9, another urgent message was communicated to government officers throughout the state. It urged each revenue officer at the block level to go on tour within the area of his immediate responsibility in the interests of collecting rapidly data relevant to the implementation of the various reforms. It also specified that a weekly progress report be sent to government showing, for example, the number of "big cases taken up" in connection with the implementation of the ceilings legislation; the number of cases encountered in which government lands had been illegally encroached upon by big landholders; the number of cases "in which the encroachments are vacated as a result of persuasion or legal action"; the amount of land available for settlement with weaker sections of the peasantry; and the amount of such land actually distributed to deserving persons. The directive emphasized government's sense of urgency concerning the implementation drive by stating that the annual confidential reports covering the performance of its civil servants in the year 1970–1971 should make special reference to work done well or poorly

[33] "Parchas" is used here to mean legal certificates.

[34] Bihar, Revenue Department, "D.O. No. 5LR-LA-224/70-5667-L.R." (unpublished: Patna, July 1, 1970). A copy of this directive was supplied to the author on July 29, 1970, through the courtesy of the Revenue Department, Government of Bihar.

during the drive. Moreover, government asked all officers to appreciate "the need of the hour to rise to the occasion and reorient the work in such a fashion that the drive is made a real success."[35]

Tensions continued to grow. Newspapers carried reports on July 17, 1970, that the land grab was already in progress and that communist-inspired mobs of peasants were taking possession of government fallow lands in the district of Purnea, north Bihar. The same reports suggested also that the communists were busily collecting data concerning other lands that might be occupied in that region and that a "Kisan Sabha" (a farmers' organization comprised, in this case, of large landholders and their representatives) had been established in Purnea to resist the land-grab movement.[36]

On July 18, government heightened anxiety among landholders by publishing the names of 125 of the largest landholders in the state. Many of these were ex-zamindars and substantial raiyats who still retained estates comprised of hundreds, even thousands, of acres of land in Patna, Shahabad, Saran, Champaran, Muzaffarpur, Darbhanga, Bhagalpur, Monghyr, Purnea, Saharsa, and Hazaribagh districts. Among the major estates named were those of Kursaila in Purnea, Dumraon Raj in Shahabad, Darbhanga Raj in Darbhanga, Hathwa Raj in Saran, and Ramgarh Raj in Hazaribagh. At the same time, government specified that the lands of all who had been named would immediately be brought within the purview of the ceilings act of 1961, and their cases disposed of "summarily."[37] Simultaneously, government let it be known that notices under the ceilings act were being served on "at least five big farmers in each of the 587 blocks in the State."[38] Their cases were to be processed in accordance with procedures set forth in the ceilings act and disposed of as quickly as possible in order to enable government to distribute at least 100,000 acres of surplus land to the landless by the end of September 1970.

[35] Bihar, Revenue Department, "D.O. No. 5LR-LA-224/70-6016-L.R." (unpublished: Patna, July 9, 1970). A copy of this directive was made available to the author on July 29, 1970, through the courtesy of the Revenue Department, Government of Bihar.

[36] *Indian Nation*, July 17, 1970, p. 1.

[37] For the names of all landholders listed by government, see *Indian Nation*, July 19, 1970, p. 1.

[38] Ibid.

The next day, July 19, brought confirmation of a disturbance near the village of Sathi in Champaran District of north Bihar. Two men were killed by the police in an incident described in the press as "part of the land grab movement launched by the Communist Party of India in order to secure Government fallow and surplus private land to hand over to the landless peasants."[39] On the same day, the Samyukta Socialist party announced that one of its land-grab targets in Bihar would be the estate of the late maharaja of Darbhanga. A spokesman of the Communist party of India, Right, Mr. Bhogendra Jha, M.P., stated that his party's Farm Labour Organization (Khet Muzdoor Sabha) would give special attention to Darbhanga District during the forthcoming land-grab exercise. Darbhanga District, said Mr. Jha, had been the scene of large-scale violations of existing land reform legislation by big landlords. According to Jha (and the evidence supports his assertions), these landlords had forcibly evicted sharecroppers, demolished the homes of landless peasants, illegally occupied the fallow government lands, and generally abused less-powerful sections of the peasantry.

July 19 also brought reports (possibly distorted) of aggressive government activity at the subdivisional level in Monghyr District. The *Indian Nation* stated that the subdivisional officer of Begusarai, Monghyr District, had announced publicly that the surplus lands of five landlords in each of eleven blocks within his jurisdiction would be seized and distributed among the landless.[40] Whether an accurate report or not, the news from Begusarai was distressing to landed interests who seemed (from their perspective) to be caught between the hammer of the land-grab activists and the anvil of a government eager to demonstrate belatedly its vigorous commitment to the implementation of land reforms.

Rumors began circulating with increased velocity. Large landholders converged on Patna and gathered in each other's town houses,[41] commiserating with one another and asking, "What can we do?" "How can we protect our interests?" "From whom can we

[39] Ibid., July 20, 1970, p. 1.

[40] Ibid., July 19, 1970, p. 5.

[41] The author was present at several such gatherings in Patna in July and August 1970.

draw support?" As if in response, political parties of the right, opposed to the land-grab movement, began issuing statements condemning those who would agitate the peasants, end rural tranquility, and create a dangerous law and order situation in the state as a whole. Bihar's conservative Bharatiya Kranti Dal issued statements labeling the incipient movement of the left as unconstitutional, unjust, and antinational. The working committee of the Bihar unit of the Bharatiya Jana Sangh passed a resolution denouncing the land-grab movement of the Communist party, ignoring the land-grab intentions of the Samyukta Socialist party and the Praja Socialist party, and charging the Congress (Ruling) led coalition government of Bihar with having encouraged the lawless activities of the Communist party of India.

The former Congress chief minister, K. B. Sahay, acting as president of the Congress (Organization), also lashed out at the land-grab movement, emphasizing his party's opposition to it. The movement, he said, would lead only to violence and anarchy and would not result in the landless receiving land. Indeed, argued Sahay, there was insufficient land for distribution to all who desired it; neither violent nor nonviolent methods could make elastic a resource which was inelastic.

There were new developments on July 23. Two thousand armed men, said to be Naxalites, the most militantly pro-Peking segment of India's fragmented Communist party, attacked the holding of a landlord of Bhagalpur District and forcibly harvested thirty-one bighas of standing crops.

Three days later, on July 26, a Jana Sangh party worker was killed in Musahari Block, Muzaffarpur District, north Bihar. Because Musahari Block (located in perhaps the most densely populated rural region of India—a region with more than nine hundred people per square kilometer) had long been considered a communist (Naxalite) stronghold, the Jana Sanghi's death was immediately interpreted by many to be a political assassination directly linked to the land-grab movement. Police reinforcements were rushed to Musahari to forestall further violence.

With the death of the Jana Sangh worker, attention shifted for a time from the Communist party of India, Right, to the Naxalites. On August 3 an anti-Naxalite meeting was held in Jamshedpur under the auspices of the Jana Sangh, and a twelve-foot effigy of Mao was burned to climax the occasion. Four days later (August 7), there was an anti-Maoist procession in Patna. As the procession moved past the main gate of Patna College and proceeded about two hundred yards to the west, a homemade bomb was thrown into the midst of it, hitting by chance a passing rickshaw and severely injuring its occupant, the principal of a local public school. Tension mounted to new heights. Government imposed a curfew on the Patna municipal area. It became more fashionable than ever to deplore the breakdown in law and order.

Meanwhile, additional voices were being raised against the growing climate of violence. Jaya Prakash Narayan had decided, before the Naxalites became a burning issue, to confront them in their Musahari stronghold. Having set up camp in Musahari in June 1970, he now issued public statements emphasizing that Bihar's land problem should be resolved by peaceful persuasion rather than by violence. He also stressed that time was running out for those who would substitute token reforms for fundamental efforts aimed at a redistribution of land resources and income. There would be no substitute for violence, he added, if there were further delays in the implementation of reforms enacted and promised.

The prospect for violence seemed immediate enough to the inspectors general of police in the states of Bihar, West Bengal, Orissa, and Andhra. They made known their plan to meet and to evolve a joint program for curbing the activities of political elements committed to socioeconomic change through acts of violence.

Demonstrating similar concern about the likelihood of violence, the government of Bihar banned the carrying in public of all weapons and instructed all district authorities to maintain law and order, using minimum force, during the formal phase of the land grab to be launched on August 9.

Government also urged the Communist party of India, Right, the Praja Socialist party, and the Samyukta Socialist party to postpone the land grab, giving government additional time to meet its pledge to speedily implement existing land reform legislation by the end of September. There was no response from the parties of the left.

Apparently fearing the worst, government issued urgent new directives on August 8 to all of its district officers, emphasizing their responsibility for preventing mob violence, if necessary by exercising police power against those engaged in land grab, or land-grab related activities.

August 9 came and went. Reports began filtering in to Patna. Violence on any significant scale had apparently been averted. The principal parties engaged in the land-grab movement issued their own progress reports on August 10. The Communist party of India, Right, and its supporters claimed to have occupied two thousand acres over the state as a whole; fifteen hundred of these acres were said to have been grabbed in Bhagalpur District alone. The Praja Socialists claimed to have assisted twenty-five Harijan families in the liberation of one hundred acres of government fallow land in Gaya District and to have initiated the movement in Darbhanga, Monghyr, Gaya, and Ranchi districts of the state. In Ranchi, the Praja Socialist party claimed to have liberated lands alleged to be held by Shri Jagjivan Ram, a Bihari member of Mrs. Indira Gandhi's cabinet. The Samyukta Socialist party announced that thirty of its workers had been arrested while engaged in land-grab activities in Palamau, Muzaffarpur, and Gaya districts.

Within a few days, hundreds of political workers, members of the Communist party of India, Right, the Praja Socialist party, and the Samyukta Socialist party, had been detained by the police, and the land-grab movement's claimed successes started to dwindle in number. Indeed, the movement became more and more symbolic in character, and some began to speculate about the capacity of any of the leftist parties to mobilize the peasantry in a movement having meaningful scale.

Politicians of the left, such as Indradip Sinha,[42] were careful to explain that their strategy had not been aimed at a comprehensive mobilization of the peasantry. The Communist party of India, Right, suggested Sinha, had had limited objectives of symbolic dimensions. "Our attention," said Sinha, "was focused on no more than fifteen big landholders, such as Ramgarh, Darbhanga, Hathwa, Dumraon and Kursaila."[43]

[42] Indradip Sinha, a leader of the Communist party of India, Right, was revenue minister in Bihar's first United Front Government, which was formed following the 1967 defeat of the Congress.

[43] Interview with Shri Indradip Sinha, Patna, Bihar, August 13, 1970.

Whether the land-grab strategy of the Communist party of India, Right, was limited in intent or not, five days after the author met with Indradip Sinha, the Bihar unit of the Communist party of India, Right, announced that it had decided to withdraw from the land-grab agitation. In withdrawing from the agitation, the Communist party of India, Right, emphasized that it would decide its future course of action after assessing the Bihar government's performance through September 30 in fulfilling agrarian reform implementation targets.

Left in the field in a movement of apparently rapidly waning immediate significance were the Samyukta Socialists and the Praja Socialists.

If the goal of any of the leftist parties had been to precipitate a full-scale peasant uprising, they had experienced frustration. But if, as is more likely, their goals had been of limited definition—designed to apply pressure on government and to engender promises of rapid implementation of land reforms previously enacted, as well as to secure publicity and to contribute further to the awakening of the peasantry—then their success could not be discounted.

Agrarian Tensions in Bihar in the Context of Government's Failure to Implement Agrarian Reforms

Neither the spate of agrarian reform legislation introduced in 1969–1970 nor the government's promises that existing legislation would be implemented were effective in preventing land-grab activity in July and August of 1970. The promises of government (together with government's police power) did provide the basis for short-term political adjustments between the political elite and the organizers of land grab. However, the short-term truce is in large measure dependent on government's carrying out its program of reforms, and it is unlikely that these reforms can be implemented in the near future.

The old obstacles to the implementation of agrarian reforms persist: (*a*) Up-to-date land records are available for only a fraction of Bihar's territory, and new records are being produced with something less than deliberate speed. (*b*) There is a dearth of relevant, trained personnel to execute the reforms, particularly at lower levels of the administrative hierarchy. The administrative procedures that determine the manner in which the reforms can be implemented are archaic, fitted to conditions of the nineteenth century but not to those of the twentieth—even when manipulated by able and dedicated administrators. (*c*) Those who oppose any change in Bihar's agrarian structure remain adept at exploiting existing loopholes in the law and at circumventing its provisions. (*d*) There is no consensus within government regarding the place and significance of agrarian reform measures in Bihar's general program for agricultural development. Indicative of this lack of consensus is the continuing administrative separation of agricultural production issues from agrarian reform issues in the central secretariat of Bihar. Dichotomous thinking on rural development is thus endorsed and nurtured. Agrarian reform, as an issue, stands divorced from agricultural development, however defined. In current government policy, agrarian reform is related vaguely to the reduction of agrarian tensions because it is supposed to address peasant demands, or at least the demands of certain political parties; agricultural development means simply the application of new technology (essentially "miracle" seeds, fertilizer, and water) in rural areas in a fashion thought to assure increases in production. The goal is to achieve increases in aggregate output. Who produces on what holdings and who benefits are questions to be set aside—or referred by those concerned with agricultural development to the Revenue Department, the unit primarily responsible for effecting agrarian reforms. (*e*) Finally, political consensus leading to the implementation of new agrarian reform measures is difficult to achieve, or maintain, among the diverse political parties that comprise the government of Bihar. This was so in the era of Congress dominance prior to 1967 when factions vied for power under the "umbrella" of that party, and it was so in 1970 with an eight-party coalition government in Bihar. Whereas caste and other factional struggles used to be carried on within the boundaries of the old Congress coalition, they are now carried on more obviously among the parties which support and buffet the Congress (Ruling). In this atmosphere, it is difficult to discern much commitment to the implementation of the new (or old) reforms, except when one faction sees political advantage over others by escalating its rhetorical commitment to radical agrarian reforms in the belief that such reforms are an increasingly significant (peasant mobilizing) issue in rural areas.

The immediate prospect in Bihar is for increasingly radical talk about the need for agrarian reforms, with little action in the field of implementation. Meanwhile, agrarian tensions will continue to build—and not only for reasons associated with the failure of government to implement its promised and legislated reforms.

Agrarian Tensions in Bihar in the Context of Social Change

In considering the growth of agrarian tensions in Bihar and in discussing the failure of government to implement various measures of agrarian reform, it is not our purpose to obscure other factors that have been instrumental in producing a climate of tension in rural areas.

Contemporary agrarian tensions are not simply of recent origin. They are associated not only with the land hunger of the poor and the failure of agrarian reforms in Bihar to meet newly articulated peasant demands, but also with a less-conspicuous struggle for power among competing elites and newly emerging groups.

The recent structure of power in Bihar has been one in which men of high caste and economic status have tended to predominate. Their power in the society has been a derivative of their social and ritual status and of their control over the source of economic power in an underdeveloped agrarian society—land. Traditionally, and particularly over the last thirty years, three castes (the Brahmans, Bhumihar Brahmans, and Rajputs) have influenced or controlled the state's decision-making processes, having achieved political dominance because they occupied the apex of both the social and economic hierarchies.

Earlier, during most of the period of British rule in Bihar, the structure of power was different. For the most part, political power was exercised by British authorities independent of the traditional system. High caste and economic status did not necessarily yield influence. Indeed, it appears that Bihari Hindus of high social and economic status were somewhat less favored by the colonial rulers than some other communities. Whether or not the British pursued a deliberate policy of favoring other groups, the historical record suggests that the Kayasthas, for example, enjoyed more influence than did higher-caste, landed Hindus by the end of the nineteenth century.

The Kayasthas are Hindus who first achieved distinctive status as the educated scribes of the Moghuls. Their status then, as under British rule and now, was based less on inherited social and economic status than on their capabilities as an educated community (with a stereotyped reputation for "cleverness") to perform services for others above them in the social hierarchy.

Additional opportunities for upward mobility and political influence were opened for the Kayasthas after 1911, when Bihar achieved separate identity from the province of Bengal. Prior to that date, the administrative services of Bihar had been dominated by Bengalis who had migrated from the Calcutta region and who had enjoyed a comparative educational advantage over Biharis. After 1911, the movement of Bengalis to Bihar diminished somewhat, and the Kayasthas of Bihar, the most literate and educated community in the region at the time, had greater access to positions of significance in public service.

It was not long after the separation of Bihar from Bengal before other castes—notably the Bhumihars, the Rajputs, and the Brahmans of Bihar—began to achieve political importance and to vie among themselves and with the Kayasthas for power. The political mobilization of these high-caste, landholding communities was not conspicuous during the early part of the twentieth century. But, as the struggle for independence from the United Kingdom gained adherents in Bihar—following Gandhi's involvement in the dispute between the peasantry and the indigo planters of Champaran District in 1917, the noncooperation movement of 1920, and successive campaigns of civil disobedience in the 1930s—each of these groups established its political identity. It was during this period that men such as Shri Krishna Sinha, a Bhumihar, and Anugrah Narayan Sinha, a Rajput, established their credentials as followers of Gandhi, supporters of the "freedom struggle," and rivals for control of the Congress movement in the state of Bihar.[44]

The Kayasthas also had their own distinguished exponents of freedom from British rule. The late former president of India, Dr. Rajendra Prasad, and Jaya Prakash Narayan, the socialist and

[44] *Illustrated Weekly of India*, March 17, 1968, p. 17. For information on the composition of Congress leadership at the all-India level, particularly in its years of political and organizational transformation, see Gopal Krishna, "Development of the Indian National Congress as a Mass Organization, 1918–23," *Journal of Asian Studies* (May 1966).

Bhoodan leader, were among the Bihar Kayasthas nationally recognized long before independence was achieved.

The shared interest in overthrowing British rule and in acquiring power for themselves bound these diverse caste groups together for a time. Each of these dominant groups recognized that it could not achieve political power in an independent Bihar, except in association with other groups. Some recognized that they were in a position to exercise power disproportionate to their numbers. Together, the Brahmans, Bhumihars, Rajputs, and Kayasthas comprised substantially less than 20 percent of the people of Bihar. Yet, representatives of these castes, in shifting alliances of convenience, ruled Bihar absolutely during the first two decades of independence and will strive to retain power during the third decade, that of the seventies.

It was this shifting coalition of elite castes that formed the Congress "monolith" in Bihar. Yet, even in periods of apparent stability, no other state government of India was so riven with internal rivalry, so replete with factions mobilizing support along lines of caste. It was this kind of government, with effective leadership distributed mainly among landholding upper castes, that was charged with responsibility for effecting agrarian reforms in Bihar. And it was this kind of government that failed to frame meaningful reforms and to implement them. To have pressed for such reforms would have been to risk changes in the agrarian structure of Bihar that would have threatened the continuing predominance of the Brahmans, the Bhumihars, the Rajputs, and, in some cases, the Kayasthas.

Whatever the interests of Bihar's ruling elites and however much they have sought to retain power in their own hands, it has now become obvious that new coalitions of lower and "backward" castes, and other interest groups, threaten the rule of the old elites. This, in essence, was the meaning of the general elections of 1967, when the Congress monolith in Bihar was shattered and, after the elections, a new government could not be formed simply by seeking a short-term consensus among the old dominant groups. The infighting for political power could no longer be confined within the old closed circle of Bhumihars, Rajputs, Brahmans, and Kayasthas. Other communities had become politically potent and either were increasing their demands to be incorporated within the existing political structure or were pressing for the destruction of that structure.

This basic competition for power between old, established elites and emerging groups seeking a role in decision-making contributes to and underlies current agrarian tensions in Bihar. It is a competition that supersedes issues and ideology. It will not be resolved in piecemeal fashion by addressing its more obvious manifestations.

During the next decade, it seems likely that there will be a continuous, though not always obvious, erosion of the power of the established high-caste and landed interests of Bihar. New demands have been articulated from below. Once generated, these demands will not cease. And, the masses of Biharis will be much less easily manipulated by a minority configuration of elite castes in the 1970s than in the 1950s, when promises of change served as substitutes for action.

The more traditional elites, striving to hold on to some vestige of power, will undoubtedly weigh alternative strategies. Some will attempt to sustain themselves in power through the more traditional Bhumihar, Brahman, Kayastha, and Rajput understandings and trade-offs. Others will seek to build alliances of convenience with newly emerging groups in the hope of maintaining indirect control over rural voters. Such a strategy implies the making of specific concessions to the demands of numerically strong lower castes, such as the Yaddavas. Still others may attempt to involve themselves directly in the mobilization of segments of the peasantry through the utilization of local issues.

It is this last strategy which some believe could lead to persistent peasant uprisings in Bihar during the next decade. While there is little evidence to suggest that revolutionary activities are likely to be initiated by the peasants themselves, such activities could be instigated—as was the land-grab movement of 1970—by minority groups (including a disgruntled, mainly high-caste, urban intelligentsia) seeking to exploit the discontent of the peasantry. Such a strategy would exploit the persisting gap between those who have ruled and the masses of the peasantry; it would exploit existing and growing tensions in rural areas between those who control land and those who want land, between those most able to benefit from new technology in agriculture and those least able to benefit from such new technology; it would build on the frustration and anger that are widespread among various classes of the Bihar peasantry, particularly those evicted from lands they once tilled as a result of shoddily framed and poorly implemented land reform legislation and those who still retain land in daily fear of losing it.

It remains possible that the ruling elites in Bihar will successfully absorb key elements of a new rural-based leadership into the old structure of power—thus broadening political participation in a fashion that undermines the efforts of any who would exploit latent discontent in rural areas.

It is also possible that would-be revolutionaries will be slow to recognize the revolutionary potential of the peasantry. The attention of those who want to change radically the Indian political system may continue to be focused on the cities rather than the countryside. Yet, the persistent intrusion of Maoist and North Vietnamese literature into Bihar and Bengal suggests that a variant on the Chinese revolutionary model may provide inspiration for those who already identify the peasantry as the critical group in India now that political mobilization is increasingly a phenomenon of the countryside. While the applicability of Maoist thought in India can be questioned, it has been amply demonstrated in Southeast Asia, and elsewhere, that "the peasants, as Furtado has observed in Brazil, are 'much more susceptible to revolutionary influences of the Marxist-Leninist kind than the urban classes, although the latter, according to orthodox Marxism, should be the spearhead of the revolutionary movement.' "[45]

Whether or not the existing tensions in Bihar will lead to peasant uprisings that can be classified as Maoist or Marxist-Leninist, the persistence of a fundamentally inegalitarian society comprised of a minority of "haves" and a majority of "have-nots" poses a threat to the orderly, constitutional development of that society. "Remove the secondary causes that have produced the great convulsions of the world and you will almost always find the principle of inequality at the bottom."[46]

Given the structure of power that has so long prevailed in Bihar —a structure that has perpetuated traditional inequalities in the social and economic system and fostered new inequities—it is easy to predict that issues such as distributive justice and land to the

[45] Samuel P. Huntington, *Political Order in Changing Societies*, p. 296.

[46] Alexis de Tocqueville, *Democracy in America*, p. 266.

tiller will again become fashionable in the days ahead as the old elites and those who oppose them wrestle for effective control over the peasantry. The results of this competition cannot be anticipated at present, but of one thing we can be certain: the competition will further the process already in motion by which the masses are being politicized. The next decade may determine whether the peasantry of Bihar will be stabilized or destabilized as a political force.[47]

It is here asserted that the peasantry is the critical group in Bihar (and in India) today. He who controls them will control the future of India. Whether or not this is already obvious to those currently in power or seeking power in Bihar is questioned by some. However, efforts on the part of leaders in the central government of India to identify their regime more closely with the plight of the peasantry are evident. The resurgent rhetoric of Mrs. Gandhi's dominant faction of the Congress—including the promises to implement existing laws on land reform by no later than 1971 and to check the rich, uplift the poor, and make the country more self-sufficient—can be seen as part of an effort both to identify with peasant interests and to respond, at least symbolically, to peasant demands. Whether or not the central government has the power to take action directly affecting the demands of the peasantry in a state like Bihar is less clear.

Agrarian Tensions in Bihar in the Context of Agricultural Production Maximization Focus

There is increasing evidence that the agrarian tensions in Bihar have been exacerbated by the strategy of production introduced in the 1960s in selected districts and regions of India. The strategy, in essence, was one of maximizing agricultural production by directing "state effort in the first instance to those areas which were best endowed for food production."[48] In Bihar, as elsewhere in India, this meant a concerted attempt on the part of government to

[47] Huntington's argument is considered to be relevant to the situation in Bihar—and compelling. "The role of the countryside is variable: it is either the source of stability or the source of revolution. For the political system opposition within the city is disturbing but not lethal. Opposition within the countryside, however, is fatal" (Huntington, *Political Order in Changing Societies*, p. 292).

[48] India, Planning Commission, *Fourth Five Year Plan, 1969–74*, p. 113.

concentrate development assistance in localities (such as Shahabad District in Bihar) which had already demonstrated high production potential. In such localities government attempted to make available to "progressive" cultivators a package of new inputs. Chemical fertilizers, high-yielding varieties of seeds, and improved irrigation facilities were the inputs given emphasis in the government program. This effort in the 1960s to introduce new technology in agriculture formed the basis of what has subsequently been lauded as the Green Revolution in India.

By 1968 it became commonplace in India to speak of an agricultural production miracle—a miracle claimed as the result of the selective introduction of improved seeds, chemical fertilizers, plant protection aids, improved implements and machinery, irrigation facilities, and agricultural credit. Indeed, after a lapse of some years, there was renewed talk in 1968 and 1969 of self-sufficiency in food production for India as a whole.

Soon, however, the enthusiasm for the production miracles made possible by the Green Revolution was tempered by more cautious observations. First, it was noted that the propagation of high-yielding varieties of seeds in India as a whole was confined to limited acreage and confined mainly to the new dwarf varieties of wheat.[49] In Bihar it was clearly premature in 1970 to speak of a Green Revolution, except in a carefully qualified sense with respect to wheat.[50] Experimentation with high-yielding varieties of wheat, paddy, bajra, maize, and jowar had taken place. However, high-yielding varieties of paddy, Bihar's principal food crop, covered only 705,558 acres in 1969–1970, and enthusiasm for the new paddy was low—due in part to the high-yielding variety's susceptibility to disease within Bihar's climatic conditions. Even the cover-

[49] "By 1967–68, 6.04 million hectares [in India] were brought within the purview of the program. On the eve of the Fourth Plan, the coverage estimated was 9.2 million hectares." The new varieties of wheat, where used, have been a notable success. "In some of the dwarf varieties, a yield of 5 to 6 tonnes per hectare has been recorded in farmers' fields as against a normal yield of about 2 tonnes in irrigated areas" (ibid., p. 114).

[50] The success of wheat relative to other Green Revolution crops was evident in the state of Bihar in 1970. This was confirmed through personal observation during 2,000 miles of touring within that state and conversations with Bihar government officials, various non-officials, extension workers in the field, and peasant cultivators.

age of new varieties of wheat was not so extensive in 1969–1970 as some Green Revolution enthusiasts had hoped. Only 1,019,369 acres (out of a net cultivated acreage in Bihar of more than 21 million acres in the state as a whole) were planted with high-yielding varieties of wheat in 1969–1970. The distribution of this acreage, by district, is shown in table 18.

Second, the production maximizing strategy was increasingly criticized in 1969 and 1970 for its principal assumption that the new technology could be widely enough disseminated among enterprising, landholding cultivators to assure spectacular increases in aggregate output—the benefits of which would percolate downward in the rural hierarchy rapidly enough to assure broadly distributed increases in income and well-being even to "weaker sections" of rural society, including agricultural laborers. To some observers, this principal assumption of the new strategy in agriculture seemed invalid in practice;[51] in many regions the benefits of increased

TABLE 18
Acreage under High-Yielding Varieties of Wheat, 1969–1970

Name of District	Coverage in Acres
Patna	63,967
Gaya	59,077
Shahabad	283,136
Saran	44,964
Champaran	194,467
Purnea	135,942
Monghyr	42,991
Santhal Parganas	3,268
Ranchi	3,580
Muzaffarpur	20,110
Darbhanga	79,183
Bhagalpur	11,101
Hazaribagh	510
Palamau	1,247
Singhbhum	209
Dhanbad	52
Total	1,019,369

Source: The data for this table were supplied by the government of Bihar, Department of Agriculture, August 1970.

[51] See, for example, Pranab Bardhan, "Trends in Land Relations, A Note,"

yields were not being widely distributed. Raiyats with holdings of five acres or less, raiyats with insecure rights in land, under-raiyats, sharecroppers, and agricultural laborers—these tended not to benefit from the Green Revolution success stories. Instead, raiyats having operational holdings of fifteen acres or more were disproportionate beneficiaries of the increased yields made possible by new inputs. This was clearly evident in Bihar in 1970 where officials of government made no effort to disguise the fact that landholders with twenty-four acres or more had been deriving the major benefits from the state's agricultural development activities.

Defenders of the new, production-oriented strategy have argued that it enables government to concentrate its limited resources on the best lands in cooperation with landholders who are most able and willing to adopt the new technology—those, admittedly, who have security of tenure over substantial landholdings. Moreover, they argue, the strategy has been validated by success—measured in dramatic increases in yields, together with the percolation downward of the benefits from increased production, particularly in selected regions of India, such as the Punjab.

Even if the above argument were verified in the Punjab, the primary problem associated with the implementation of the same strategy in Bihar stems from the fact that Bihar is not the Punjab. The differences between the Punjab and Bihar are too numerous to elaborate here. But it must be emphasized that a whole constellation of favorable factors have combined to benefit the Punjab—factors incidentally which pre-date the Green Revolution and are related in part to programs initiated by the British long before independence. "So because Punjab had a conjunction of favorable factors in the past, in the present it has been able to plan on sounder lines, and the outlook for increasing production is far more promising."[52] If Bihar had less population on the land, twice as much land irrigated, more medium-sized agricultural holdings on which the cultivators had security of tenure, human resources with the apparent motivation and agricultural tradition of the Sikhs, a more effective government, and a less volatile political system—if Bihar had these things then, perhaps, we could sit back comfort-

---

Economic and Political Weekly 5 (January 1970); Francine Frankel, "Agricultural Modernisation and Social Change," *Mainstream* (November 29, 1969).

[52] Doreen Warriner, *Land Reform in Principle and Practice*, pp. 211–212.

ably, make fertilizer available, improve administrative and agricultural extension services, and watch the situation take care of itself.

It is most unlikely, however, that anyone can establish in Bihar in the near future the conjunction of favorable factors that seem to have applied in the case of the Punjab. In Bihar, without the required constellation of favorable physical factors, the introduction of new technology in agriculture will be less successful, even with respect to the lands of cultivators having twenty-four acres or more. Furthermore, even if the strategy were successfully applied to increase production in the aggregate in Bihar, the benefits of increased production are likely to flow to and be contained within the top levels of the rural hierarchy. Indeed, this seems to be what is happening in contemporary Bihar, a development process in which the traditional, landholding elites derive the main benefits from economic development while the masses of the peasantry derive few benefits and experience declining social and economic status relative to the elites.[53] The result is an acceleration of political and economic polarization.

We have many examples in the world outside India of the dangers inherent in the situation one encounters in contemporary Bihar. The demands placed on the political and economic system by the American Negro have increased as he noted the disparity between what was produced in the United States and what was permitted to "trickle down" to him. Indeed, his demands have become more urgent as he increasingly perceived that those above him in the hierarchy have derived proportionately greater benefits from the growth that has taken place. It is the recognition that his position in the hierarchy relative to others is static or declining that contributes to his politicization and mobilization.

The pathetic poor of rural Bihar[54] are no less equipped than the American Negro to perceive the meaning in personal terms of an

[53] During field investigations in Bihar in regions of the state experiencing increases in agricultural output attributed to "new technology in agriculture," the author noted numerous instances in which wages for labor had remained static since 1957. Increased wages for labor, when reported, generally reflected the prevailing inflated market price for wages in kind, and did not represent an increase in real income for agricultural laborers living at subsistence levels.

[54] Pranab Bardhan has determined that the percentage of rural people living below a minimum level (defined by Bardhan as Rs. 15 per month at 1960–1961

agricultural development strategy that benefits the ex-zamindars, the large raiyats, and others enjoying superior rights in land, but which does not benefit the majority of the peasantry.

Agrarian Tensions in Bihar in the Context of Rapid Population Growth

Among the least discussed aspects of the problem of agrarian unrest in Bihar is the rapid population growth in a state in which 92 percent of the people live in villages, in which 77 percent of all workers are employed in agriculture, in which employment opportunities outside of agriculture are extremely limited due to the slow pace of industrialization, in which the net cultivated area per capita is only .42 acres, in which (in 1961) average landholdings were 2.94 acres, and in which more than 80 percent of all holdings were below five acres in size and splintered into a bewildering number of often noncontiguous fragments.

In Bihar, rapid population growth implies a growth rate of roughly 2.7 percent per annum. It means increasing the population from 46.46 million in 1961 to roughly 57 million in 1970. It poses the further prospect of 63.15 million Biharis in 1974 at the end of the Fourth Five Year Plan. It means a need for 113.11 lakh tons of food by 1974 in order to meet the estimated minimum per capita food requirements in that year, when the state anticipates producing only 90.6 lakh tons in 1969–1970 and sees no scope for increasing acreage under food crops by 1974.

In other words, the struggle for life in Bihar has been reduced to basic elements. The population explodes while land resources remain static. The hunger for land and for food becomes more urgent, the rural masses more restless, and the inherited system of government and administration less able to cope.

Clearly, rapid population growth is associated with the present increase in agrarian tensions. Unless this growth can be curbed—and who can suggest that it will be in the near future?—the struggle for survival will become more and more elemental until it becomes a grotesque joke perpetrated on the people of Bihar.

---

prices) has increased within Bihar from 37.64 percent in 1960–1961 to 42.80 percent in 1964–1965 to 80.50 percent in 1967–1968 (Pranab Bardhan, "The So-Called Green Revolution and Agricultural Labourers" [unpublished, 1970], p. 21).

9. *The Future of Bihar: Revolutionary Ferment or Evolutionary Change?*

A Modified Rural Development Strategy for Bihar

Bihar faces an agrarian crisis of great complexity and enormous proportions, a crisis which is pervasive in its potential effects on the fabric of Bihar society. As mentioned earlier, new coalitions are being formed in rural areas to challenge the political and economic power of the traditional, landholding elites. The essence of the challenge centers on the control of scarce land resources in a society that remains predominantly agrarian. It is by no means certain, in the near term, that those who challenge the landholding elites will succeed in overthrowing them. What does seem certain is that the tension and conflict among traditional and emerging groups will, in time, produce change in the political economy of the state. The remaining question is whether political and economic change will be achieved through means that are mainly orderly and evolutionary or through processes that are essentially chaotic and revolutionary.

What is increasingly clear is that there is no escaping the dilemma posed by the prospects of continuing social, economic, and political change in a climate of group conflict and tension. There is no turning back to a society in seeming equilibrium where intermediaries, raiyats, under-raiyats, sharecroppers, and landless laborers interact within a structure imposed by tradition. Indeed, Biharis of disparate persuasions know that an awakening has already occurred in rural Bihar. The peasantry are less subservient to established authority. They do not vote as they are told. No longer can they be described as stolid and stunned, brothers to the bullocks in the fields. Instead, the peasantry are seen increasingly as people capable of placing demands on Bihar's economic and political system. Already, the ruling elites (and the institutions of government in Bihar) are being asked to respond to the newly awakened or face the prospect of demands that are backed by militant action. The situation is one of revolutionary portent, foreshadowed dimly by events such as the land-grab movement of 1970.

For the present, the choice remains open to those who hold power in Bihar to facilitate or hinder the processes of change that are under way. For these elites, to encourage change is to cooperate in paradoxical alliance with groups seeking to supplant them; to facilitate change is to engage in activities that threaten to erode the power and prestige they would like to retain. Yet, for the elites to hinder change may mean attaching themselves irrevocably to an increasingly isolated minority in an ultimately fruitless effort to deny the demands of a militant majority coalition of small landholders, sharecroppers, and some landless laborers (led by opportunistic politicians of the right or left).

If the ruling elites fail to respond to the legitimate interests of the Bihar peasantry, they risk losing all opportunity to guide and direct a process of orderly social, economic, and political change, thus leaving the field exclusively to those who believe in the legitimacy of violence—on the one hand those who would act violently to promote change and on the other those who would act violently to forestall it.

In these circumstances, the involved observer tends to look in despair for a way to resolve Bihar's agrarian crisis. No easy answers to the crisis can be projected. No textbook provides simple formulae that can be readily applied to meet the complexities of the dilemma facing contemporary Bihar. Similarly, there are few, if any, guidelines to be found in conventional ideological discourse. Nor can one demand that the pluralistic people of Bihar establish instant symbiosis leading to quick consensus concerning their problems of economic development and social change. The needs and fears of the people of Bihar are so diverse that conflict is more easily assured than consensus on almost any issue that confronts them. One cannot conjure up a representative, wise, and powerful government having political and administrative capacities sufficient to implement all the necessary reforms (including agrarian reforms) long delayed or still needed. And, one cannot expect the central government to come up with a prescription to banish poverty in Bihar or to satisfy the already escalating demands of those who press for change in the agrarian structure of the state.

If there is no panacea that can be invoked to resolve the agrarian crisis, this need not imply that there is no scope for constructive programming in Bihar to meet the needs and demands of newly mobilized sections of the peasantry. There are now men in Bihar (and elsewhere in India), including members of the political and landed elites, who see that their own self-interest, as well as the whole enterprise of rural economic development, will be served by engaging in activities that hold some prospect of reducing tensions, building confidence in government in rural areas, and improving tangibly the living conditions among those in the lower ranks of the rural hierarchy. Such men see their own survival as being inextricably linked to the success of development programs that are not divorced from the concept of distributive justice. If men such as these acquire followers and sufficient power, it will be easier to envisage Bihar as a viable economic and political unit within the Republic of India. Those who recognize the necessity for constructive action (whether motivated by self-interest or altruism) must now move to establish a modified strategy of rural development. The critical element of such a strategy of rural development would be official commitment to the simultaneous fulfillment of twin goals: an increase in agricultural production and a lessening of the disparities between Bihar's haves and her have-nots. This would represent a departure from past and present policies in the field of rural development which have tended to emphasize the need to increase agricultural production and to ignore the need to assure improved distribution of the benefits of increased output. It has now become a policy imperative to recognize that the goals of increased production and better distribution are inseparable in contemporary conditions in rural Bihar. It is here asserted that economic growth in rural areas of Bihar will become impossible if social justice continues to be denied to the masses of the peasantry. Conversely, social justice will prove an illusory target unless economic growth can be achieved.

Even to enunciate such a two-fold goal is to contradict established dogma and to reject the conventional wisdom. The literature concerning economic development is filled with references to the self-contradictory nature of these goals. It has been customary to argue that the goals of increased production and social justice must be approached in sequence, first one and then the other, and to suggest that economic growth, by definition, implies growing inequalities among classes within a region, growing inequalities among regions within a country, and growing inequalities among nations. John Mellor has observed that "the development process, while providing the long-term basis for amelioration of poverty and economic inequality, may in the short run exacerbate it."[1] In similar vein, Albert Hirschman has stated that "the development process means that international and interregional [and intergroup] inequality of growth is an inevitable concomitant and condition of growth itself."[2]

Such views are the product of dichotomous thinking about the development process: thinking that separates artificially and quite unrealistically economic from social and political processes. By separating these processes, it is possible to escape (in an economic theory) the complexities of the real world and to have faith that economic growth (defined narrowly in terms of growth in income per capita) implies development (defined more broadly to include structural changes in a social system permitting difficult to measure increases in distributive and social justice) by means of a trickling down process from haves to have-nots. This is the kind of thinking that permits us to emphasize the attainment of food production targets in a state such as Bihar (by working almost exclusively with the established landed elites and by covering only a fraction

[1] John Mellor, et al., *Developing Rural India, Plan and Practice*, p. 359.

[2] Albert O. Hirschman, *The Strategy of Economic Development*, p. 184.

of the cultivable area) while not addressing directly the problems of distribution and social justice. And we rationalize not addressing those problems either by emphasizing that they are beyond the purview of development economists or are resolvable automatically, albeit with a time lag, if economic growth can be sustained at a given rate. The plea here is for the recognition that the situation in Bihar does not permit such dichotomous thinking—unless the development goal is the production of revolution or anarchy. As earlier stated, the goals of increased production and a lessening of various disparities between Bihar's haves and have-nots are mutually dependent: neither can be achieved in artificial isolation from the other.

Yet, to modify the rural development strategy and to adopt the twin goals enunciated in preceding paragraphs are not to imply development without pain or instability—given the situation in contemporary Bihar. Painful social, economic, and political adjustments will be inevitable, whatever the strategy and however ideally it could be implemented. Adherence to the modified strategy—embracing the twin goals—offers only the hope of reducing tensions to proportions that may be manageable and of permitting the maintenance of an environment in which continuing development in the economic, social, and political spheres is possible. It is implicit that, in implementing any plan for development in rural Bihar in the 1970s, the government will have to use some coercive power: it will have to use coercive power to control outbreaks of violence resulting from tensions in the agricultural sector and which threaten to preclude the possibility of peaceful change; it will have to use coercive power to implement change. It is to be hoped that such force will be exercised by a democratically constituted authority.

Clearly, there are no simple solutions to the problems that confront Bihar, but some concrete steps—consistent with the twin goals—can be taken. These are outlined in the succeeding section.

A Minimum Program of Agrarian Reforms

Agrarian reforms in Bihar have been rather extravagant in verbiage, but almost meaningless in fact. Such reforms as have been legislated have served mainly to raise peasants' expectations rather than to fulfill them. A yearning for land is now expressed almost uniformly by all classes of rural society. If a peasant holds land with a recognized right of permanent occupancy, he wants more land similarly protected by law. If a peasant holds land as a non-occupancy raiyat, he wants his "right" to land made permanent. Similarly, those who have held dwarf (one acre or less) holdings through verbal agreement, sometimes on a yearly basis, together with those who are landless wage laborers want land distributed to them so that they can reap the multiple benefits thought to accrue from possession of land, irrespective of the size and economic viability of the holding. In short, the most consistently emphasized viewpoint of peasant respondents (interviewed by the author in Bihar in a period extending from 1956 through 1970) was that they should have land for personal cultivation.[3]

So long as the economy of Bihar remains fundamentally rural and agrarian (with 92 percent of the people living in rural areas),[4] the possession of land will continue to assume primary significance. Land owned is wealth; it is prestige; it is power.

Any government of Bihar, regardless of its political composition and ideological orientation, must now be cognizant of the peasantry and their hunger for land. The evidence of agrarian tensions in recent years, together with the land-grab movement of 1970, has emphasized the political need to put into effect without further delay a minimum program of agrarian reforms.

This minimum program must have meaning that extends beyond the rhetoric of the next general elections. It must be a program capable of being implemented without the delays that have accompanied all other reforms. In essence, the minimum reforms must include the following: (*a*) completion of Survey and Settlement operations for the state as a whole by 1974, the revised date for the ending of the Fourth Five Year Plan; (*b*) linking of consolidation of holdings operations to the Survey and Settlement, and the utili-

[3] The term "personal cultivation" is used loosely; peasants of high caste seldom touch the plow or engage in the actual work of cultivation, whereas peasants of lower status are generally actual tillers of the soil.

[4] The 92 percent figure is quoted frequently in various government documents, e.g., Bihar, Planning Department, *Brief Outline of the Revised Fourth Five Year Plan (1969–74)*. A substantial reduction in the percentage of people living in rural areas of Bihar is not anticipated in the near future, though the 1971 census should record a reduction of a few percentage points, reflecting some migration from rural to urban areas.

zation of modern survey techniques (including aerial photography, if possible) to speed the implementation of these programs; and (*c*) provision of security of tenure for those small farmers—raiyats, under-raiyats, and, in some cases, sharecroppers—who can demonstrate that they are the actual tillers of the lands they claim to hold.

We are not suggesting here a drastic "land to the tiller" land reform program, a program, for example, which would imply providing some land even for Bihar's landless wage laborers. The pressure of population on Bihar's land resources precludes such a comprehensive program. The issue of population pressure on existing land resources clouds the whole subject of agrarian reforms to the extent that such reforms include attempts at more equitable distribution of land. The limitations imposed by the pressure of population on existing land resources have been evident for some time. In 1951, prior to an adjustment in the state's boundaries that later reduced its total land area from 45,011,072 to 42,823,000 acres, the land area per capita was 1.12 acres and the "topographically usable" area was considered to be only .89 acres per capita.[5] By 1961, Bihar's population having increased by 19.78 percent in the decade, the land area per capita had been reduced to .928 acres, and the area of actual cultivation had diminished on a per capita basis from .57 acres to .44 acres. By 1970, the per capita availability of the net cultivated area was reduced still further to .42 acres for the state as a whole and .35 acres in the most densely populated agricultural division.

Even allowing for gradual changes in agricultural practices (in-

[5] The topographically usable area was determined for Bihar in accordance with the following schedule in the *Census of India, 1951*.

Topographical Class	*Proportion Considered Usable*
Mountains	5 percent
Hills	25 percent
Plateaus	75 percent
Plains	95 percent

"This method of classification of topographically usable area should not be taken to furnish a precise estimate of the topographically usable area in a relatively small area like a natural division." Thus, the ratio of 75 percent for plateaus may be misleading; it is low for an area like the north Deccan (in central India), but high for the south Bihar plateau region (India, Census Operations, *Census of India, 1951*, I, Parts I-A and I-B, Appendix I, p. 5).

cluding the introduction of more intensive cultivation techniques, the wider dissemination of new inputs, and the better utilization of labor), the preceding facts impose limits on any possible solution of Bihar's land problem: clearly, the land-hunger issue cannot be resolved simply by redistributing existing agricultural holdings or reclaiming vast areas of uncultivated lands. Even if the total area of the state could, somehow, be brought under cultivation, it is most doubtful whether the existing rural population could be given economic holdings. What is more, it seems clear that the area under cultivation cannot be increased in any meaningful fashion. The net area sown in Bihar has been remarkably constant over many years, even with the rapidly growing pressure of population on land resources. Indeed, "[a]lthough the population of Bihar has increased by more than 70 percent since the beginning of the century there has been no extension of either the net or gross area cultivated."[6] Such uncultivated lands as might be considered topographically usable are mainly in the south Bihar plateau region; and it is unlikely that any meaningful amount of this land, or, for that matter, such unused lands as may exist in the plains regions north or south of the Ganges, can be reclaimed for agricultural purposes, even with heavy investments of capital for general development purposes, including irrigation.[7]

In the light of the above evidence, the land problem of Bihar cannot be resolved even theoretically through a utopian program of "land to the tiller," if "land to the tiller" implies providing land to

[6] S. R. Bose, "The Changing Face of Bihar Agriculture" (unpublished manuscript). Professor S. R. Bose, the former director of the Central Bureau of Economics and Statistics, Government of Bihar, is now associated with the A. N. Sinha Institute of Social Studies, Patna, Bihar. He has estimated that the net cultivated area may actually have diminished somewhat as the land lost to the state in 1956 "contained a higher proportion of cultivated land compared to the residual area left in the Dhanbad District of Bihar."

[7] Perhaps the most optimistic assessment is that as many as 2.2 million acres of "culturable waste lands" in Bihar can be reclaimed for cultivation (Bihar, Public Relations Department, *Bihar 1955–56*, p. 97). However, it is noteworthy that Bihar's agricultural development program, as outlined in the Bihar Department of Agriculture's "Draft Outline of the Fourth Five Year Plan 1969–74 (Agriculture)" (unpublished document: 1968), makes no such claim with respect to the possibility of extending the area under cultivation through reclamation projects. Indeed, land reclamation projects (with the possible exception of a land-leveling project in the Kosi canal region of north Bihar) have no priority in the Fourth Plan set forth by government.

all who desire it. There is clearly insufficient land available for distribution to meet the growing demand for this crucial resource. What we are proposing in our minimum program of agrarian reforms is not a redistribution of land to all who want it, but rather the provision of security of tenure to those who already hold at least tenuous rights in land.

The program recognizes both the political and the economic necessity to provide security of tenure to legions of small cultivators (whether classified as raiyats, under-raiyats, sharecroppers, or those fitting into more than one of these classifications, as is often the case). For it is these small cultivators who hold the key to the success of any agricultural production program in Bihar. Small farmers with holdings of 9.9 acres or less now cultivate roughly 62 percent of the cultivated acreage of Bihar.[8] Such cultivators are in the overwhelming majority in a land of dwarf holdings—a state in which 90 percent of all rural holdings are below 9.9 acres in size and the average holding is 2.94 acres. It is the small cultivator who has not participated in any meaningful fashion in the state's agricultural production programs, including those associated with new inputs such as the high-yielding varieties of seeds. And, while it can be admitted that the inaccessibility of assured water supplies, fertilizer, and agricultural credit is a constraint on the spread of the new technology, there can be no greater impediment to the dissemination of that technology than a pervasive climate of fear and insecurity regarding rights in land. Such a climate limits the

[8] We have no reliable statistics showing the degree to which holdings in the state are tilled by cultivators lacking legally recognized rights in land. Once again it must be emphasized that, in the absence of up-to-date Survey and Settlement records and given the calculated attempts by some to obfuscate such records as do exist, we have a most imperfect picture of the nature of rights in land in contemporary Bihar. Nonetheless, the term "security of tenure" as used in our statement of a minimum program of agrarian reforms implies some redistribution of rights in land through the conferring of occupancy-raiyat status to all tillers who can prove a direct, physical relationship to the lands in their cultivating possession. Should the rights in land claimed by thousands of under-raiyats and sharecroppers be legally recognized and guaranteed, the small farmers of Bihar might actually control even more than 62 percent of the cultivated area of the state. For additional information concerning estimates of the size and distribution of landholdings in Bihar, see Bihar, Directorate of Economics and Statistics, *Bihar Statistical Handbook, 1966*, Table 3.14, p. 50; S. R. Bose, "Levels of Poverty in Rural Bihar," *Searchlight* (April 21, 1970): 4.

readiness of any Bihari cultivator (whatever size holding he commands) to accept risk and to engage in production innovations, and it has a particularly negative effect on the small cultivator whose socioeconomic status is weak. The provision of security of tenure to Bihar's small cultivators is seen as a vital step in the direction of reducing fear among the majority of the peasantry and encouraging agricultural innovations among a vast segment of the rural society. In addition, security of tenure would encourage increasing numbers of peasants to invest in fixed improvements on land and to secure credit. This would facilitate both the wider dissemination and adoption of new technology in agriculture. In the process, Bihar's agricultural production potential would be enhanced at the same time that political tensions might be reduced somewhat as new elements of rural society participated, many for the first time, in the economic growth process. In the long term, beneficent changes set in motion hopefully through the provision of security of tenure to small cultivators would serve the twin goals that we earlier enunciated: a lessening of disparities between Bihar's haves and have-nots and increased agricultural production.

It must be emphasized that the minimum program of agrarian reforms that we have set forth has economic validity in a region of small holdings such as Bihar. Indeed, there is increasing evidence[9] throughout the world "that production per acre is generally higher on small holdings than on large—that there is an inverse relationship between size of holdings and output per unit of land, in terms of both gross output and net income. This is not to say that output *per man* is greater on small holdings, but that output per man is not the relevant criterion in the majority of [underdeveloped countries] . . . where labor is abundant, cheap and underemployed, arable land is scarce, and capital is both expensive and scarce."[10] Moreover, there is much evidence to suggest that agrarian reforms (even those involving the breaking up of large holdings and their distribution among small cultivators) have "not generally resulted in production decreases. On the contrary, production has usually increased. In some cases, temporary production decreases have re-

[9] U.S., Department of State, *Spring Review of Land Reform June 2–4*, volumes I–XII and "Findings and Implications for A.I.D" (a subsidiary pamphlet for volumes I–XII).

[10] Ibid., "Findings," p. 5.

sulted from initial political instability or poor reform administration—not inability of peasants to manage their own land; but alleged decreases in production resulting from land [agrarian] reforms have usually proved to be either decreases in deliveries to traditional market channels, and use of new channels, or a reflection of higher peasant consumption of their own products and hence a reduction in marketing."[11]

Thus, the program of agrarian reforms we have set forth accepts the persistence in Bihar of peasant family agriculture on small holdings. Such holdings, even those in the range from 2.5 acres to 5.0 acres, can be made economically viable, particularly under conditions of security of tenure where an effort is also made to assure the supply of other necessary inputs.

In summary, the minimum program of agrarian reforms outlined above would stress the provision of security of tenure to the small landholder in Bihar. It would stress the need for consolidation of holdings, recognizing that the economic viability of small holdings is enhanced when fragmented, non-contiguous plots are consolidated. It would emphasize the need for completion of Survey and Settlement operations, recognizing that neither consolidation nor the conferring of secure rights in land is possible without accurate up-to-date land records.

It is anticipated that the implementation of our minimum agrarian reforms will involve the utilization of summary procedures (including the by-passing of civil courts) by the government of Bihar. In other words, nothing short of new approaches and radical measures, sometimes involving the use of the government's coercive powers, will be necessary in the days ahead if the minimum program is to be implemented.

A Minimum Program of Assistance for Small Farmers

During the Fourth Five Year Plan (1969–1974), the government of Bihar is attempting officially to attain "self-sufficiency" with respect to the production of foodgrains. That is to say, by 1974 (when the population of Bihar is likely to exceed 63 million, according to official estimates) government hopes that the agricultural sector will be capable of producing approximately 11,311,000 tons of foodgrains to ensure 18.3 ounces of foodgrains per person

[11] Ibid.

per day. To meet this target the production of foodgrains must be increased by at least 3,200,000 tons from an estimated production of 8,300,000 tons at the outset of the Fourth Plan to 11,500,000 tons in 1973–1974. This implies annual increases in production of around 7 percent, as against an average annual increase over the first three plans of around 3 percent (if one accepts the validity of earlier production statistics).

Few officials of the government of Bihar are sanguine about meeting the Fourth Plan food production target. Even those who maintain official optimism have recognized that a modified rural development strategy will be required if the production target is even to be approached. However, those who argue for a modified approach to rural development seldom emphasize the need for fundamental agrarian reforms. Instead, they persist in hoping that the spread of new technology in agriculture (high-yielding varieties of seeds, pesticides, etc.) alone will produce an agricultural production revolution. A few officials admit that the primary focus of programming in rural areas must be shifted from large landholders to small if the state is to make progress toward self-sufficiency in foodstuffs. Such men recognize that rural extension and development programs in Bihar (and in India generally) have mainly benefited substantial landholders (defined arbitrarily by them and the author to include both ex-intermediaries and raiyats with secure rights in 24 acres or more of land). Such men realize that their rural development efforts have not "trickled down" to small cultivators (defined arbitrarily here to include cultivators with holdings between 2.9 and 9.9 acres). Whether or not they accept the thesis that government's efforts have directly contributed to a widening of the existing social and economic gaps among the peasantry, such officials are beginning to appreciate the fact that the state's food production efforts require the widest possible participation among cultivators. They are beginning to recognize that a production-oriented rural development strategy that has ignored such small cultivators is self-limiting to a degree that appears questionable (in 1970), to say the least.

The importance of small cultivators to the success of a production-oriented development program is underlined when one recognizes that (*a*) there is little, if any, possibility of increasing the production of foodstuffs by bringing meaningful amounts of new acreage under the plow and that (*b*) there is little possibility of attacking the production problem simply by increasing the area of the state that is cultivated more than once in an agricultural year—unless major investments are made in minor irrigation works. Concerning the former point, we have already emphasized elsewhere in this study that the net cultivated area of the state has remained remarkably constant over many years, notwithstanding dramatic increases in population concentrated in rural areas. Concerning the latter, it must be emphasized that double cropping is already extensive in Bihar (with 39 percent of the cultivated acreage double cropped, as compared with only 15 percent of India's cultivated acreage).[12] Available evidence suggests that to extend the acreage under double cropping will require more major and minor irrigation facilities than are currently projected.[13]

Given the above limitations on any production-oriented development strategy, government must increasingly commit itself to the most intensive utilization of the lands of small cultivators—especially lands in north and south Bihar that are within the Gangetic Plains region. These small holdings, so long outside the scope of the rural development program, are generally of excellent quality (the soil is better than that of the Punjab throughout much of the Gangetic Plains region of Bihar) and are capable of being irrigated by minor irrigation works, including diesel pumps, which can make available a perennial water supply simply by lifting water from the subsoil at depths (in most instances) of no more than fifty feet. Government must also devise more effective means of relating to the needs of small (as well as large) cultivators in dry farming regions of the state, where single cropping patterns will prevail for some time to come.[14]

Already, some officials, notably S. K. Chakraverty, the agricultural development commissioner, in 1970 have begun to promote pilot projects designed to determine the best means of disseminat-

[12] See S. R. Bose, *A Study in Bihar Agriculture*, p. 36.

[13] The government of Bihar has estimated that "with the best efforts it would be difficult to bring more than 40 percent of the area under irrigation by the end of the Fourth Five Year Plan period" (Bihar, Planning Department, *Brief Outline of the Revised Fourth Five Year Plan [1969–74]*, p. 4).

[14] The government of Bihar has estimated that 60 percent of the cultivated area will remain dependent on "dry farming" and the vagaries of the monsoon for many years (ibid.).

ing new technology in agriculture among peasant cultivators with small holdings. These pilot projects will test the proposition that small holdings (between 2.5 and 5 acres in the first instance) can be made economically viable if various inputs, including agricultural credit, are made available to the landholders.[15]

It is, of course, one thing to endorse a program for small farmers in Bihar and another to implement it on a scale that would be meaningful in its impact on agricultural production in the state as a whole. Moreover, it seems doubtful whether the small farmers' pilot projects can themselves be successful when they are being initiated prior to the implementation of the minimum program of agrarian reforms that we consider essential to the development of an environment in which agricultural innovation on small holdings can take place. In other words, no attempt is being made to link pilot schemes for small farmers with minimal programs of agrarian reforms (notably the provision of security of tenure for small cultivators who presently lack secure rights in land). Indeed, even within the administrative hierarchy of government, few, if any, attempts have been made to assure that agrarian reform and agricultural development programs are made complementary.

Even if the agrarian reforms suggested earlier were implemented, there are other problems that must be addressed if programs for small farmers are to be successful. First, massive improvement and a change in focus are needed in the state's

[15] These programs for "small farmers" have been endorsed by the central government and are to be implemented in selected districts of Bihar during the Fourth Plan period. It is the author's understanding that "Small Farmers Development Agencies" are being established at the district level to effectuate these pilot projects. As of August 1970, one "small farmers" scheme had been made operative in Purnea District, north Bihar, but it was too early to evaluate the results of the program. Similar attempts to provide assistance to "small farmers" are slated for Ranchi, Patna, Shahabad, and Champaran districts. The draft programs for these districts appear in the following documents of the Bihar Department of Agriculture, *A Pilot Project on the Agricultural Development of the Small Farmers of Purnea District*; *Problems of Small Farmers of Kosi Area (Purnea and Saharsa Districts)*; "Project for Development of Small Farmers in Champaran District" (unpublished document, July 1970); "Special Project for Marginal Farmers and Agricultural Labourers of Shahabad District" (unpublished document, 1970); and "Pilot Scheme for Marginal Cultivators and Agricultural Labourers for the District of Ranchi" (unpublished document: 1970).

agricultural extension program. One cannot assume, for example, that existing forms of new technology will trickle down to lower levels of the rural hierarchy and be adopted by small farmers if the peasant cultivator is expected to experiment "on his own" with new inputs. The cultivator with a small holding may lack sophisticated understanding concerning interrelationships among new inputs; he will not automatically understand that his output will be determined by the manner in which he plants potentially high-yielding seeds and by the timing of applications of related inputs of fertilizer, pesticides, and water—even if we make the unrealistic assumption that he has access to adequate and timely supplies of these inputs. Lacking this sophistication regarding the best means of making use of new inputs, the small cultivator courts disaster if he dares to experiment without advice and supervision. To employ an inappropriate mix of new inputs on one occasion and to experience low yields is only to reinforce the small cultivator's belief in the efficacy of traditional agricultural practices. Why should he attempt to emulate the successes of cultivators above him in the rural hierarchy who (enjoying greater security of tenure on larger holdings, easier access to credit at favorable rates, and other necessary inputs) may be prepared to assume greater risks associated with breaking with traditional practices of cultivation?

Because he lacks the multiple advantages of those above him in the rural hierarchy, the small cultivator is unlikely in the first instance to assume risks inherent in experimentation with new methods—and he is much less likely to assume those risks again, having tried and failed. He would prefer to persist in the utilization of traditional practices, anticipating traditional returns, rather than to gamble on much higher returns and to end up with output that may be less than the traditional. If he is to be induced to change his traditional methods of cultivation, he must be helped pointedly in many ways. This suggests, in part, the need not only to strengthen Bihar's agricultural extension services but also to require extension workers to address, as never before, the diverse needs of the small cultivator.

While some attempt is being made to improve the state-wide machinery for agricultural extension operations,[16] those actually

[16] Mention must be made of the efforts of the "Bihar Agricultural Production Program" (a combined effort of the University of Missouri and the Department

involved in strengthening existing services and the development of new ones would be the first to admit that trained and appropriately motivated manpower—men capable of establishing working rapport with small cultivators in village situations—is either lacking or being misused. The personnel attached to the state's Community Development blocks, for example, have been overloaded with multiple revenue and general administrative functions, few of which can be said to be linked to rural agricultural development efforts.[17] Only in selected districts of the state, such as Shahabad, has government endorsed the separation of developmental functions from general administrative responsibilities. In such districts, where there are special intensive development programs (for example, the Package Program, the Shadow Package Program, and the Applied Nutrition Program), an effort has been made to avoid diverting personnel from developmental to general administrative duties. This division of labor must extend to the state as a whole if the Community Development block infrastructure is to contribute in any substantial manner to the fulfillment of agricultural production-oriented programs. This will require the kinds of administrative and structural reforms within government that are threatening to bureaucrats in the best of circumstances. In Bihar's situation, where the Community Development blocks have never been strong, it is difficult to perceive how these institutions can be transformed to perform as effective instrumentalities of rural extension attentive to the needs of small farmers. Nonetheless, an effort must be made to achieve new agricultural extension capacity in Bihar if any program for small farmers is to succeed.

Second, there is a need to establish more effective means of providing credit to agriculturists generally and small farmers in particular. It is widely recognized within Bihar that the institutions that have been entrusted to meet rural credit needs have been un-

---

of Agriculture, Government of Bihar) and its multi-faceted efforts to improve extension work. Men associated with this program have established various "Field Problems Units": a "State Extension Information Council" (comprised of heads of concerned sections of the Department of Agriculture and Animal Husbandry, but not encompassing those sections or divisions of government concerned with agrarian reforms); a "Seed Improvement Field Problems Unit"; a "Plant Protection Field Problems Unit"; etc.

[17] Bihar, Department of Community Development and Panchayats, *Report of the Committee on Community Development.*

equal to the task. The state's cooperative credit institutions, especially, are so weak that they are probably dysfunctional as instruments of rural development. Even though government claimed in 1965–1966 that 85 percent of Bihar's 68,000 villages "were covered by primary agricultural credit societies,"[18] it is noteworthy that the list of allegedly viable societies was reduced in number from 30,000 to 16,500 during the following fiscal year, 1966–1967. And, few would claim in 1969–1970 that there are more than a handful of cooperative credit societies that are worthy of being preserved. In general, the cooperative credit movement in the state cannot be relied on to meet rural credit needs associated with the broader dissemination of new technology in agriculture.[19] The government of Bihar has estimated that rural credit needs will grow from roughly 2 billion to 4 billion rupees per annum from 1969 through 1974. Existing rural credit institutions are anticipated to be able to make credit advances of only up to 1 billion rupees per annum during the same period.

Thus, while cooperative credit institutions will persist in providing short-term and medium-term credit to cultivators and institutions such as the State Land Development Bank will continue to dispense long-term credit to cultivators with large landholdings, a massive new program is being organized to meet the anticipated expansion of rural credit needs during the Fourth Five Year Plan.[20] The new program involves the utilization for the first time of commercial banks as credit-dispensing institutions in rural areas. These banks are to direct their attention to "the needs of the weaker sections of the population" (essentially cultivators with small holdings) who have largely been neglected by other credit-dispensing institutions, excepting the traditional village moneylenders.[21]

[18] Ibid.

[19] As indicated, the cooperative credit movement in Bihar is probably worthy of being scrapped. Yet, the word "cooperation" retains its symbolic potency. Cooperative institutions of all descriptions (credit, marketing, processing, joint cooperative farming, etc.) have been given a place in the Fourth Five Year Plan for Bihar.

[20] For elaboration, see N. K. P. Sinha, *Measures Taken So Far by the State Government to Help Steady Flow of Institutional Finance in the Agricultural Sector.*

[21] See Bihar, Development Commissioner N. P. Mathur, "Financing of Agriculture by Commercial Banks" (unpublished document, June 12, 1970).

By August 1970, certain Lead Banks (designated by the Reserve Bank of India) were being pressed to address the rural credit needs of specified districts of the state. In Patna District, for example, the Punjab National Bank[22] was being urged to open branch offices at the block level, having completed a survey of credit needs and banking development opportunities in the district. Eventually, it is hoped that branch offices of various banks will be opened at the block level throughout the state, often in direct competition with existing cooperative institutions. Indeed, it is anticipated by some officials of the government of Bihar that the diffusion of banking institutions in rural areas will either drive the credit cooperatives out of business or cause them to do more effective work than they have done in the past.[23]

Clearly, a major attempt is being made to assure that agricultural credit is made available to agriculturists with small holdings. While it is premature to assess the quality of the effort by various banking institutions to address the needs of new clients, the effort itself deserves commendation.

Third, attention must be given to the rapid development of minor irrigation programs that benefit agriculturists with small holdings. Adding to the area under perennial irrigation will be critical to the dissemination of high-yielding varieties of seeds (particularly wheat) and their adoption by peasants with secure rights in land.

In 1970, it was estimated that between 20 and 30 percent of the net area sown was irrigated by major and minor irrigation projects.[24] Assuming the full operation of major irrigation schemes,

[22] The Punjab National Bank is one of those nationalized in 1969 by the government of India. It has been assigned Lead Bank responsibility in Patna, Gaya, and Shahabad districts in Bihar.

[23] As a means of coordinating the activities of various institutions involved in providing agricultural credit, the government of Bihar has established a special committee chaired by the development commissioner (Shri N. P. Mathur in 1970) and including representatives of various departments of government and key banking institutions, such as the Agricultural Finance Corporation, which initiated its first project in Bihar in 1969–1970 in the Kosi region—a project valued at Rs. 70,400,000 and focused mainly on the credit needs of small farmers. The managing director of the Agricultural Finance Corporation, Shri B. Rudramoorthy, is a man of competence who is committed to the development of many such projects in India.

[24] Estimate given in an interview by Dr. D. N. Ram, deputy director of agriculture, Government of Bihar, August 13, 1970.

including the Kosi and Sone, and taking into rough account the acreage covered by minor irrigation projects, we might conclude that between five and six million acres out of twenty-one million acres (the approximate net area sown) were irrigated in 1970.

How much more land can be brought under perennial irrigation in Bihar is not known with any precision. However, it can be assumed that many small holdings, even in areas in which irrigation is common, are not irrigated because small cultivators have had neither the security of tenure nor the access to capital necessary to the establishment of fixed improvements on their holdings. If government could assure security of tenure to cultivators with small holdings (in the 2.5 to 9.9 acre range) and also give them access to new sources of credit, as currently planned, our findings suggest that a whole new segment of the peasantry would be much more likely to invest in fixed improvements (including minor irrigation works) on lands in their cultivating possession.

Though the provision of complementary programs (such as security of tenure and agricultural credit) for small cultivators is not assured, Bihar's Fourth Plan does seem to give appropriate emphasis to the development of minor irrigation works in various districts. Selected blocks in Patna, Darbhanga, Purnea, and Saharsa districts are to receive tube wells. Some of these are to be financed by the Bihar Relief Committee (an organization established during the Bihar famine of 1967); others are to be financed by the Agricultural Finance Corporation and commercial banks. Still others will be drilled and financed by international voluntary agencies that have retained an interest in Bihar following involvement in famine-relief activities in 1966–1967.[25]

Much more can be done in the field of minor irrigation with minimum cost by continuing public works projects designed to repair traditional irrigation facilities (for example, bundhs, ahars, and pynes) which have been neglected since the 1950s when zamindari abolition legislation was enacted.[26]

[25] There is an Indo-German project in Ranchi District, a Norwegian tube-well drilling project in Champaran District, and the Freedom from Hunger Campaign retains interest in fulfilling minor irrigation programs in several districts.

[26] Some have attributed the harshness of the famine of 1966–1967 to the neglect by government (and the ex-intermediaries) of traditional minor irrigation works following zamindari abolition and the lack of incentive among

While it seems evident that the government of Bihar placed too much hope in the past on major projects of flood control and irrigation (such as the Kosi), the new commitment to the rapid extension of minor irrigation works in the five-year period beginning in 1969 represents an appropriate shift in emphasis. As usual, however, there are problems associated with implementing the projected program. Even if the program were implemented, it is one thing, for example, to propose to install thirty thousand tube wells during the Fourth Plan and quite another to fulfill the target in a fashion that does not further widen the existing gap between haves and have-nots (large landholders and small) and thus exacerbate existing tensions in rural areas.[27]

Fourth, the extension of minor irrigation facilities in Bihar will be facilitated if the government is able to press ahead with its rural electrification program. By the summer of 1970, only 7,538 villages (out of roughly 68,000 in the state as a whole) were listed among those having access to electricity. The 7,538 figure is misleading, of course, because it cannot be assumed that there are multiple outlets in those villages. In many instances electricity is available in only a few households, and the distribution of electricity in the villages is as biased in favor of large landholders as has been the distribution of other inputs that can contribute to increases in agricultural output. The need, therefore, is not simply to expand the coverage of the rural electrification program during the Fourth Plan so that 125,000 pumps (for minor programs of lift irrigation as well as tube wells) are energized and 12,500 additional villages receive electricity.[28] The need, as far as 90 percent of Bihar's cultivators are concerned, is to assure that cultivators with small holdings are not shut out from the progress in rural electrification that has been achieved and will be achieved. This suggests the need, in part, for

---

under-raiyats and sharecroppers to invest in such works. See, for example, B. G. Verghese, *Beyond the Famine: An Approach to Regional Planning for Bihar*, p. 27.

[27] The demand for tube wells is increasing, particularly among ex-intermediaries and others with substantial landholdings. The politics associated with the final placement of tube wells are convoluted. Needless to say, the haves and have-nots engage in unequal competition for both diesel pumping sets and tube wells.

[28] Bihar, Planning Department, *Brief Outline of the Revised Fourth Five Year Plan (1969–74)*, "Power."

concessional rates for small cultivators where electricity is available. It also suggests the need for a general modification in the focus of the rural electrification program and the evaluation of its future success in terms that transcend the recording of increases in the number of villages receiving electricity in at least one outlet.

Fifth, agriculturists with small holdings must have access to government certified high-yielding varieties of seeds. During more than two thousand miles of traveling within Bihar in the summer of 1970, the author encountered numerous instances in which small cultivators had dared to experiment with new seeds that they had procured at high prices (often from ex-intermediaries who have recently taken to seed farming) only to find that the seeds were of mixed quality, the result of willful adulteration or careless growing and certification. To assume risk is difficult enough for the small landholder without having to worry about being cheated by those who provide him seed. Of course, even if one could assure that small landholders were given access to adequate amounts of certified high-yielding varieties of seeds, the broadest dissemination of the new seeds among small landholders would not be automatic. Large landholders with more secure rights in land and easier access to credit would continue to enjoy advantages over the small—unless the whole range of programs outlined in preceding pages were implemented in a fashion that consciously discriminated in favor of the peasantry with holdings in the 2.5 to 9.9 acre range.

Sixth, there is a need to assure that the distribution of fertilizer in the state is regulated in a fashion to assure that small cultivators have access to it. While it is encouraging that the consumption of fertilizer has been increasing in recent years, as shown by table 19, government must recognize that existing fertilizer distribution procedures do not complement a modified rural development strategy in which cultivators with small holdings are to have an important role. In this connection the decision of the government of Bihar (in 1968–1969) to permit the private sector to enter the fertilizer trade is a step in the wrong direction. One need not have illusions about the efficiency of the government or its incorruptibility to suggest that the prospects of small cultivators receiving some fertilizer (at reasonable prices) would have been enhanced had government continued to monopolize the fertilizer trade. Instead, government has reduced whatever capacity it had to control the

TABLE 19
Use of Fertilizer in Bihar, 1966–1970[a]

	1966–1967	1968–1969	1969–1970[b]
Nitrogen	25,553	49,257	75,000
Phosphoric acid	4,544	13,719	18,000
Potash	2,384	3,808	10,000

[a] All data are in tons. Figures for 1967–1968 were not available to the author.
[b] The 1969–1970 data are projections of government and therefore reflect anticipated consumption of fertilizer, rather than actual consumption.
Source: The table uses information from Government of Bihar, Planning Department, *Brief Outline of the Revised Fourth Five Year Plan (1969–74)*, "Agricultural Production."

distribution of fertilizer by permitting an increasing number of private traders to become active in the field. These private traders are in no sense attempting to gear their operations to the needs of small cultivators. Indeed, they are setting up distribution machinery in rural areas that relies almost exclusively on the traditional landholding elites. These local dealers (referred to even by government as "progressive farmers"),[29] some of whom are ex-intermediaries, can be expected to dispose of their limited supplies of fertilizer to large landholders at prices that small landholders will be unable, generally, to meet. Thus, the government of Bihar seems to have erred in relinquishing control over fertilizer distribution operations just prior to committing itself officially to a rural development strategy in which small farmers were to have some prominence. A corrective decision must now be made and implemented if government is to regain strategic control over the distribution of fertilizer in the state.

Seventh, there is a need for continuing research (linked to extension services) on existing and new technology in agriculture to assure that the introduction of technological reforms is made compatible, to the extent possible, with the need to utilize a growing rural labor force. Bihar's population is growing at roughly 2.7 percent per annum. It now seems likely that the state's labor force will

[29] The *Brief Outline of the Revised Fourth Five Year Plan (1969–74)* actually refers to the need to encourage traders in fertilizer to "appoint progressive farmers as their dealers" (ibid., "Agricultural Production").

grow rapidly until the end of the century at least. Most of this burgeoning labor force will have to be absorbed in the rural sector, rather than in a modernized sector of large-scale and small-scale manufacturing enterprises.

Some years ago it seemed possible to hope that a program of industrialization and exploitation of the state's natural resources might be important in relieving the growing pressure of population on land, both by drawing off presently under-utilized labor and by providing new employment opportunities for the growing labor force. Optimism in this respect seemed in order because the state was not totally lacking in a modernized industrial sector and was endowed with rich natural resources.[30] However, the industrial development of the state has lagged (notwithstanding the gradual implementation of a number of major public-sector projects in the 1960s),[31] as has the exploitation of natural resources. As a result employment opportunities outside of agriculture have grown very slowly. Between 1957 and 1967, for example, employment in factories[32] rose only from 179,693 to 237,178.[33] Such new industries as

[30] The Chota Nagpur Division of Bihar has the most important concentration of mineral resources in India. In 1951, that region produced 82 percent of India's coal, 57 percent of her mica, 46 percent of her iron ore, the entire output of copper ore, and fairly significant quantities of manganese, graphite, bauxite, limestone, and other minerals. By 1970, Bihar's production of most of these minerals had increased, though the state's percentage share of all-India production had in most instances declined. In addition, major deposits of uranium ore had been discovered in south Bihar and were being exploited at a processing plant at Jadugudda in Singhbhum District. Finally, it is noteworthy that a comprehensive geological survey of the state had not been completed. Until such a survey has been done, estimates of the state's mineral endowment will remain imprecise. For supplemental information, see Bihar, Directorate of Statistics, *Bihar through Figures, 1967*, pp. 128–132.

[31] Among these major projects are the following: a heavy machine building project in Ranchi District in collaboration with the Soviet Union; an oil refinery at Barauni in Monghyr in collaboration with the Soviet Union; a high-tension insulator factory in Ranchi District in collaboration with Czechoslovakia; the Sindri fertilizer establishment in Dhanbad; a uranium processing plant in Singhbhum; and the Soviet-assisted steel mill at Bokaro (ibid., p. 153).

[32] The word factories, as used here, applies to manufacturing institutions registered under the Factory Act of 1948 and employing 50 or more workers with the aid of power and 100 or more workers without aid of power.

[33] Bihar, Directorate of Economics and Statistics, *Bihar Statistical Handbook, 1966*, p. 307.

were being developed tended to economize on labor. For example, public-sector projects such as the superphosphate factory at Sindri (Dhanbad District) employed only two hundred workers and the Czechoslovakian-assisted high-tension insulator factory at Namkum (Ranchi District) employed only five hundred. Also, the worker skills demanded by such projects necessitated the procurement of labor on an all-India basis, and few Biharis were trained to meet successfully the out-of-state competition for the scarce opportunities being generated locally. Moreover, the state's diverse mining operations (including coal, copper ore, iron ore, mica, etc.) have not been rapidly expanding their demand for labor in Bihar. In 1957, there were 239,799 workers in mining operations. Nine years later, in 1966, there were only 253,731 workers engaged in mining activities.[34] As against these totals, the number of workers in agriculture was estimated to be almost 15 million in 1961 and represented 76.84 percent of the state's labor force.[35] In short, the evidence suggests that Bihar will continue to rely on her agricultural sector to provide employment for her growing labor force. For many years to come, opportunities for employment outside of agriculture will remain limited relative to the size of the labor force. Indeed, as Gunnar Myrdal has recently observed for the South Asia region as a whole, "the hope, so commonly expressed, that a large proportion of those who will join the labor force in decades to come will become productively employed outside agriculture is illusory."[36]

In the circumstances outlined, it becomes imperative to introduce new technology in agriculture in forms that are labor utilizing rather than labor displacing. Fortunately, not all technological reforms in agriculture need be labor displacing. The utilization of high-yielding varieties of seeds and fertilizers requires an increased number of plowings, more weeding, more applications of water, and additional labor in the harvesting period. And greater labor input is needed not only in the planting, irrigation, harvesting, and processing of crops; the need for labor is increased as multiple cropping becomes possible on lands favored by dependable water

[34] Ibid., pp. 78–79.

[35] Bihar, Directorate of Statistics, *Bihar through Figures, 1967*, p. 26.

[36] Gunnar Myrdal, *Asian Drama: An Inquiry into the Poverty of Nations*, p. 1242.

supplies. There is an increased need for labor in connection with the maintenance (and refurbishment) of irrigation works, including the traditional pynes and ahars of Bihar. Even "the killing of rats and flies and the undertaking of other measures to protect the crops—and the health of the people—against insects, pests and diseases are tasks requiring manpower."[37]

In the pursuit of technological reforms that are labor utilizing, care must be exercised not to rule out forms of mechanization that at one stage of production may be displacing of labor, but which provide substantially increased opportunity for labor at a later stage. Agricultural conditions vary enormously within Bihar. Tractors in some regions may be necessary to enlarge the gross area sown and, when used in combination with high-yielding varieties of seeds, fertilizers, and pesticides, may increase the local demand for labor. In other regions, tractors may be introduced by raiyats and ex-intermediaries with large holdings explicitly for the purpose of reducing their dependence on sharecroppers and casual laborers.[38] This suggests the need for a flexible, yet controlled, approach to the introduction of new technology in rural Bihar. At issue is not whether mechanization is good or bad. What should be at issue is whether mechanized techniques, as well as other forms of new technology, can be made consistent with a program of support for labor intensive farming.

Also at issue is whether new technology in agriculture (including mechanized techniques) can be adapted for use on Bihar's hundreds of thousands of small holdings. This, in turn, suggests an increasing need for research, linked to extension services, to discover forms of new technology that are operative on small holdings under varying soil and climatic conditions. Beyond this creative adaptation of new technology, there is the need for government to recognize and change the current pattern of distribution of existing forms of technology, which has thus far favored large landholders

[37] Ibid., pp. 1295–1296.

[38] In 1970 in Champaran, Shahabad, Muzaffarpur, and Purnea districts, the author encountered large landholders who openly stated that their commitment to "tractorization," as well as other forms of mechanization, was based on the hope that they could thus become less dependent on sharecroppers and casual laborers.

with holdings of twenty-four acres and above,[39] and may even have provided additional incentive for such landholders to enlarge their holdings at the expense of raiyats (who were unable to prove occupancy raiyat status), under-raiyats, and bataidars. This pattern of distribution of high-yielding varieties of seeds, fertilizers, tube wells, and tractors must be reversed if government is sincere about directing attention, for the first time, toward the majority of small cultivators. If the pattern is not reversed, then we must anticipate that large raiyats and ex-intermediaries, who are beginning to experience increasing incomes following their utilization of new technology and precise timing of farming operations, will continue to benefit disproportionately from government's promotion of modern methods of agriculture. If government wishes to mitigate rural tensions; to diminish the existing socioeconomic gap between rural haves and have-nots; to include small landholders in its agricultural production program; to provide rural employment, rather than to pursue policies that transform under-utilized rural labor into unemployed urban labor—if government wishes to do these things, it must emphasize the development of labor intensive forms of new technology as well as the adaptation of new technology for use on small holdings. It must establish better control over the dissemination of all forms of technology. It must be aware of the potential negative and positive effects of the technology, depending on where it is applied, by whom, and for what purposes. While the technology itself may appear to be neutral—favoring neither the large nor small landholder—where and how it is used in Bihar will determine whether it contributes to the fulfillment of the twin goals of the agrarian program we have outlined or limits the prospects of their fulfillment.

One cannot suggest that the modified strategy of rural development endorsed in preceding pages, and the associated programs of agrarian reforms and assistance to small farmers, will be implemented in Bihar in the near future. Nor can one suggest that these

[39] The tendency for technological reforms to "provide their benefits to the peasant farming class roughly in proportion to landholdings" has been observed elsewhere in India by Professor John Mellor. This phenomenon, suggests Mellor, can be associated with attempts by large landholders "to displace some labor with the most efficient types of mechanization." The whole process,

APPENDIX

Case Studies—Descriptions of Selected Villages

There are approximately 68,000 villages in the state of Bihar; of these, only a handful have been intensively surveyed by the author and visited periodically in the period beginning in 1956 and ending in 1970.[1] The personally selected and surveyed villages are not considered representative of either "typical" or "atypical" villages within their respective districts and regions.

The following criteria were used in selecting the villages subsequently surveyed. First, it was considered important to select at least one village in which a single zamindari interest had been maintained for several generations within one family—a village in which the zamindar had traditionally enjoyed broadly developed socioeconomic privileges, together with rights associated with the collection of rent from his "tenants." Second, it was considered appropriate to select a village in which a number of small, resident zamindars were prominent. Third, it was considered appropriate to select a village in which intermediary interests had been divided among a number of absentee zamindars. Fourth, it was considered useful to select a village in which Bhoodan (land gift) workers had attempted to implement their nonofficial program of agrarian reforms. Fifth, it was considered appropriate to select a village in which rural extension activities of the government of Bihar were conspicuous. Finally, it was considered essential that the selected villages be distributed among the various geographic regions of the state (the North Gangetic Plain, the South Gangetic Plain, and the South Bihar Plateau) and be graded according to their accessibility from urban centers or lines of communication.

Among the five villages chosen for intensive study in 1956–1957,

[1] Complete enumeration surveys—involving the interviewing of the headman of every household—were conducted in five villages by the author in 1956–1957.

none represented an ideal, hypothetical village for which selection criteria have been listed. Yet each selected village fulfilled a combination of the selection criteria.

A description of the villages as they were when they were first surveyed in 1956–1957 follows.[2]

Village A: Muzaffarpur District—North Gangetic Plain

Village A is situated on a fertile plain in the district of Muzaffarpur, forty-five miles north of the Ganges. It is eighteen miles northeast of the principal city of the district, Muzaffarpur. It is not easily accessible. A fairly reliable, but apparently nonscheduled, rural bus service extends over deeply rutted kacha[3] roads to within seven miles of Village A. The remaining seven miles can be covered by using foot paths or by following the cross-country marks of bullock carts. While eighteen miles is not a significant distance under ideal circumstances, during the months of April and May, when temperatures are high, and at the time of the monsoon, when intermittent streams overflow their banks, it is difficult to negotiate the same distance.

Though there is little foliage to obstruct the view, the village is "invisible" at less than a mile; it is a naturally camouflaged and dispersed collection of reed and thatch huts. The arrangement of the huts is such that large tracts of land separate them. In fact, Village A can be described as a series of hamlets, each a semiautonomous unit of the main village. This physical fragmentation of the community, a relatively common feature in many sections of the North Gangetic Plain region, partially coincides with differences in caste. However, it does not seem to be common for villagers of a single caste to live within a single hamlet or detached unit of the village. What seems to be more characteristic, judging from the residential pattern of Village A as well as from that of other villages of the same district, is for people of roughly the same economic and social position to be grouped in one of the semi-independent units of the village.

There are 73 households in Village A; 61 are landed, 12 are landless. The average size of a landed household is 6.18 persons; that of a landless household, 4.75 persons.[4] The total number of persons in the village is 434.

[2] The descriptions presented here are, substantially, those in F. Tomasson Jannuzi, "Agrarian Problems in Bihar" (Ph.D. dissertation, London School of Economics and Political Science, 1958).

[3] "Kacha," as applied to a road, indicates a nonmetalled, dirt-surfaced road.

[4] The fact that the joint family institution is stronger among the landed than the landless could account for the difference in the average sizes of the households for the two groups.

The principal castes of the village are Awadia, Chamar, Dhusad, Kurmi, Lohar, Teli, and Yaddava.[5] According to the villagers, none of the castes is of high traditional status. There is also a single Muslim family. There seems to be little tendency for any group to assume leadership in the village. This may be due to the subordination (for several generations) of the villagers' interests to those of a powerful absentee zamindar. The current zamindar, until the enactment of the Bihar Land Reforms Act, 1950, as amended in 1954, had been one of the most powerful in the North Gangetic Plain region. He, and his ancestors before him, had been the supreme authority in Village A. As of August 1957, even after the abolition of intermediary interests in Bihar, the ex-zamindar retains legal interest in 500 of Village A's 600.625 cultivable acres. Similarly, he has other holdings in other villages of the district.

Excluding the ex-zamindar and his holdings, the landed households in Village A have average holdings per household of 1.65 acres. As compared to the unfragmented holding of 500 acres cultivated under the direction of the ex-zamindar's estate manager, the 100.625 acres held by villagers are divided into 361 noncontiguous plots. The average holding of 1.65 acres per household is divided into an average of 5.92 noncontiguous plots. The largest holding in the village, excluding the holding of the ex-zamindar, is 6.87 acres, divided into eleven noncontiguous plots. The villagers' lands are not of such quality or size as to allow the landed to derive the major portion of their incomes from their own land. It is customary, therefore, for the landed, as well as the landless, to work for wages[6] on the lands of the ex-zamindar. Thus, someone from each of the seventy-three households works as a wage laborer on the ex-zamindar's estate during part of each agricultural year. Moreover, only six respondents, representing a similar number of households, claimed to earn the major portions of their incomes by some means other than working on the lands of the ex-zamindar. The villagers' dependence on the ex-zamindar is increased by the "monopoly" he holds as the only source of cash income in the village. In Village A cash wages are paid by the ex-zamindar's estate manager,

[5] For this village, as for villages B, C, and D, the caste groups are listed in alphabetical order.

[6] Since the abolition of his intermediary interests, the ex-zamindar has claimed that he can no longer afford to pay wages at pre-abolition rates and has reduced the wages paid for labor on his fields. The pre-abolition rate was 1 rupee, 2 annas, per day for male laborers; the post-abolition rate per day for men is 10 annas. Female laborers work for less, usually 8 annas per day. A working day usually starts at sunrise and ends at sunset.

only. This man, the former patwari, is also the principal moneylender of the community.

The water supply of the village is limited. Only the fields of the ex-zamindar are irrigated. Two water tanks exist in the village: one on the estate of the ex-zamindar, the other in the village proper. Of the two, the ex-zamindar's is made usable for irrigation purposes by means of an electric pumping system run by a portable generator. The system is not perfect, but is useful during the dry season. The village tank is used for watering animals.

Under ideal conditions, the villagers expect to trap enough water within their paddy lands at the time of the monsoon to enable them to begin a good crop. Dry cultivation is the accepted method for the second crop. At the height of the dry season the shallow pit wells of the community yield a meager supply of turbid water, sufficient only for the daily needs of the people.

Despite the similarity of soil, the lands of the village cultivators and those of the absentee ex-zamindar are cropped differently. Yields per acre in the latter far exceed those of the former. This results from the ex-zamindar's effective use of irrigation, his use of intensive labor together with a tractor on lands which are unfragmented, and his use of ammonium sulphate fertilizer, crop dusting, and improved seeds.

It is the practice in Village A to do subsistence farming, i.e., to grow pulses, cereals, and rice for personal consumption. There are six cultivators who attempt to raise cash crops, tobacco and sugar cane, but they seldom succeed in producing marketable quantities. The ex-zamindar devotes his entire acreage to tobacco and sugar cane. For the year immediately preceding the survey, his annual net gain from the sale of his produce was Rs. 50,000, according to records made available by his estate manager.

The standard of living of the villagers is low. Excepting the ex-zamindar's estate manager, none own pacca[7] homes; the usual home is of reed and thatch. The villagers' diet is meager throughout the year; all exist daily on two meals, or less, consisting mainly of poor-quality rice with little seasoning; only one family can afford ghee.[8] The per capita gross annual income among the landed is Rs. 76.[9] The landless are even less well off, having per capita gross annual income of only Rs. 51.

As of June 1957, Village A had not been incorporated in an active

[7] "Pacca" as used here indicates "mud or mud-brick."

[8] "Ghee" is clarified butter, usually made from buffalo butter.

[9] All income statistics used in this text and pertaining to the surveyed villages were computed for the year preceding the survey.

Community Project development block, nor had it benefited from the work of rural social workers associated with the Bhoodan movement or any similar movement.

In Village A there is no school or library. Neither is there an active village council. The village is not electrified.

Indigenous language newspapers are not delivered as part of a normal service; they are brought to the village occasionally by those who travel to Muzaffarpur City.

The village is seldom visited by outsiders, though its members now look forward, periodically, to the lectures of traveling politicians.

The major interest shared by the villagers is resentment of the ex-zamindar and his patwari. The respondents were not asked questions pertaining to their political affiliations. However, the majority (approximately 80 percent) volunteered the information that they planned to vote for the local Communist candidate in the 1957 general election. The ex-zamindar was, at the time of the survey (January 1957), a member of the Bihar State Legislature and a prominent member of the Congress party.

Village B: Darbhanga District—North Gangetic Plain

Village B of Darbhanga District on the North Gangetic Plain, benefiting from the government-sponsored rural development program, graduated in 1956 from the Community Project "intensive phase" of rural development to the "post-intensive" state of development. The village is situated twelve miles from the nearest railway station and three miles from the Community Project Block Headquarters of the Pusa-Samastipur-Sakra Community Project. A kacha road, graded in 1955 by the villagers under the direction of the Community Project village-level worker, connects the village with two neighboring villages and the Community Project Block Headquarters.

The principal castes of the village are Bhumihar Brahman, Chamar, Dhom, Dhusad, Kahnu, Koirii, Kurmi, Lohar, Malaah, Musahar, Tatawan, Teli, and Yaddava. There are ten Muslim households in the village.

There are 93 families within the village, a total population of 599. Among the families, 52 are landed and 41 are landless. The landed are mainly Koiriis and Brahmans; together, they represent 37 households and have holdings totaling 203 acres. The 15 remaining landed households have holdings totaling 18 acres. Thus, the village's 221 cultivable acres are divided among 52 landed households with an average holding per household being 4.25 acres.

Among the landed householders, 30 had been small zamindars or tenure-holders. Of these, 28 were Brahmans; two were Koiriis. When Village B was surveyed in November–December 1956, the zamindari classes had been divested of the zamindari right, as intermediaries of the state, to collect rent from tenants and had been informed of the legal vesting of their interests in the state. The zamindars' notification, in accordance with provisions of the Bihar Land Reforms Act, 1950, as amended in 1954, had been in December 1955 and January 1956.

The average size of a landed household is 7 persons, while the average number of persons per landless household is 5.73. The fact that the joint family institution is stronger among the landed than the landless could account for the difference in the average sizes of the households for the two groups. It was suggested by some villagers that whereas the poorer (usually the landless) could not indulge in the luxury of encouraging several "real" families to live under one roof for fear of further depressing the standard of living of the household, the richer (especially the landholders) could more easily presume that the joint dependence of more than one "real" family would strengthen the group. In other words, where landless families seemed to view the joint family as a producer of collective insecurity and poverty, the landed tended to view it as a means of pooling resources for common strength.

The differences in standard of living between landed and landless households of the village are pronounced. Generally, the homes of the landed have tile roofs and mud walls, while those of the landless have thatch roofs and reed walls. The diet of a landed household is, generally, more varied than that of a landless household, though neither landed nor landless households usually have sufficient food for more than two meals daily. Another indication of the relative strength of the landed and landless communities may be seen in the income statistics for the two groups. The per capita gross annual income of the landed is 115 rupees, as compared to a per capita gross annual income of 47 rupees for the landless.

The villagers are mainly agriculturalists and produce a variety of crops. Wheat and rice are grown as staples, while maize, tobacco, and chillies are grown in small quantities. Also, the villagers catch and consume small numbers of fresh-water fish from a stream approximately three miles north of the community. It is customary for a single caste, the Malaah, to do the fishing.

The villagers' agricultural practices are of high standard relative to other surveyed villages (Villages A, C, D, and E). Eighty percent of the landed cultivators fertilize their lands with cow dung or ammonium sulphate. Contour plowing on plots subject to seasonal erosion has been encouraged by the Community Project village-level worker.

Improved seeds and improved implements have been introduced to the villagers by Community Project workers. The Japanese Paddy Method of developing better-quality rice and increasing yields of rice per acre has been demonstrated to the community and three households have used the new technique.[10]

Government funds, administered through the Community Project block to which Village B belongs, have supplemented the resources of the villagers in the construction of a village school, the construction of a village library, the grading of the main kacha road leading to the village, and the improvement of a number of village wells. The preceding projects were initiated and completed during the First Five Year Plan, the last official project being completed in 1955.

The Community Project block evaluation officer suggested that Village B's record of accomplishment had been high, relative to other villages in the block. During the intensive stage of Community Project development work in Village B, a nonstatutory gram panchayat was developed; night literacy classes were held in the newly constructed village library; and "community spirit seemed to be at a high level. . . . However, when aid from government ceased, there was a corresponding decline in the villagers' enthusiasm for community or self development." In the judgment of the evaluation officer, Village B has deteriorated economically and socially since leaving the Community Project level and being placed in a National Extension Service block for post-intensive development.

The evaluation officer stated that the most serious shortcoming of development work in Village B had been its failure to benefit all segments of the community equally. "The gap in standards of living between the landed and landless has increased as one result of government's development effort." The former have, more often, benefited from government projects because they have had the resources to permit them the luxury of experimentation and the surpluses for investment in new seeds and implements necessary for progress beyond experimentation. The latter have not had even the primary resource of an agricultural community—land on which to experiment. The impression of the broad effect of the Community Project program in Village B is that the division of the community into opposing groups has gone beyond the stage when the primary differences rested on whether a family owned or did not own land. In other words, as an indirect

[10] "Japanese Paddy Method" is used here to indicate the method by which young sprouts are carefully cultivated in compact plots, then transplanted, in rows, in other plots so that each plant has growing space sufficient to assure its maximum growth.

result of the Community Project effort, local economic, social, and political rivalries have been intensified.[11]

According to the Community Project block evaluation officer, "the only improvement in the living condition of the under-privileged people [of Village B] has been the repair or construction of wells." However, not all segments of the underprivileged (mainly landless laborers) have benefited from the new wells. Though certain wells were constructed for specific castes of the community, the Dhoms (of "untouchable status") have been debarred (by other untouchables) from drawing water from a well assigned to them. "Thus there is untouchability even between two groups of untouchables."

Village C: Gaya District—South Gangetic Plain

Nineteen miles east of Gaya City within the District of Gaya on the South Gangetic Plain of Bihar is Village C. It is a community of tightly clustered mud homes standing in nonconformity to the plains that stretch in every direction around it. In the distance, northward, another village can be seen confronting the horizon with an irregular silhouette. Patches of billowing dust to the south may indicate the location of the metalled Gaya road as government lorries or rural buses rattle along. There are no other roads nearby, nor is there a railway station nearer than nineteen miles. To the east and west the view is one of seemingly endless plains, partially disrupted by patches of scrub vegetation.

The villagers' homes are mud walled and have roofs of thatch or tile—the thatch-roofed homes being inhabited generally by the lower castes, and the tile-roofed homes by the upper castes of the community. Living conditions are similar in the homes of all classes. The houses are sparsely furnished, without exception. One or two wooden articles, a charpoy or a small stool, are occasionally to be seen, but there is seldom more than one charpoy per household and stools are exceptional. Because little wood is available for the construction of household utilities, the use of wood is confined mainly to certain necessities: the single-pronged plow or the single supporting beam of a roof or doorway.

The houses of the village are closely grouped in concentric circles around a central house, the home of the patwari and his family. This

[11] The increase in the intensity of the rivalry between landed and landless was corroborated by means of interviews (with the village headman, the Community Project village-level worker, and the Community Project block evaluation officer) and inspection of the Community Project block evaluation officer's report for Village B.

home differs from the rest in having cement portions and being approximately thirty feet high whereas the other homes of the community are less than ten feet high.

The predominant position of the patwari's home is symbolic of the position of influence maintained by a single absentee ex-zamindar, the patwari's employer, who owns the home and two hundred acres of land in the village.[12]

The principal castes in Village C are Barhi, Cahar, Chamar, Dhusad, Lohar, Manghi, Rawani, Teli, and Yaddava. There are 516 people divided among 88 households in the village. Until recently, 30 households were landed and 58 landless. However, at the time of the survey (April 1957), 74 households could be numbered among the landed, while 14 remained landless. The changes in the numbers of landed and landless households occurred in December 1955 when 44.75 acres of fallow land were donated by the zamindar and distributed in equal portions to 44 of the landless households by Bhoodan workers.

There are, altogether, 343.81 acres of cultivable land in the village. The ex-zamindar's estate is 200 acres. The 30 landed households (excluding those who have received Bhoodan lands) have holdings totaling 99.06 acres; the 44 Bhoodan landed households have a total of 44.75 acres. The average holding per landed household (excluding the Bhoodan landed and their holdings) is 3.30 acres; the average holding per Bhoodan household is approximately 1.017 acres.

For the village as a whole, the average household size is 5.86 persons; for the landed (excluding the Bhoodan landed), 7.37 persons; for the Bhoodan landed, 5.16 persons; and for the landless, 4.85 persons.

Though there is little noticeable difference in the standard of living among landed, Bhoodan landed, and landless, income statistics for the three major groups of the village show a major difference in per capita income between the 30 landed households (excluding the Bhoodan landed) and the remaining 58 households.[13] The differences in per capita income among the groups can be seen in table 20.

The landless laborers, and even the Bhoodan landed (who have yet to demonstrate that a subsistence living can be earned from their small, poor-quality holdings), earn the major portion of their incomes by

[12] The ex-zamindar retains the home and the 200 acres in accordance with provisions of the Bihar Land Reforms Act, 1950, as amended in 1954, permitting ex-zamindars to retain homestead lands and certain buildings.

[13] The fact that differences in per capita income between landed and landless households do not appear to result in an appreciable difference in the living standards for the two groups may be due to the fact that landed households (which have, generally, a higher proportion of adults than do the landless) seem to have higher consumption needs for subsistence.

working as laborers in the fields of the ex-zamindar or in those of the few villagers who can afford to hire workers during the sowing or harvesting seasons. Peak season wages for men are one rupee (or an equivalent value in kind) daily, twelve annas for women, and six annas for children. In the slack seasons, if they find employment, men earn twelve annas, women eight annas, and children four annas, daily. A day's work starts at sunrise and ends at sunset.

The villagers' diets are restricted, quantitatively and qualitatively. Only two meals daily seems to be common, regardless of season or family status. Meals consist of little more than rice prepared without ghee or spices.

TABLE 20
Gross Annual Income per Capita in Village C, 1955–1956

	No. of Households	No. of People	Per Capita Income
Landed	30	221	Rs. 95.11
Bhoodan landed	44	227	Rs. 50.74
Landless	14	68	Rs. 48.67

Source: All income statistics used in this text and pertaining to the surveyed villages were computed for the year preceding the survey.

Though rice is the staple food and main crop of the village, the village has no dependable water supply for irrigating the rice fields.[14] There are no streams or rivers in the vicinity; an ancient water tank, built by a former zamindar over one hundred years ago, is no longer serviceable. Pit wells are few and the water table is low. None of the existing wells have Persian Wheels or any other means by which water can be collected or distributed easily. For these reasons, the waters of the monsoon must be stored in the fields themselves by means of the careful bunding of each plot. Under such conditions the success of a second crop may be doubtful.

Village C has not been incorporated in a government-sponsored rural development program. The village is not electrified. There is no school, library, or active village council.

Communication with the outside is maintained by means of bullock

[14] Village C may be an exception to the rule for Gaya District where, traditionally, irrigation by means of pynes (small canals) and ahars (shallow catchment basins) has been common. According to Dayal, 70 percent of Bihar's irrigated lands are in Gaya and Patna districts (P. Dayal, *Bihar in Maps*).

carts or rural bus (available at irregular intervals at a place three miles distant from the village). However, it is not common for the villagers to travel beyond the village limits.

A number of the villagers seemed to associate the Bhoodan movement's interest and assistance with the Praja Socialist party's political activity. Approximately seventy percent of the respondents submitted their preference for the Praja Socialists in the 1957 Indian general election. Their political views were unsolicited.

Village D: Patna District—
South Gangetic Plain

Village D is located in the district of Patna on the South Gangetic Plain of Bihar. The plains surrounding the village allow an unobstructed view of agricultural lands, except in the north where a fringe of bamboo trees borders the Ganges, approximately 400 yards from the nearest homes of the village.

The village is a conglomerate of sun-baked mud homes with twisting irregular lanes among them. There is little space separating one home from another, and, except for an occasional kitchen garden, there is scant vegetation in the village proper. The settlement is compact, but divided partially into three informal compartments by kitchen gardens and a watering hole for livestock.

Though Village D is more than twenty miles from the nearest city, Patna, the capital of Bihar, its location within one mile of a pacca road leading to that city and its nearness (two miles) to a station on the trunk railway connecting Patna and Calcutta allow the villagers access to urban centers. Contacts with the outside are many and diverse, resulting from travel by train or bus to other parts of Bihar and Bengal, from reading newspapers printed in Urdu and Hindi and available at the nearby railway station, and from listening to the battery radio owned by the village schoolteacher.[15] Among the villages surveyed, Village D showed the highest degree of measured awareness of people and events outside the village.

The ease of communication with metropolitan areas has influenced life in the village, increasing the numbers of people whose opinions apparently reflect contact with the outside and diverting men from agriculture into public service (i.e., mainly, government work for the literate and work on the railways and buses for others). No attempt was made to measure the degree to which outside influences may have changed the villagers' way of life, except as such change may be rep-

[15] Village D is the only one of the surveyed villages in which a radio was found. The teacher in Village D is a Rajput; the Rajputs of the village tend to have greater access to the radio than do the other caste groups.

resented in reporting the numbers of people who, having been resident agriculturalists, now have nonagricultural employment outside the village. There are twenty-one such people, all of whom (though they are not now residents of the village) contribute to the maintenance of their families in the village.

Despite outside influences, the community of 727 persons is predominantly agricultural; among 96 households, 81 derive the major portion of their incomes from agriculture; the remaining 15 households operate stalls in the railway bazaar. The community can be divided into three segments: 60 landed households, 15 landless noncultivating households (shopkeepers), and 21 landless cultivating households (whose working members are engaged as laborers in the fields of the landholders).

The difference in standard of living between landed and landless cultivators is marked. This is partially indicated by the fact that the annual gross per capita income for the landed was 209 rupees, as compared to 125 rupees for the landless cultivators. Despite differences in standard of living, both groups have higher incomes as well as apparently higher standards of living than their opposite numbers in Villages A, B, and C. The annual gross per capita income of the landless noncultivators (shopkeepers) was 211 rupees.

The principal castes in Village D are Agrarhi, Barhi, Dhobii, Dhusad, Jaishwar, Kurmi, Pasi, Rajput, Rawani, Thakur, Vish, and Yaddava. There are six Muslim households in the village. The predominant caste of the village is the Rajput. Its predominance results from a variety of factors:[16] (*a*) the traditionally high position of the Rajputs in this village; (*b*) the caste's numerical superiority (there are 182 Rajputs in 20 households, while the nearest caste, numerically, is the Yaddava with 169 persons in 20 households); (*c*) the Rajputs' economic superiority (the Rajputs have an annual per capita gross income of 337 rupees, while the Yaddavas have an annual per capita gross income of 158 rupees); (*d*) the head man of the village is a Rajput; (*e*) the village schoolteacher, holder of a degree from Patna University, is a Rajput; (*f*) the largest landholder in the village is a Rajput; and (*g*) every Rajput household holds land.

None of the households of Village D held intermediary interests in

[16] Though there seems to be some relationship between the current status and the traditional position of a caste, a caste's prestige and position in the community are results of multiple factors other than (but including) the traditional or "religious" caste position. The economic status of a caste, for instance, may be as much a determinant of its place in the society as is its traditional position. This may be the cause of frequent anomalies; a scheduled caste in one village may have its low position partially confirmed by its poverty and landlessness while households of the same caste may enjoy relatively high

the village when general notification of the vesting in the state of all intermediary interests in Bihar was made on January 1, 1956. Thirty absentee zamindars and tenure-holders held the intermediary interests in the village lands.

The village's nearness to the Ganges does not normally affect it adversely during the rainy season because, at this point, the river is usually contained within its banks and because the village is on relatively high ground. When an overflow occurs, resultant damage to homesteads is largely offset by the addition of rich layers of alluvium to the soil. Erosion of the soil in the vicinity is not evident.

The village's location near the Ganges must be responsible for the continuously high level of the water table in the community's lands. Even during the dry season, the water table is sufficiently high to allow for the tapping of water for irrigation purposes by means of a number of Persian Wheels attached to pit wells. However, only about fifty acres of the village's lands are irrigated in this manner. On the remaining lands, the cultivators do wet farming by erecting barriers around their fields for the retention of water during the monsoon; they do dry farming for the winter crop. A cultivator who owns lands suitable for both wet and dry farming is considered to be ideally situated. Since "wet" and "dry" lands are seldom adjacent, a cultivator's desire for lands of each type contributes to the fragmentation of holdings in the village.

There are 364.5 acres of cultivable land in the village. These acres are divided into 612 separate units for cultivation. The average holding per landed household is 6.075 acres.

The villagers attempt to double-crop all of the cultivable land. Rice, cereals, and pulses are the principal crops. There are no cash crops grown in marketable quantities. The general pattern is one of subsistence agriculture.

Only three cultivators (Rajputs) use animal manure to fertilize their lands. None use chemical fertilizers, though the Rajput schoolteacher has spoken to members of his own caste, at least, of the "advantages of chemical fertilizers." Because alternative fuels are scarce and costly, it is the custom to use cow dung for fuel. Even cultivators who use cow dung for fertilizer, therefore, employ small quantities (approximately 25 pounds per acre for each growing season).

Though Village D has not been incorporated in a government-sponsored development program, it has been touched by the work of the Bhoodan movement. Vinobha Bhave and his followers worked in the village for one day in 1954.

---

status in a neighboring village in which their caste is associated with economic stability and ownership of land.

The village maintains its own school.

There is no village council or panchayat, though vague powers rest with several of the village elders and larger landholders.

Although the political affiliations of the majority of the respondents were not known at the time of the survey, the village elders, in conversations after the general election of 1957, indicated that the villagers split their votes between the Congress and the Praja Socialist parties.

Village E: Ranchi District—South Bihar Plateau

Village E is a remote aboriginal village in Ranchi District of the South Bihar Plateau region. It is forty miles from the nearest city of the district (Ranchi), forty miles from the nearest railway station (Ranchi), seventeen miles from the nearest hard-surface road, and four miles from the nearest dirt road. There are no towns in the immediate vicinity.[17]

Village E is situated in an area of rough terrain. The hills surrounding it are partly forested; those which are not are used for grazing of livestock or are crudely terraced for the cultivation of paddy.

The irregular nature of the land together with the absence of contour plowing or proper terracing have contributed to severe erosion damage through the years. Monsoon waters are uncontrolled and gully erosion seems to be common. Water runoff during each monsoon continues to do damage. The rapidity of the runoff prevents easy storage of water for the growth of paddy or for other purposes. Since the water table is low, the villagers' pit wells (seldom sunk to a depth of more than twelve feet) are useless for irrigation purposes.

As in most areas of monsoon climate, high temperatures and precipitation combine to affect adversely the quality of land for agricultural purposes. The soils of the district are leached of organic matter and are mainly ferruginous.[18] Because of the combination of negative factors (poor quality land and lack of irrigation facilities), the possibility of effective double-cropping is eliminated. It has become traditional for the people to consider agriculture a subsidiary means of earning a living. The villagers' principal means of subsistence come from their livestock and from foraging for edible roots and flowers in the nearby jungle. Some men go annually to Assam to work as seasonal laborers on the tea plantations, though this practice has diminished due to transport difficulties caused by the partition of India and Pakistan. In recent years a number of men have supplemented their incomes by

[17] For our purposes, a town is a community having a population of between 5,000 and 50,000; a city, more than 50,000.

[18] India, Census Operations, *Census of India, 1951*, I, 25.

moving temporarily to the district capital to serve on construction gangs employed on government of Bihar projects. Forms of migrant labor are the major sources of cash income.

The village is small compared to the plains villages surveyed (Villages A, B, C, and D). Forty-one families, a population of 275, live in scattered settlements. Their homes are of mud with tile roofs; some have courtyards enclosed by mud walls or by less-substantial barriers of thatch or reed. There is no standard house design. There is uniformity only in that none have windows; within all there is seldom more than subdued light even on the brightest day.

The interiors of the homes provide crowded quarters for families. Normally, there is one large room that serves as living room, kitchen, and bedroom. There is an average of 5.63 people per room in the village.[19]

Among aborigines, the absence of caste distinctions precludes the growth of factionalism based on caste stratification as may be found in nonaboriginal villages in Bihar. The absence of caste, however, is but one of the apparent reasons for the unity of purpose that is so evident in the village. The fact that the community is not primarily agricultural and that there are no landless laborers in it eliminates sources of friction that are usual elsewhere in Bihar.

The people of Village E are remarkably homogeneous. This homogeneity is especially evident when the community unites around its nonstatutory gram panchayat to administer village justice and to discuss problems affecting the community or any part of it. These meetings, though directed by the village elders, include the entire adult population of the village. Decisions are arrived at by unanimous agreement only. The nonstatutory panchayat seems to be as effective as a statutory panchayat could be.

The villagers demonstrate a "community of interest" in other ways also. The people show special concern for the aged and children, and an elementary kind of social security is provided for the unemployed and destitute. The unemployed and aged are allocated foodstuffs from village stores. Orphaned children are given new homes. In these matters, each decision is made by the villagers in plenary session.

Though food is scarce, the people of the village have a varied diet; they lack agricultural produce, but no religious taboos prevent them from having variety. The aborigines eat the flesh of the cow, the pig, the chicken, and the goat. They use the milk of the goat and cow. In the lean season, especially in February and March, it has been cus-

[19] An "average family" (household) in Village E is composed of 6.7 persons. However, because a few of the homes have more than one room, the average number of persons per room is smaller than the average family size.

tomary to forage in the jungle for wild vegetables or fruits. A special favorite and staple of diet has been the mahua flower, which grows wild abundantly in the forests. That the aborigines of Village E appear to be more sturdy, as a group, than the plains people of the more northerly portions of Bihar may be a result of their unusual (for India) eating habits.

The villagers own 227 acres[20] of land divided into 346 separate plots. The average household holding is 5.53 acres. There is no scarcity of land, and a family has customary right for grazing purposes over a larger area than it owns.

Income statistics computed for the village indicate a per capita gross annual income of 45 rupees. The gross annual income of the average family is 304 rupees. Among the variables affecting these statistics, there is one which deserves special mention: it is the extreme difficulty of determining income derived from foraging and hunting, for which no estimate was made. For this reason, the income statistics for this village are somewhat lower than they would be if all sources of income for the villagers were included.

There was no cash indebtedness in the village for the year preceding the survey. Though fourteen families among forty-one had incurred debts in kind, the debts were at a relatively low rate of interest (25%).[21] All except two of the loans had come from and were administered by the village council. The cash equivalent of these debts per indebted family for the year preceding the survey was approximately 47 rupees.[22]

The physical remoteness of the village is not offset by easy communication with the outside world. Visitors are uncommon. There are no current indigenous language newspapers available. There is no village library. There is no school in the village, although several families send their children to a Jesuit Missionary School located approximately seven miles from the village. Despite these disadvantages, the people show an awareness of people and events beyond the village and in the whole of India.

One indication of the degree to which the people were conscious of

[20] The figure includes land for which the villagers pay rent to the state or for which rent will be assessed after Survey and Settlement operations are concluded. "Owned land" includes land where the proprietary right rests with the state. "Owned land" is also used here to include those lands in the possession of a cultivator whether or not he has a right of permanent occupancy.

[21] It was noted in several districts of Bihar that interest rates on loans varied from 5 to 75 percent per annum.

[22] The cash value of the loans was determined by noting the local bazaar prices of the commodities during the "lean" or high price months.

current issues is their voting record in the last general election (1957). According to the village elders, the villagers voted as a group, unanimously, for the Jharkand party[23] which stood in opposition to the government of Bihar and the Congress party for fear that the Congress government would use clauses included in the Bihar Land Reforms Act, 1950, as amended in 1954, to restrict the aborigines' right to forage in forested areas. There is no simple explanation for the villagers' developed political consciousness or their general awareness. However, since migrant labor has been a consistent feature of the village's employment pattern and since there are children who attend school outside the village, it is assumed that these factors provide sources of information and enlightenment partially offsetting the factors of isolation.

At the time of the survey, Village E had not been actively incorporated in a Community Project Development program or in a National Extension Service scheme. It had not been visited by social workers connected with the Bhoodan experiment. It is likely, however, that Roman Catholic missionaries have exerted indirect influence in the village through the children they instruct.

[23] The village elders were re-interviewed after the election. At this time they provided information about the voting record of the village as a whole. Their views and information on this topic were not solicited.

The Jharkand party is a local party that represents aboriginal interests. Its political strength is restricted mainly to the tribal areas of Bihar.

SELECTED BIBLIOGRAPHY

Allen, J., T. Wolseley Haig, and H. H. Dodwell, eds. *Cambridge Shorter History of India.* Cambridge: Cambridge University Press, 1934.

Anstey, Vera. *The Economic Development of India.* 4th ed. London: Longmans, Green and Company, 1957.

Baden-Powell, B. H. *Indian Village Community.* London: Longmans, Green and Company, 1896.

———. *Land Revenue and Tenure in British India.* 2nd ed. Oxford: The Clarendon Press, 1913.

———. *Land Systems of British India.* London: Clarendon Press, 1892.

Bailey, F. G. *Caste and the Economic Frontier.* Manchester: University Press, 1957.

Balogh, Thomas. *Some Aspects of Economic Growth of Under-Developed Areas.* 2nd ed. New Delhi: National Council of Applied Economic Research, 1962.

Bardhan, Pranab. "The So-Called Green Revolution and Agricultural Labourers." Unpublished. 1970.

———. "Trends in Land Relations, A Note." *Economic and Political Weekly* 5, nos. 3, 4, and 5. Annual Number (January 1970).

Bhave, Vinobha. *Bhoodan Yajna (Land-Gifts Mission).* Ahmedabad: Navajivan Publishing House, 1953.

———. Personal interview at the Sarvodaya Sammelan, Kerala. June 13, 1957.

———. *Principles and Philosophy of the Bhoodan Yagna.* Tanjore, India: Sarvodaya Prachuralaya, March 1956.

———, K. G. Mashruwala, and J. C. Kumarappa. *Planning Commission and Sarvodaya Approach.* Muzaffarpur: Bihar Khadi Samiti, n.d. [1956?]

Bhoodan as Seen by the West. A collection of articles and radio talks on Bhoodan by the friends of the West. Tanjore, India: Sarvodaya Prachuralaya, May 1956.

Bihar. Department of Agriculture. "Draft Outline of the Fourth Five Year Plan 1969–74 (Agriculture)." Unpublished document. Patna, Bihar: 1968.

———. *A Pilot Project on the Agricultural Development of the Small Farmers of Purnea District.* Patna, Bihar: October 1969.

———. "Pilot Scheme for Marginal Cultivators and Agricultural Labourers for the District of Ranchi." Unpublished document. Patna, Bihar: 1970.

———. *Problems of Small Farmers of Kosi Area (Purnea and Saharsa Districts).* Patna, Bihar: Secretariat Press, 1969.

———. "Project for Development of Small Farmers in Champaran District." Unpublished document. Patna, Bihar: July 1970.

———. "Special Project for Marginal Farmers and Agricultural Labourers of Shahabad District." Unpublished document. Patna, Bihar: 1970.

Bihar. Department of Community Development and Panchayats. *Report of the Committee on Community Development.* Patna, Bihar: Secretariat Press, 1969.

Bihar. Department of Finance. *Season and Crop Report of Bihar for the Year 1953–54.* Patna, Bihar: Secretariat Press, 1956.

Bihar. Development Commissioner N. P. Mathur. "Financing of Agriculture by Commercial Banks." D.O. No. DIF(SD) 06/70–2490. Unpublished document. Patna, Bihar: June 12, 1970.

Bihar. Directorate of Economics and Statistics. *Bihar Statistical Handbook, 1957.* Patna, Bihar: Superintendent, Secretariat Press, 1958 [?].

———. *Bihar Statistical Handbook, 1966.* Patna, Bihar: Superintendent, Secretariat Press, 1970.

Bihar. Directorate of Statistics. *Bihar through Figures, 1967.* Patna, Bihar: Secretariat Press, 1969.

Bihar. Laws, statutes, etc. (Bills). *Bihar Agricultural Lands (Ceiling and Management) Bill, 1955.* Patna, Bihar: Secretariat Press, 1955. (Includes "Statement of Objects and Reasons" by K. B. Sahay.)

———. *Bihar State Acquisition of Zamindaris Bill, 1947.* Patna, Bihar: Secretariat Press, 1947.

Bihar. Laws, statutes, etc. (Notices). "Notice Issued to the Assembly Secretariat for the Introduction and Consideration of the Bihar Public Land Encroachment (Amendment) Bill, 1970." Unpublished document. Patna, Bihar: June 22, 1970.

———. "Notice Issued to the Assembly Secretariat for the Introduction and Consideration of the Bihar Tenancy (Amendment) Bill, 1970." Unpublished document. Patna, Bihar: June 12, 1970.

Bihar. Laws, statutes, etc. (Reports). "Report of the Select Committee on the Bihar Agricultural Lands (Ceiling and Management) Bill, 1955." Patna, Bihar: Secretariat Press, 1955.

Bihar. Planning Department. *Brief Outline of the Revised Fourth Five Year Plan (1969–74)*. Patna, Bihar: Secretariat Press, March 1970.

Bihar Provincial Government. *Bihar in 1938–39*. By S. M. Wasi, Director of Publicity. Patna, Bihar: Government Printing Office, 1942.

Bihar. Public Relations Department. *Bihar 1955–56*. Patna, Bihar: Secretariat Press, 1956.

Bihar. Revenue Department. "D.O. No. 5LR-LA-224/70-5667-L.R." Unpublished document. Patna, Bihar: July 1, 1970.

———. "D.O. No. 5LR-LA-224/70-6016-L.R." Unpublished document. Patna, Bihar: July 9, 1970.

———. Gazetteer Revision Section. *Bihar District Gazetteers—Gaya*. Patna, Bihar: Secretariat Press, 1957.

———. Land Ceiling Section. "Statement Showing Demand and Collection of Rent, Cess, Education Cess and Miscellaneous Incomes, Rate of Rent, Rent Potential, Compensation and Establishment Costs, Etc." Patna, Bihar: Government Printing Office, June 30, 1967.

Bihar Herald, 1957–1970.

Bihar Local Acts, The. Vols. I–VII. Allahabad: Bharat Law House, 1962+. Vol. I: "Bihar Bhoodan Yagna Act, 1954." "Bihar Consolidation of Holdings and Prevention of Fragmentation Act, 1956." "The Chota Nagpur Tenancy Act." 1964+. Vol. III: "Bihar Land Reforms Act, 1950" (Bihar Act 30 of 1950). "Bihar Land Reforms (Amendment) Act, 1953" (Bihar Act 20 of 1954). "Bihar Land Reforms (Fixation of Ceiling Area and Acquisition of Surplus Land) Act, 1961."

Bose, Saroj Ranjan. *Bihar Population Problems*. Calcutta: Firma K. L. Mukhopadhyay, 1969.

———. "The Changing Face of Bihar Agriculture." Unpublished manuscript made available to the author on August 19, 1970.

———. "Levels of Poverty in Rural Bihar." *Searchlight*, April 21, 1970.

———. *A Study in Bihar Agriculture*. Calcutta: Firma K. L. Mukhopadhyay, 1967.

Boserup, Ester. *The Conditions of Agricultural Growth: The Economics of Agrarian Change under Population Pressure*. London: George Allen & Unwin, 1965.

Brayne, F. L. *The Remaking of Village India*. London: Oxford University Press, 1929.

Brown, Lester R. *Seeds of Change*. New York: Praeger, 1970.

Brown, W. Norman. *The United States and India and Pakistan*. Cambridge: Harvard University Press, 1958.

Buchanan, Francis. *Bihar and Patna in 1811-1812.* Vol. 2. Patna, Bihar: Bihar and Orissa Research Society, n.d.

———. *Journal . . . Kept during the Survey of the Districts of Patna and Gaya in 1811–1812.* Edited by V. H. Jackson. Patna, Bihar: Superintendent of Government Printing, 1925.

Cambridge History of India. Cambridge: University Press. Vol. IV: "Mughul Period." Edited by Sir Richard Burn. 1937. Vol. VI: "Indian Empire, 1858–1918." Edited by H. H. Dodwell. 1932.

Chatterjee, Bishwa B. "Bhoodan Changes Life." *Yojana*, January 26, 1967.

Chou, Ya-lun. "Chinese Agrarian Reform and Bolshevik Land Policy." *Pacific Affairs* 25, no. 1 (March 1952): 24–39.

Dandekar, V. M. "Economic Theory and Agrarian Reforms." *Oxford Economic Papers* 14, no. 1, new series (February 1962): 69–80.

Dantwala, M. L. "Agricultural Credit in India—The Necessary Link." *Pacific Affairs* 25 (December 1952): 349–359.

———. *India's Food Problem.* Bombay: Asia Publishing House, 1961.

———. "Land Reforms in India." *International Labor Review* 66, nos. 5, 6 (November–December 1952): 618–643.

———. "Land Tenure Problems in Countries with Heavy Pressure of Population on Land." In Wisconsin University, *Conference on World Land Tenure Problems—Proceedings*, pp. 49–61. Wisconsin: Parsons, Penn and Raup, 1951.

———. "The Problem of a Subsistence Farm Economy: The Indian Case." In *Subsistence Agriculture and Economic Development*, edited by Clifton R. Warton, Jr. Chicago: Aldine Press, 1969.

———. "Prospects and Problems of Land Reform in India." *Economic Development and Cultural Change* 6, no. 1 (October 1957/58): 3–15.

Darling, Malcolm L. *Punjab Peasant in Prosperity and Debt.* London: Oxford University Press, 1925.

———. *Report on Certain Aspects of the Co-operative Movement in India.* New Delhi: Government of India Publishers, 1957. Under the auspices of the Government of India Planning Commission.

———. *Rusticus Loquitur.* London: Oxford University Press, 1930.

Dasgupta, Sugata. *A Great Society of Small Communities: The Story of India's Land Gift Movement.* Varanasi: Sarva Seva Sangh Prakashan, 1968.

Dayal, P. "The Agricultural Geography of Bihar." Ph.D. dissertation. London School of Economics and Political Science, 1947.

———. *Bihar in Maps.* Patna, Bihar: Kusum Prakashan, 1953.

Del Vasto, Lanza. *Gandhi to Vinoba.* Translated from the French by Philip Leon. London: Rider and Company, 1956.

Deva, Acharya Narendra. *Socialism and the National Revolution.* Edited by Yusef Meherally. Bombay: Padma Publications, 1946.

Dhadda, Siddharaj. *Gramdan (The Latest Phase of Bhoodan).* Wardha, India: A. W. Sahasrabuddhey, General Secretary of Akhil Bharat Sarva Seva Sangh, September 1957.

Dore, Ronald Philip. *Land Reform in Japan.* London: Oxford University Press, 1959.

Driver, Peshotan Nasserwanji. *Problems of Zamindari and Land Tenure Reconstruction in India.* Bombay: New Book Company, 1949.

Frankel, Francine. "Agricultural Modernisation and Social Change." *Mainstream,* November 29, 1969.

———. *India's Green Revolution.* Princeton: Princeton University Press, 1971.

Frykenberg, Robert E., ed. *Land Control and Social Structure in Indian History.* Madison: University of Wisconsin Press, 1969.

Gandhi, Mohandas K. *An Autobiography: The Story of My Experiments with Truth.* Boston: Beacon Press, 1957.

———. *Satyagraha (Non-violent Resistance).* Ahmedabad: Navajivan Publishing House, 1951.

———, et al. *Sarvodaya—Its Principles and Programme.* Ahmedabad: Navajivan Publishing House, 1954.

Grant, James. *An Inquiry into . . . Zamindari Tenures in the Landed Property of Bengal.* London, 1790.

Hardgrave, Robert L. *India: Government and Politics in a Developing Nation.* New York: Harcourt, Brace & World, 1970.

Hauser, Walter. "The Indian National Congress and Land Policy in the Twentieth Century." Mimeographed paper prepared for the December 1962 meeting of the American Historical Association. As quoted by George Rosen in *Democracy and Economic Change in India.* Bombay: Vora and Company, 1966.

Hirschman, Albert O. *The Strategy of Economic Development.* New Haven: Yale University Press, 1958.

Hoselitz, Bert F. "Non-Economic Factors in Economic Development." *American Economic Review* 47, no. 2 (May 1957): 28–42.

Huntington, Samuel P. *Political Order in Changing Societies.* New Haven: Yale University Press, 1968.

Illustrated Weekly of India, March 17, 1968.

India. Census Operations. *Census of India, 1951.* Delhi: Manager of Publications, 1952+. 17 volumes. Vol. I: "India." Parts I-A and I-B. Report and appendices. 1953. "India." Part II-B. Economic tables, general population. 1954. "India." Part II-C. Economic tables, rural and urban population. 1954. Vol. V: "Bihar." Part II-B. Economic tables. 1953.

———. *Census of India, 1961*. Delhi: Manager of Publications, 1962+. Vol. IV: "Bihar." Part II-A.

India. Home Ministry, Research and Policy Division. "The Causes and Nature of Current Agrarian Tensions." Unpublished report. 1969.

India. Ministry of Community Development and Cooperation. *Report on India's Food Crisis and Steps to Meet It*. Delhi: Manager of Publications, 1959.

India. Ministry of Food and Agriculture. *Agricultural Legislation in India*. Issued by the Economic and Statistical Adviser. Delhi: Manager of Publications, 1950+. Vol. I: "Regulation of Money-lending." 1951. Vol. II: "Consolidation of Holdings." 1950. Vol. III: "Agricultural Production and Development." 1952. Vol. IV: "Land Reforms—Abolition of Intermediaries." 1953. Vol. V: "Village Panchayats." 1954. Vol. VI: "Land Reforms—Reforms in Tenancy." 1955. (Includes Bihar Tenancy Act of 1885.)

———. *A Bibliography of Indian Agricultural Economics*. Issued by the Economic and Statistical Adviser. Delhi: Manager of Publications, 1952.

———. *Co-ordination of Agricultural Statistics in India (September 1949)*. Delhi: Manager of Publications, 1950.

———. *Indian Agriculture in Brief*. 2nd issue. Issued by the Economic and Statistical Adviser. Delhi: Manager of Publications, 1956.

———. *Report of the Committee on Large-sized Mechanical Farms: First Report, 1961; Second Report, 1964*. Delhi: Manager of Publications, 1961 and 1964.

———. *Report of the Indian Delegation to China on Agricultural Planning and Techniques*. Delhi: Manager of Publications, 1956.

———. *Report of the Working Group of the Government of India and Food and Agriculture Organization of the United Nations on Methods for Evaluation of Effects of Agrarian Reform*. Delhi: Manager of Publications, 1958.

———. *Report on Intensive Agricultural District Programme, 1961–63*. New Delhi: Manager of Publications, 1964.

———. Directorate of Economics and Statistics. *Indian Agricultural Atlas*. Issued by the Economic and Statistical Adviser. Delhi: Manager of Publications, 1952.

———. Directorate of Economics and Statistics. *Report on the High Yielding Varieties Programme: Studies in Eight Districts, Kharif, 1966–67*. New Delhi: Manager of Publications, 1968.

India. Ministry of Food, Agriculture, Community Development and Cooperation. "Chief Ministers' Conference on Land Reform—Notes on Agenda." Mimeographed report. New Delhi: Department of Agriculture, 1969.

India. Ministry of Information and Broadcasting. *Acharya Vinobha Bhave*. Delhi: United Press, 1955.

India. Ministry of Labor. *Agricultural Labour*. By B. Ramamurti. Delhi: Manager of Publications, n.d. [1952?].

India. Ministry of Law. *Constitution of India*. As modified up to October 1969. Delhi: Manager of Publications, 1970.

India. Planning Commission. *First Five Year Plan*. New Delhi: Manager of Publications, 1952.

———. *Review of the First Five Year Plan*. New Delhi: Manager of Publications, 1957.

———. *Second Five Year Plan*. New Delhi: Government of India Press, 1956.

———. *Appraisal and Prospects of the Second Five Year Plan*. New Delhi: Manager of Publications, 1958.

———. *Third Five Year Plan*. Delhi: Manager of Publications, 1962.

———. *Fourth Five Year Plan—A Draft Outline*. New Delhi: Manager of Publications, 1966.

———. *Fourth Five Year Plan, 1969–74*. New Delhi: Manager of Publications, 1970.

———. *Implementation of Land Reforms: A Review by the Land Reforms Implementation Committee of the National Development Council*. New Delhi: Government of India Press, 1966.

———. *Land Reforms in India*. New Delhi: Manager of Publications, 1959.

———. Programme Evaluation Organisation. *Evaluation Report on Working of Community Projects and N. E. S. Blocks*. P.E.O. Publication No. 10. New Delhi: Government of India Press, April 1956.

———. Programme Evaluation Organisation. *Fourth Evaluation Report on the Working of Community Projects and N. E. S. Blocks*. I, P.E.O. Publication No. 19. New Delhi: Government of India Press, April 1957.

———. Programme Evaluation Organisation. *Fourth Evaluation Report on the Working of Community Projects and N. E. S. Blocks—Summary of Conclusions and Recommendations*. New Delhi: Government of India Press, April 1957.

———. Programme Evaluation Organisation. *Studies in Co-operative Farming*. P.E.O. Publication No. 18. New Delhi: Government of India Press, December 1956.

———. *Progress of Land Reform.* New Delhi: Ministry of Information and Broadcasting, January 1955.

———. *Progress of Land Reform.* New Delhi: Manager of Publications, 1963.

———. *Report of the Indian Delegation to China on Agrarian Cooperatives.* New Delhi: Government of India Press, May 1957.

———. *Reports of the Committees of the Panel on Land Reforms.* New Delhi: Government of India Press, 1959.

India. Reserve Bank, Agricultural Credit Department. *Review of the Co-operative Movement in India 1952–54.* Bombay: Reserve Bank of India, 1956.

India. Supreme Court. *Ramranvijoy Prasad Singh et al.* v. *Bihari Singh.* C.A. 195 (1961), decided on April 25, 1963.

Indian Nation, Patna, Bihar, 1947–1970.

Indian Society of Agricultural Economics. *Indian Journal of Agricultural Economics 1940–1964: Selected Readings.* Bombay: Indian Society of Agricultural Economics, 1965.

———. *The Indian Rural Problem.* By M. B. Nanavati and J. J. Anjara. Bombay: Vora and Company, March 1951.

"Indian Villages in Trust." *The Economist*, September 28, 1957, pp. 1037–1038.

International Labor Office. *Development of the Co-operative Movement in Asia.* Geneva: International Labor Office, 1949.

———. "Land Reforms in India." *International Labor Review* 66, nos. 5, 6 (November–December 1952): 419–443.

———. "Report on India's Policy and Action on Behalf of Tribal Populations." *International Labor Review* 73, no. 3 (March 1956): 241–251, 284–298.

Jannuzi, F. Tomasson. "Agrarian Problems in Bihar." Ph.D. dissertation. London School of Economics and Political Science, 1958.

———. "Land Reform in Bihar, India: The Agrarian Structure in Bihar." In *Land Reform in India.* A.I.D. Spring Review of Land Reform, June 1970, 2nd ed., vol. 1, Country Papers. Washington: Agency for International Development, 1970.

Krishna, Gopal. "Development of the Indian National Congress as a Mass Organization, 1918–23." *Journal of Asian Studies*, May 1966.

Krishna, Raj. "Agrarian Reform in India: The Debate on Ceilings." *Economic Development and Cultural Change* 8, no. 3 (April 1959): 258–278.

———. "Some Aspects of Land Reform and Economic Development in India." In *Land Tenure, Industrialization and Social Stability*, edited by Walter Forelich. Milwaukee: Marquette University Press, 1961.

Ladejinsky, Wolf. "Agrarian Reform in Asia." *Foreign Affairs* 42 (April 1964): 475–487.

Lelyveld, Joseph. "India Finds Gandhi Inspiring and Irrelevant." *The New York Times Magazine*, May 25, 1969.

Lewis, J. P. *Quiet Crisis in India.* Washington: Brookings Institution, 1962.

Long, Erven. "The Economic Basis of Land Reform in Underdeveloped Economies." *Land Economics* 37, no. 2 (May 1961): 113–125.

Malaviya, H. D. *Land Reforms in India.* 2nd ed. New Delhi: All India Congress Committee, 1955.

Malenbaum, W. *Prospects for Indian Development.* New York: Free Press of Glencoe, 1962.

Mann, Harold H. *The Social Framework of Agriculture.* Edited by Daniel Thorner. Bombay: Tri Printers, 1967.

———, and N. V. Kanitkar. *Land and Labour in a Decan Village—Study No. 2.* London: Oxford University Press, 1921.

Martin, Kingsley. "The Gandhi Way." *The Atlantic Monthly*, August 1960.

Mashruwala, K. G. *Gandhi and Marx.* Reprint, with an introduction by Vinoba Bhave. Ahmedabad: Navajivan, 1954.

Meherally, Yusef, ed. *Socialism and the National Revolution.* Bombay: Padma Publications, 1946.

Mellor, John W. *The Economics of Agricultural Development.* Bombay: Vora and Company, 1969.

———, Thomas F. Weaver, Uma J. Lele, and Sheldon R. Simon. *Developing Rural India, Plan and Practice.* Ithaca, New York: Cornell University Press, 1968.

Menon, V. K. N. "The New Anchal Adhikari System in Bihar." *Indian Journal of Public Administration* 2, no. 2 (April–June 1956).

Misra, B. R. *Land Revenue Policy in the United Provinces.* Benares: Nand Kishore and Bros., 1942.

———. *V for Vinoba—The Economics of the Bhoodan Movement.* Bombay: Orient Longmans, 1956.

Moreland, W. H., and Atul Chandra Chatterjee. *A Short History of India.* London: Longmans, Green and Company, 1936.

Morris-Jones, W. H. *The Government and Politics of India.* London: Hutchinson and Company, 1964.

Morse, R., and M. L. Dantwala. "Agrarian Reforms in India." *Far Eastern Survey* 19 (1950): 233–243.

Mukerjee, Radhakamal. *Land Problems of India.* Calcutta University Readership Lectures. London: Longmans, Green and Company, 1933.

———. *The Rural Economy of India.* London: Longmans, Green and Company, 1926.

———, et al. *Inter-caste Tensions.* A survey under the auspices of UNESCO. Lucknow, India: Institute of Sociology, Ecology and Human Relations, University of Lucknow, 1951.

Mukerji, Karuna Moy. *The Problems of Land Transfer: A Study of the Problems of Land Alienation in Bengal.* Santiniketan, Birbhum: Santiniketan Press, 1957.

Myrdal, Gunnar. *Asian Drama: An Inquiry into the Poverty of Nations.* New York: Pantheon Press, 1968.

Nair, Kusum. *Blossoms in the Dust: The Human Element in Indian Development.* London: Gerald Duckworth and Company, 1961.

Narayan, Jaya Prakash. "The Bhoodan Movement in India." *Asian Review* (October 1958): 271–274.

———. Personal interview with in Patna, Bihar, December 1956; Sarvodaya Ashram, Sukhodeora, Bihar, January 1957; Patna, Bihar, March 1968; and Muzaffarpur, Bihar, August 1970.

———. *A Picture of Sarvodaya Social Order.* Tanjore: Sarvodaya Prachuralaya, 1956.

Neale, Walter C. *Economic Change in Rural India: Land Tenure and Reform in Uttar Pradesh, 1800–1955.* New Haven: Yale University Press, 1962.

———. "The Limitations of Indian Village Survey Data." *Journal of Asian Studies* 17, no. 3 (May 1958).

Nehru, S. S. *Caste and Credit in the Rural Area.* Calcutta: Longmans, Green and Company, 1932.

O'Malley, L. S. S. *Bengal District Gazetteers.* Calcutta: Bengal Secretariat Book Department. Vol. III: "Gaya." 1906. Vol. IV: "Muzaffarpur." 1907. Vol. VI: "Darbhanga." 1907. Vol. VIII: "Patna." 1907.

———. *Bihar and Orissa District Gazetteers—Patna.* Revised edition by J. F. W. James. Patna: Bihar Government Printing Office, 1924.

"Panchayat Raj as the Basis of Indian Policy, an Exploration in the Proceedings of the Constituent Assembly." *AVARD Newsletter* 4, no. 1 (January–February 1962).

Parsons, Kenneth H., Raymond J. Penn, and Philip M. Raup, eds. *Land Tenure.* Conference on World Land Tenure Problems, University of Wisconsin, 1951. Madison: University of Wisconsin Press, 1956.

Patel, Govindlal D. *Agrarian Reforms in Bombay: The Legal and Economic Consequences of the Abolition of Land Tenures.* Patel Collection, Mogal Lane, Matunga, Bombay.

———. *The Indian Land Problem and Legislation.* Bombay: N. M. Tripathi, 1954.

"Planning for Sarvodaya (Draft Plan)." Issued under the auspices of the Bhoodan movement. New Delhi: Ananda Press, 1957.

Prasad, Kedarnath. *The Economics of a Backward Region in a Backward Economy*. Vol. I. Calcutta: Scientific Book Agency, 1967.

Raj, K. N. *Indian Economic Growth, Performance and Prospects*. New Delhi: Allied Publishers, 1965.

Ram, Dr. D. N. (Deputy Director of Agriculture, Bihar.) Personal interview in Patna, Bihar, August 1970.

Ramabhai, Suresh. *Vinoba and His Mission*. Sevagram (Wardha), India: Akhil Bharat Sarv Seva Sangh, 1954.

Ranga, N. G., and P. R. Paruchuri. *The Peasant and Co-operative Farming*. New Delhi: Indian Peasants' Institute, July 1958.

Rao, V. K. R. V. "India's First Five Year Plan." *Pacific Affairs* 25, no. 1 (March 1952): 3–23.

Rochester, Anna. *Lenin on the Agrarian Question*. New York: International Publishers, 1942.

Rosen, George. *Democracy and Economic Change in India*. Bombay: Vora and Company, 1966; and Berkeley: University of California Press, 1966.

Roy, Ramashray. "The Congress Party in Bihar." Centre for the Study of Developing Societies, Delhi, India.

———. "Dynamics of One-Party Dominance in an Indian State." *Asian Survey*, (July 1958).

Saha, K. B. *Economics of Rural Bengal*. Calcutta: Chuckerverty, Chatterjee and Company, 1930.

Sahay, K. B. (Revenue Minister in Bihar 1955–1966.) Personal interviews in Patna, Bihar, November 1956; April, May, and November 1957; December 1967; and March 1968.

Sarvodaya Planning and the Second Five Year Plan. Calcutta: Bhoodan Yajna Prachar Samiti C-52, College St. Market, 1957.

Sen, Bhowani. *Indian Land System and Land Reforms*. Delhi: People's Publishing House, 1955.

Sen, S. R. (Editor of the *Indian Nation*.) Personal interview in Patna, Bihar, December 1956.

Sharma, Jagdish Saran. *Vinoba and Bhoodan—A Selected Descriptive Bibliography*. New Delhi: Indian National Congress, May 1956.

Shea, Thomas J., Jr. "Implementing Land Reform in India." *Far Eastern Survey* 25, no. 1 (January 1956): 1–8.

Singh, Tarlok. *Poverty and Social Change*. 2nd ed. Delhi: Orient Longmans, 1969.

Sinha, Indradip. (Official of the Communist party of India.) Personal interview in Patna, Bihar, August 13, 1970.

Sinha, N. K. P. *Measures Taken So Far by the State Government to Help Steady Flow of Institutional Finance in the Agricultural Sector*. Patna, Bihar: Secretariat Press, 1969.

Sinha, Ram Narain. *Bihar Tenantry, 1783–1833.* Bombay: People's Publishing House, 1968.

Sivaswamy, K. G. "Indian Agriculture—Problems and Programmes." *Pacific Affairs* 23, no. 4 (December 1950): 356–370.

———. *Legislative Protection and Relief of Agriculturist Debtors in India.* No. 6. Poona: Gokhale Institute of Politics and Economics, 1939.

Smith, Vincent A. *The Oxford History of India.* 2nd ed. as revised by S. M. Edwards. Oxford: Clarendon Press, 1923.

Spate, O. H. K. *India and Pakistan.* 2nd ed. London: Methuen and Company, 1957.

Srinivas, M. N. "Caste in Modern India." *Journal of Asian Studies* 16, no. 4 (August 1957): 529–548.

Strachey, John. "Zamindar into Kulak." *New Statesman and Nation* (London), September 29, 1956, pp. 366–367.

Streeter, Carroll P. *A Partnership to Improve Food Production in India.* A special report from the Rockefeller Foundation printed by S. D. Scott, New York, 1969.

Tennyson, Hallam. *India's Walking Saint: The Story of Vinobha Bhave.* New York: Doubleday and Company, 1955.

Thorner, Daniel. *The Agrarian Prospect in India.* Delhi: Delhi University Press, 1956.

———, and Alice Thorner. *Land and Labor in India.* New York: Asia Publishing House, 1962.

Times of India Directory and Yearbook, 1967. Edited by N. J. Nanporia. Bombay: Times of India Press, 1967.

Tocqueville, Alexis de. *Democracy in America.* New York: Vintage, 1954.

United Nations. Department of Economic Affairs. *Land Reforms: Defects in Agrarian Structure as Obstacles to Economic Development.* New York: United Nations, 1951. Sales No. 1951 II B.

United Nations. Department of Economic and Social Affairs. *Progress in Land Reform.* New York: United Nations, 1954.

United Nations. Food and Agriculture Organization. *Bibliography on Land Tenure.* New York: United Nations, 1955.

———. *Bibliography on Land Tenure in Asia, the Far East and Oceana.* Rome: United Nations, 1969.

———. *Progress in Land Reform, Fourth Report.* New York: United Nations, 1966.

United States. Department of State. Agency for International Development. *Spring Review of Land Reform June 2–4.* Vols. I–XII. Washington, D.C.: U.S. Government Printing Office, 1970. "Findings and Implications for A.I.D." Subsidiary pamphlet for vols. I–XII.

Verghese, B. G. *Beyond the Famine: An Approach to Regional Planning for Bihar.* Published under the auspices of the Bihar Relief Committee. New Delhi: Super Bazaar, 1967.

Warriner, Doreen. *Land Reform and Development in the Middle East.* 2nd ed. London: Oxford University Press, 1962.

———. *Land Reform in Principle and Practice.* Oxford: Clarendon Press, 1969.

Wunderlich, Gene. *Land Reform in Western India: Analysis of Economic Impacts of Tenancy Legislation, 1948–63.* United States Department of Agriculture Economic Research Service, Resource Development Economics Division, Agriculture Series, no. 82. Washington, D.C.: U.S. Government Printing Office, 1964.

Zinkin, Taya. "Collective Villages of Orissa." *Manchester Guardian,* October 24, 1957, p. 9.

INDEX